W9-CPF-924

TOUCHSTONES OF REALITY

TOUCHSTONES
OF REALITY

Existential Trust and
the Community of Peace

Maurice S. Friedman

E. P. DUTTON & CO., INC. | NEW YORK | 1972

Published simultaneously in Canada
by Clarke, Irwin & Company Limited, Toronto and Vancouver

Library of Congress Catalog Card Number: 74-165598
SBN 0-525-22160-3

The author wishes to acknowledge the permission of the John Day Company, Inc., to quote verses from Witter Bynner, *The Way of Life according
to Lao-tzu*, copyright © 1944 by Witter Bynner; of Simon & Schuster, Inc.,
to quote from Bertrand Russell, *The Autobiography of Bertrand Russell*
(vol. III), copyright © 1969 by George Allen and Unwin Ltd.; and of
Fellowship Publications, Nyack, N.Y., to quote from Kenneth Boulding,
There Is a Spirit: The Naylor Sonnets, copyright 1945.

To the Memory of
My Teacher Joachim Wach
and
My Friend William H. Cleveland, Jr.
and
To All My Comrades
On the Opening Way

O world invisible we view thee.
O world intangible we touch thee.
O world unknowable we know thee.
Inapprehensible we clutch thee.

Not where the wheeling systems darken
And our benumbed conceiving soars,
The drift of pinions, would we hearken,
Beats at our own clay-shuttered doors.
Francis Thompson
"In No Strange Land"

Discoverers of love's opening way
recognize one another, whatever their affiliations.
Dan Wilson
An Opening Way

Preface

Although none of my books is more my own than this one, it might not have come into being had not Philip Scharper, at that time editor-in-chief of Sheed & Ward, suggested to me that I write a book on "A Faith for Modern Man." To try to write a book of that sort seemed to me presumptuous, yet I was so touched by this confirmation coming to a committed Jew from the head of a distinguished Catholic publishing house that I responded as I could—with a series of outlines that were the forerunners of the present book.

I do not recall how I evolved the metaphor of touchstones of reality—certainly not under the influence of Matthew Arnold, whose essay on literary touchstones I only recalled when someone pointed out that my book and his essay had that word in common. But I was truly amazed when, after completing this book, Paul Riley, a graduate student of mine, showed me the following from the 13th century Sufi mystic, Jalálu'ddin Rúmí:

> Inasmuch as truth and falsehood have been mingled, and the good and bad coin have been poured into the travelling-bag. Therefore they need a picked touchstone, one that has undergone [many] tests in [assaying] realities,
> So that it may become a criterion for these impostures; so that it may be a standard for these acts of providence.[1]

[1] Jalálu'ddin Rúmí, *The Mathnawi*, trans. by Reynold A. Nicholson, E. J. W. Gibb Memorial New Series, Vol. IV, 2 (1926) (London: Messrs. Luzac

It was clear to me from the first that if I could not presume to spell out "a faith for modern man," I might make a witness to touchstones as the immediate product of those events that underlie each man's working faith. To claim that each man has touchstones of reality, even when he is not aware of it, is not, of course, to claim that he has the same touchstones as others. On the contrary, the very meaning of touchstones necessitates each man's touchstones being unique. At the same time, this is a uniqueness that we can share and witness.

The only form in which I can communicate what is more attitude than specific content is that of personal witness, including an autobiographical journey that fills the second to fifth chapters and that runs, in however small a vein, throughout. Touchstones of reality can only be existentially communicated if they evoke answering touchstones in each reader—from the events and depths of his own life. It is concrete, personal sharing which is most likely to call forth this response. My autobiographical journey is confined for the most part to a small segment of my life that best shows my movement from touchstone to touchstone as "an opening way." The way touchstones meet is illustrated by the fact that I have taken this phrase, which I use as the title of Part I, from Dan Wilson's autobiographical pamphlet *An Opening Way*.[2]

Once I believed Gerald Heard's statement that one could become a saint through twelve years' practice of spiritual discipline. Even after this naive notion had been shattered, I wrote an M.A. thesis entitled, "From Inquisitor to Saint: The Search for Faith in Ten Modern European Novels." Eventually I dropped the idea of spiritual perfection altogether as neither possible nor desirable and took as my goal the difficult and problematic task of becoming a human being. In this pro-

---

& Co. Ltd., 1960), Book II, verses 2966-2968, from a chapter entitled, "On Making Trial of Everything So That the Good and Evil Which Are in It May Be Brought to View."

[2] Wallingford, Pa.: Pendle Hill Publications, 1961.

gressive moderation of my hopes and expectations I may not be atypical of modern man. I have suggested in my book *To Deny Our Nothingness* that a truly modern "saint" would have to be someone who takes on and embodies within himself the contradictions of contemporary existence rather than transcends them through his personal holiness. Even if we need not set out like Tarrou in Camus' novel *The Plague* to be "saints without God," God, holiness, and above all man himself have become questionable in our age. The "death of God" is not a metaphysical or theological proposition but a recognition of the absence of personal and social guidelines that might help us simply to be human. Before the vogue of the "God is dead" theologians, I wrote in my book *Problematic Rebel:*

> The "death of God" does not mean that modern man does not "believe" in God, any more than it means that God himself has actually died. Whether or not one holds with Sartre that God never existed at all or with Buber that God is in "eclipse" and that it is we, the "slayers of God," who dwell in the darkness, the "death of God" means the awareness of a basic crisis in modern history—the crisis that comes when man no longer knows what it means to be human and becomes aware that he does not know this. This is not just a question of the relativization of "values" and the absence of universally accepted mores. It is the absence of an image of meaningful human existence, the absence of the ground that enabled Greek, Biblical, and Renaissance man to move with some sureness even in the midst of tragedy.[3]

We have been engaged in a prolonged and disastrous war in Indochina from which we seem helpless to disengage ourselves despite the fact that there is almost no one in our society

---

[3] Maurice Friedman, *Problematic Rebel: Melville, Dostoievsky, Kafka, Camus,* 2nd revised, enlarged, and radically reorganized ed. (Chicago: The University of Chicago Press, Phoenix Books, 1970), p. 456. The first edition was published in 1963 with the subtitle "An Image of Modern Man."

who will not affirm the necessity of ending the war and bringing back American troops. The Middle East mirrors Indochina as the potential mirrors the actual. No one imagines that the desire on the part of the great powers to avoid a general conflagration there will in itself prevent that conflagration from taking place. Our means and our ends have come apart, and in the process the idealism of our goals is so far from self-evident that we must ask whether we have any rational direction at all. The same thing can be said about the domestic scene. The "crisis in black and white" is getting steadily worse, not better; yet our heightened awareness of this crisis and of the related urban and ecological crises does nothing to allay them.

What is at stake is not the *names* of things—God, church, society, respect for the family, "dialogue"—but the wind of the spirit that once blew over them and gave them life. If today's youth are turning to the "new religions," [4] just as I did myself a quarter of a century ago, it is because they see the emptiness of the professed goals and values of their parents and their society. But the awareness of emptiness is not in itself a guarantee of finding meaning. The fact that youth know "where it is *not* at" does not necessarily make them good judges of those charismatic figures and revolutionaries who claim that *they* know "where it *is* at." Neither are today's youth likely to find much guidance from the professionally trained educators whom they encounter in their colleges and universities. "Meaning" is being hedged in by teachers of philosophy all over the United States and England in the formulas of an ever more precise linguistic analysis, the positivism and psychologism of which are in many cases all too evident. The "illogical negativism of logical positivism," to use my own phrase, is not confined to philosophy. It has found its way into the bastions of social and political science, psy-

[4] Cf. the fine study and analysis by Jacob Needleman: *The New Religions* (New York: Doubleday & Co., 1970).

chology, and educational theory and method. Still more deadly, because it is far more widespread, is the universal misconception that one becomes educated through learning to abstract what others say from the personal ground from which they speak.

What modern man needs is not "faith" in the traditional sense of that term but a life-stance—a ground on which to stand and from which to go out to meet the ever changing realities and absurdities of a techtronic age. Touchstones of reality have to do above all with our life-stance—with that personal and social ground that might enable us to withstand bureaucratization and surveillance—the innumerable incursions of military, industrial, ecological, economic, and political forces into our personal lives.

Touchstones of Reality might serve as a text for a wide-gauge introductory religion course, as a graduate student who read the manuscript suggested. But that is only because such a wide-gauge course would be oriented not around religion as a special study in itself, but as a source of our understanding of man and in particular of the man of our time. One might even use it as part of a comparative religion course or of a course in religion and ethics, since it touches on all these subjects. Yet it is not primarily an objective text as much as it is an address to the seeking and concerned reader of whatever age, vocation, and life situation and of whatever persuasion or lack of one—so long as that reader is concerned with the depth-dimension of being human. So, far from being about "religion," its chief focus is the substitution of "touchstones of reality" for that special sphere of religious feelings, experiences, creeds, and institutions that Martin Buber once called "the great enemy of mankind" because such "religion" confirms us in that dualism in which what really matters in our lives remains untouched and unconcerned.

The final chapter of *Touchstones* is entitled "A Meaning for Modern Man." Touchstones of reality may fairly claim to be concerned with the wholeness of man—of his personal and social existence. Not that we all have or should have the same touchstones, but that we share them, that we grow from one to another, including our meeting with those of others. Our "opening way" is personal and communal at once. As it opens, we may come to recognize that immediacy of trust is meaning enough for modern man—that we can live without a "world view." "In that which convinced you," George Fox wrote to William Edmunson, "wait, that you may have that removed you are convinced of . . . and nothing may rule in you but the life. . . ." "Moshe," the Hasidic rebbe Shneur Zalman of Ladi asked when his disciple entered the room, "what do we mean when we say 'God'?" Moshe said nothing even when asked a second and third time. When asked the reason for his silence, he replied, "Because I do not know." "Do you think I know?" said the rebbe. "But I must say it, for it is so, and therefore I must say it: He is definitely there, and except for Him nothing is definitely there—and this is He."

I wish to thank my wife Eugenia for the invaluable criticisms she has given me out of our "community of otherness." I am also indebted to my editor Ned Arnold for his helpful suggestions concerning restructuring, to my typist Myrtle Keeny for her patience through numerous versions of the text, and to my friend Marie Vallanie for the retreat which the hospitality of her cabin in the Adirondacks gave me at a crucial juncture in my writing.

Maurice Friedman

Swarthmore, Pa.
April, 1971

Contents

17

PART ONE

An

Opening

Way

Chapter 1

Where Touchstones Meet

"He who knows that what is true in his heart is true for all men is a genuis," said Ralph Waldo Emerson. One might with equal validity say, "He who assumes that what is true for himself is true for all men is a fool." Being neither, I cannot imagine that what has been true for me is necessarily true even for the contemporary men of my time and culture, much less for all men. I may hope, nonetheless, that the touchstones of reality that have emerged in the course of my encounters with the world of our time may speak, in one way or another, to the condition of many who have also had to encounter this world and to search, in its confusion, for their personal way. These "touchstones of reality" do not claim to add up to a philosophical system or a comprehensive world-view. They are responses to the real questions that have arisen for me as I have found myself claimed and challenged during the past thirty years.

In speaking of "touchstones of reality," I imply no separate and prior definition of "reality." On the contrary, I presuppose that it is not possible to speak of reality directly. Therefore, I cannot answer the traditional philosopher who asks what I mean by "reality" by pointing to a set of Platonic ideas or to any metaphysical absolute. But neither can I go along with those in our age who will want to reduce my "touchstones" to one or another form of subjectivism— whether it be the cultural relativist who says that since customs differ from one place to another, there really are no values, there are simply the needs and interests of a particular group; or the behaviorist psychologist who wishes to reduce values to a collection of reactions or chemical formulations; or the Freudian psychoanalyst who wants to reduce values to the superego introjected from the father through the fear of punishment; or the Sartrian existentialist who claims that values do not exist and we must invent them; or the linguistic analyst who says, "It is all right for you to feel all these things about God and ethics and reality, but you should not make the false inference that your feeling refers to anything outside itself." In contrast to all of these "points of view," I offer no "reality" independent of "touchstones," but also no "touch" independent of contact with an otherness that transcends my own subjectivity even when I respond to it from that ground and know it only in my contact with it. What I am concerned with is glimpses of a way at once uniquely personal and, I believe, broadly human. These glimpses have come to me in a series of separate yet not unconnected events and meetings of my life—meetings with persons, with situations, with the characters of literature, the scriptures of religions, and the writers who have spoken to me through their thoughts. In the residues of these events and meetings a way in the present and into the future has opened up for me. For these residues, I claim what cannot be claimed for any objective metaphysics or subjective inspiration. They are "touchstones of reality."

What is most needed by the bewildered man of today is not theological systems or linguistic analyses but "an opening way." [1] The way does not always move easily like a boat drift-

[1] Dan Wilson, *An Opening Way, loc. cit.*

ing down the stream. More often it is a path through a forest which at times leads through the densest thickets and at times opens on to glades of breathtaking beauty. Certainly my own way has known as many pitfalls and roadblocks as break-throughs and illuminations. When we try to hold on to our touchstones, moreover, we often lose that impact of otherness that gave them their weight of reality. Pascal sewed the word "fire" into his coat to remind him of his hour of mystical ec-stasy, and much in his life and thought testifies to his faithful-ness to that memory. But many of us are like the children in Maurice Maeterlinck's play, who find the bluebird and put it into a cage only to see it turn before their eyes into a black-bird. We retain our touchstones only by plowing them back into our lives.

A coloration that we take on from the culture or *Zeitgeist* but have not made our own is not a touchstone: it is only fool's gold. A touchstone cannot be passively received. It must be won by contending, by wrestling until dawn and not let-ting the nameless messenger go until he has blessed us by giv-ing us a new name. Touchstones only come when we have fought our way through to where we are open to something really other than our accustomed set of values and our ac-customed ways of looking at the world. I came to my touch-stones not through the values that I already had but through the conflict between those values—a conflict that was only resolved by reaching continual new positions and with them new or transformed values.

Touchstones have a history. They live with us. More than that, they enter into other touchstones that we have along the road. They do not always enter easily. There is sometimes great conflict and deep confusion. Touchstones have a two-sidedness which is at the same time a form of immediacy. Nothing can be so deeply confusing as to have known that immediacy and then to find your touchstone shattered or no longer there, replaced by another or perhaps by none at all.

Then you ask yourself, "Was that a delusion? Was there anything real there? What is left that I may be faithful to?"

A touchstone of reality is either present or it has ceased to
exist. Insofar as it is renewed or is taken into another touchstone, it is present. Insofar as two touchstones clash, that is real
too. I cannot speak of a "progressive revelation" or unbroken
evolution of touchstones. I can only witness to life as I and my
contemporaries have known it: discontinuous and broken,
walking over abysses, encountering the absurd, and finding, at
the same time, moments of meaning, moments of trust. Walking on our path, we encounter something that lights up for us
—an event perhaps, but it might also be the teaching of the
Buddha if that speaks to our condition. We cannot rise above
our culture, but neither are we hermetically sealed within it.
A Greek tragedy or a Rig Veda may say something to us just
as any contemporary happening may.

Along with its other connotations, the word "touchstone"
suggests probing, testing, proving—but in an existential sense;
that is, as something we take back with us into the new situation that we meet. It helps us relate to that new situation, but
the situation also modifies the touchstone. On us is laid the
task, as long as we live, of going on probing, proving, testing,
authenticating—never resting content with any earlier formulation. However true our touchstone, it will cease to be true if
we do not make it real again by testing it in each new situation. This testing is nothing more nor less than bringing our
life-stance into the moment of present reality. In contrast to
the scientist who is only interested in particulars insofar as
they yield generalizations, we can derive valid insights from
the unique situations in which we find ourselves without having to claim that they apply to all situations. We take these insights with us into other situations and test the limits of their
validity. Sometimes we find that these insights do hold for a
particular situation and sometimes that they do not or that they

have to be modified. Yet that does not mean that they cannot be valid insights for other situations.

Touchstones of reality are like insights, except that they are closer to events. An insight arises from a concrete encounter, but we tend to remove it too quickly and completely to a plane of abstractions. Any existential truth remains true only insofar as it is again and again tested in the stream of living. We have no secure purchase on truth above this stream. If we are going to walk on the road from touchstone to touchstone, we will have to wrestle painfully with the problem of when it is right to move in the direction of insight and philosophical abstraction and when we must move back into the living waters. The simple formulae—the either-ors—will not help. I cannot, for example, be either for the "verbal" or for the "non-verbal" in the abstract. There is a time for words and a time for silence, and a time for words which have between them thick silence. Every form of intellectual, philosophical, theological, psychological, sociological, economic, or political "party line" that tells us in advance how we ought to regard a situation gets in between us and the possibility of a fresh, unique response.

As we move through life, our relation to the events of our past changes and with it our interpretation of their meaning. Sometimes these changing interpretations derive from new touchstones that we have acquired along the way. Sometimes it is the other way around: our new touchstones derive from our testing of the old ones and from our reinterpretation of the events of which they are the residue. This does not mean that we begin with raw experience and later add meaning or interpretation to it. We never have experience by itself. Our attitude toward experience is always present along with the experience itself, even at the moment we are having it. As we keep growing, however, our attitude changes—not only toward present experience but toward the experiences we have had in the past.

I claim for touchstones what I claim for touching. In touching you do make contact. Even if it is only a partial contact, like that of "The Blind Men and the Elephant," that contact itself is a reality and a form of direct knowing, however illusory the inferences from the contact may be. We cannot say with what we make contact minus the touching, but the touching itself *is* a contact. It is not just that we have the *experience* of touching. On the contrary, to touch is to go through *and beyond* subjective experiencing: if I touch, if we touch, then there is a communication which is neither merely objective nor merely subjective, nor both together. The very act of touching is already a transcending of the self in openness to the impact of something other than the self. When two people really touch each other as persons—whether physically or not—the touching is not merely a one-sided impact: it is a mutual revelation of life-stances.

Equally as important as the question of how we continue to remain faithful to our touchstones without objectifying them or taking them for granted is the question of how we communicate them to others. Indeed, many of our touchstones come to us precisely through such communication. Real communication means that each of us has some real contact with the otherness of the other. But this is only possible if each of us has related to the other's touchstones in his unique way. If instead I take on the role of the "objective observer" or even of the sympathetic "receptive listener" and fail to respond, then I have not even heard you, much less having learned anything myself. We can only really listen if we are willing both to be open and to respond personally. The product of such communication will be something different from what either you or I intend. But it will be real communication, in contrast to that habitual misunderstanding in which we are all too often imprisoned—closed circuits in which we make a little voyage toward the other and then come back.

We have no right to judge the touchstones of others,

whether we mean by judging to evaluate them objectively or morally to condemn them. They are personal revelations and witnesses to existential truth. If we pretend to judge their adequacy by some objective, universal criteria, it simply means that we have not really listened to the other, that we have used what he said as a pawn in our own mental chess game rather than entering into genuine dialogue with him. If we morally condemn them, then we are excluding the other's reality with his touchstones. We are saying, in effect, "You have no right to make a witness. We have already defined your witness out of existence before it is made." But there is a third sort of "evaluation" which we cannot rightfully escape: we must hear the other and we must respond. He needs to know that he is really coming up against us as persons with touchstones and witnesses of our own. Sometimes the strongest opposition is more confirming by far than someone who defends your right to your opinion but does not take it seriously. The real "dialogue of touchstones" means that we respond from where we are, that we bring ourselves into the dialogue.

To communicate a touchstone is to witness. When we really witness, we hold the tension of the event out of which we witness *and* of the words, gestures, and actions through which we witness. We do not abstract what we have to say from the event in which it took root nor do we imagine that we can hand the event over as an objective fact minus the interpretation that we have made of it. For this same reason we have the right to ask that those to whom we witness do not limit themselves to the words that we use minus the person using them and what we are witnessing to in our own life. If we are making a witness, we are sharing something really unique with a unique person in a unique situation. Only in this way can we share our witnesses with one another. Because this sharing is real, it often happens that more than one witness, more than one touchstone is real to us at the same time.

When this is so, we cannot exclude either voice, even when they seem to contradict each other.

Although each of us has his own viewpoint, we are not completely alone. We are able to share what is uniquely our own and, each of us in his own way, bring it into a common reality. The sad thing is that so much of our sharing is pseudo-sharing because we lift it to a plane of objective discourse. In order to have real contact with one another, we must overcome our "education"; for we are programmed to "hear" in such a way that we rarely really hear. Most of our education is an education in the methods of abstracting. Consequently, we do not hear the person who speaks but only his "opinion" or "point of view." We put him into this or that category—a "phenomenologist," an "existentialist," a "realist," a "pragmatist," or a "linguistic analyst"—and this putting into categories we call being educated.

True education is an education in the communication of touchstones. No human happening that issues into touchstones of reality can be described or articulated in such a way that either it or the touchstone that derives from it can be objectively handed over. Touchstones of reality always include the component of our unique response to them. John Dewey and Sigmund Freud rejected mysticism on the ground that it cannot become common public knowledge. The logical positivist and the linguistic analyst tend to reject all touchstones of reality on the same ground. Yet from the beginning of his existence as man, man has always been trying to share with his fellow man events and images that cannot be quantified, defined, and spelled out, but only pointed to. Some of the greatest literature, art, and thought of all ages has been of this nature. This is not esotericism—a knowledge for the élite few. It is simply saying that much that cannot be delimited can nonetheless be indicated. Once in answer to a question, the Buddha silently held up a blue flower. Only one man, Maha-

kasyapa, understood what the Buddha was "saying." According to legend he became the founder of Zen Buddhism.

We think we communicate when we set ourselves aside as persons, agree on definitions, and meet on the high plane of abstractions. But this is really another form of subjectivism since only a few people, if any, will agree with our terms and what we propose that they should mean. For the rest, most of what we call communication is simply mismeeting and misunderstanding—people using words in different ways and not even caring enough to ask the other person what he means by what he says.

For many years I have sought ways of pointing to realities that I cannot satisfactorily define or objectify. From this search arises my conviction of the importance of "touchstones of reality." Because of this conviction, I invite you to a "dialogue of touchstones." There is a sense in which the very confusions and complexities of our way are a part of the way. If our way is a true way, it has to be unique, and if it is unique, it cannot serve as a model. Yet we help one another along the road when we share our touchstones *and* the confusion that sometimes accompanies them. We evolve our touchstones in relation with one another; we witness to one another. We have an impact on one another through which we grow in our own touchstones. Growing in this way, we come to recognize that a "dialogue of touchstones" is itself a touchstone.

[Chapter 2]

The Making of a "C.O."

An opening way means more an attitude and approach than a finished conclusion. For this reason, it may add a dimension of depth and concreteness to my "touchstones" if I set down some of the less finished, crude, and at times just plain naive ways of thinking that were part of my "opening way" twenty-five and even thirty years ago. This means not only a *description* of the stages on my life's way but also some of the actual formulations in which I expressed those stages at the time I was living through them. If faith is faithfulness to the memory of the moments of awareness of the ineffable, to paraphrase Abraham Heschel, then even these youthful expressions —from the time when I was a senior in high school to seven years later when I had just begun graduate school—have their place as markers on the way that my life and thought, confusion and search, despair and hope have opened for me.

My parents both came to the United States from Europe in their early teens, my father from a traditional Jewish family in Poland, my mother from a Hasidic family in Lithuania. According to my great uncle, both of my maternal great grandfathers belonged to the Lubavicher dynasty of Hasidism,

which laid more stress upon Talmudic and mystical study than many of the other Hasidim. My mother's father spent most of his time in prayer and study, leaving the support and care of his family to his wife, who ran an inn. Nine out of thirteen of my grandmother's children died in childhood because of poverty, hardship, and disease. I believe that it was largely in reaction against my grandfather's other-worldliness and the heavy burden carried uncomplainingly by my grandmother that my mother turned to Reform Judaism after her marriage to my father and their settling in Tulsa, Oklahoma, where I was born and grew up. Perhaps, being a brilliant woman, she reacted too against the role assigned to women in the East European culture. Jewish girls learned only how to read Hebrew, not how to understand it. When my mother was eleven and went out of town to visit a friend, her father burned the few books on mathematics and other secular subjects that she had managed to get hold of.

When I went to Reform Jewish Sunday School in Tulsa, I learned much Jewish history and legend and took to heart the predominantly moral emphasis of Reform Judaism of the 1930s. But I learned almost nothing of traditional Rabbinic Judaism or of the *mitzvot* (commandments) and observances that made up the life of my Hasidic grandfather in Lithuania. I never even heard of Hasidism, in fact, and never received more than a taste of that rich culture of traditional Jewish music, dance, and legend that is now the heritage, at least in its cultural forms, of Jewish children in almost all Sunday Schools.

One thing that my confirmation teacher said impressed and puzzled me so that I never ceased to wonder as to its meaning. This was his statement (adapted I later learned, from Terence): "Nothing Jewish is alien to me." This statement seemed to me simply untrue, and as I grew older and came into contact with cultural and religious manifestations of Judaism largely absent in the small southwestern Jewish community in which I grew up, it seemed still more untrue than before. An enormous amount that was Jewish was alien to me while much that was not Jewish was not. I came eventually to understand that what was false as a statement of fact might be true as an intention. Perhaps what my teacher really meant was that in the deepest part of his being, he identified himself as a Jew and that as long as he lived he wanted to realize this identification through engrossing himself in Jewish tradition and spirit. It was this intention, this striving, that he desired to implant in us.

Another thing that he taught us was that Judaism is "an ethical monotheism." Although I had never heard of ethics in the sense of moral philosophy, like many young Reform Jews I had a deep and unquestioning feeling for peace, justice, brotherhood, and social righteousness. If I had been asked for the connection between the ethical part of Judaism and its monotheism, I would undoubtedly have referred to the Ten Commandments. Yet I also remember that at the age of twelve, I became an agnostic since it seemed to me that what I had heard about heaven was too selfish to be worthy of God. Evidently my moral ideals could stand by themselves and had no need of theological or religious underpinning! When it came time to give our confirmation speeches, I was the one child who insisted on writing my own (the rabbi wrote the rest), and I bored or diverted the adults among whom I had grown up with a blatantly rationalistic credo that I had recently picked up from Bill Cleveland, then a teacher in my high school. All moral problems could be reduced to removing prejudice, arriving at clear thinking, making rational decision, and acting on that decision. I began my confirmation speech with a quotation from the poet John Oxenham (d. 1575), which I had also got from Bill Cleveland, a quotation which expressed the "inspiration" appropriate for "high moral endeavor":

To every soul there openeth
A high road and a low.
The high soul takes the high road,
The low soul takes the low,
And in between, on misty flats,
The rest drift to and fro.

Little did I imagine then that I would spend my life drifting to and fro "on misty flats"!

During high school I was mostly concerned with literature, history, and international relations and not at all with religion. Yet there is one short story dating from my junior or senior year in high school that now seems to me striking in its anticipation of my later mysticism—with its rejection of the physical in favor of the spiritual—and my much later concern with the absurd and the need to confront and contend with it, a central motif later in my books. I should add that, in contrast to today's high school youth, I had never even heard of Nietzsche, Dostoievsky, Sartre, Camus, Freud, or anything else that could account as an intellectual "influence" for the mind-body dualism at the heart of this story, a few excerpts from which I give here.

REVERY

. . . It was not so hard to imagine the extreme in physical totality, as the ordinary animal represented that very well. What puzzled Professor Ammerman was how to get a mental image of the mind completely divorced from the body, the spiritual separated from the material. How much time could be saved if we did not have to eat and sleep? How much more pleasant life would be if we did not have to spend our existence "cramming" for dollars! How much better to surrender to dreamy meditation and philosophy than to be always in such a mad rush to get nowhere and to get nothing done!

The professor pictured himself as engaged in a horrible conflict between body and mind. His flesh lost all semblance of looseness, and his bones became so prominent that he closely resembled a man dying from starvation. Decaying and crumbling bit by bit, the figure deteriorated until nothing but the horrible, glaring, magnificently bright eyes showed a sign of life in the crumpled heap of animal matter. Gradually, everything faded away except the eyes, which kept getting brighter and brighter until it seemed they must burst asunder with their very radiance. Finally, the light in the eyes narrowed down and the outer part of the eyes faded away, leaving nothing but two infinitely small, infinitely bright points of light, which came together, the whole becoming even smaller as they joined. Eventually, the light became so small that it was imperceptible, and the professor, as if a load were lifted from him, felt it rise into space.

But lo, instead of the cheerful meditation and philosophy promised the mind upon its separation from the body, there was only nothingness, a horrible, binding, gripping inescapable nothingness: no dimensions, no objects, no light, no darkness, no feeling, no emotions, no sound, no smell, no taste, no thought—no finite thing of any kind. The nothingness was trying to close in and envelop the little spark of consciousness. He suddenly sensed a new power seeping into him, but at the same time he felt the forces of nothingness press closer and closer upon him. The stronger he became, the tighter he was pressed. Finally, in one awful second all the power in the universe seemed to rush into him, and all the finite forces of nothingness to close in on him. Instantaneously, there was an explosion and a blinding flash.

When I graduated from Tulsa Central High School, I won a four-year scholarship to Harvard and a trip to Europe as First Prize for the National High School League of Nations Examination. The wonder and joy that my 1939 summer in England, France, and Switzerland engendered in me turned to the blackest gloom as Europe plunged into war. It was on the *Ile de France*, on the way back, that I first thought about the possibility of becoming a conscientious objector. America was not at war yet, but in the months and years that followed —with the fall of France and the conversion of my League of Nations Association friends into the Committee to Defend America by Aiding the Allies—I saw us drawing step by step toward it. When the Harvard Student Union split over the issue, I remained the only member of both the groups, finally resigning from them both in equal protest against the "imperialist" cries of the Harvard young communists and the self-deception of the liberals.

This split, repeated all over the country, was the end of the "popular front." The years that immediately followed were bitter years of facing harsh realities that I hardly knew existed before. When I came home to Tulsa after my first year at Harvard, France had just fallen to the Nazis, an event which I predicted to my unconcerned high school girl friend would come to weigh heavily on us all before we were through. The period that followed was for me a period of unrelieved blackness where any happiness or joy seemed the surface cover over the endless reality of pain. "But one star shining in a wilderness of night,/One ray of hope across the darkening seas" I wrote in a poem of my sophomore year at Harvard, a poem which ended, like my hymn to the League of Nations on returning from Europe, by sounding the note of the hope for brotherhood. If we did not have the social awareness of today's youth, we had the political, the historical, and the economic. Certainly Eliot House still had its menus, its waitresses, its three desserts for those who wanted it, and its common room where one sipped demitasse and played the piano. The wife of the headmaster of Eliot House deplored the plight of the refugees on the roads of France while we young boys stood around her balancing our tea cups and making polite conversation. No one could be served breakfast, even on the hottest summer day, if he was not dressed in jacket and tie, while monthly House dances and all the concerts of the Harvard Glee Club required white tie and tails.

In the midst of all this I remained deadly serious and felt little respect for the clubmen who did not. I majored in history and literature of nineteenth-century Europe my sophomore year, as background, I hoped, for work in international relations. At the end of the year I reregistered for the same major, but at the end of the summer, after the "work with mind and heart and hand" of an International Student Service work camp, I became a socialist and switched to economics, concentrating in labor economics and social reform, and planned to become a labor organizer or educator.

Despite the stunned shock that we all felt on December 7, 1941, with the news of Pearl Harbor, it never occurred to me not to continue with the plan to pass out the Harvard Pacifist League questionnaire at dinner at Eliot House that night till a member of the League begged me not to!

I did not derive my morality and my social consciousness from the war. Far from it! I was all too moral even before then: full of a morality of peace, brotherhood, justice—values inculcated in me by liberal Judaism perhaps, but needing no religious base on which to stand. These values, combined with the antimilitaristic slant of social studies in the 1930s, gave me an active social conscience which applied itself to problems of social reform and international relations. It gave me, too, a strong feeling for peace and a keen hatred of war. But it did not give me the moral foundation for making a real value decision when I found myself in a situation where I felt as if I had to choose between my concern for social reform, on the one hand, and my feeling for peace, on the other. It was only then that I came to understand ethics from within, for it was only then that I faced the basic problem of how I discover what I ought to do in a concrete situation that demands decision and response.

This decision was an extremely painful and difficult one for me since my deepest values were in conflict. The spread of Nazism and fascism filled me with horror; yet I could not believe that a destructive means such as war could lead to a constructive end. I feared instead that we ourselves might become fascist if we went to war. I arrived at a resolution of this conflict only through a year and a half of agonized indecision and intense inner struggle. I felt that never again in my life would I have to make a decision as important as this, and I sometimes felt that I would prefer suicide to making a wrong choice. In order to come to a decision I had to discover what were my fundamental moral and emotional values and try to work out a rational point of view consistent with these values. I demanded absolute honesty of myself as to my own motives and an unrelenting concentration on the question. In the course of reaching a decision I came to realize that reason was only of value in enabling one to be consistent with fundamental values but could not of itself determine or affect those values, except through helping one to know which was the most basic. After listening and talking to men like Bertrand Russell and Pitirim Sorokin, I also reached the clear conviction that I could not let myself be swayed just by my respect for these men, who knew so much more than I ever would, since it was I—a nineteen-year-old—and not they who had to make the decision. In this I anticipated the meaning of a real moral and existential decision.

For a long while I would not allow myself to read any books on pacifism for fear of prejudicing myself, but finally got out all the books on the subject in the Widener library and went through them. Of these, the books connecting pacifism with socialism, labor, and nonviolent resistance were the most important since they seemed to point to a way in which my concern for social change and my concern for peace might work together. My decision to become a conscientious objector was integrally tied up with my social philosophy. I had by that time decided that the only way in which we could get peace was through socialism and domestic reform and hoped that the American labor movement would prove the spearhead of that reform. While I believed in socialism, I had rejected entirely the Marxist ideas of a violent revolution and dictatorship of the proletariat. I was convinced that only democratic socialism brought in by democratic means could possibly last as socialism. I did not side with the communists, therefore, who remained for peace until Germany attacked the Soviet Union, but neither could I join with the liberals who were quite content with ideas of gradual reform and progress. From my studies of economics and my knowledge of the causes of war, I was convinced that we did not have forever in which to make our social reforms, but that changes would have to come quickly and on a large scale if fascism of some form were to be averted.

I was influenced at that time by Aldous Huxley's *Ends and Means*, but also by Tolstoy's *War and Peace*—that moment when Prince André lies on the ground on the battlefield, looks up at the patch of blue sky, and feels himself lifted out of the strife and killing into the peace of eternity. Of great importance also was Dostoievsky's novel *The Brothers Kara-mazov*. I was much impressed by his emphasis on growth through suffering. I felt that the American people were unwilling to suffer for their democracy, that democracy to them still had a negative meaning of *laissez faire* rather than a positive meaning of cooperation and brotherhood; that government is always at least by the negative consent of the people and that the Nazis could not impose fascism on our country for more than a generation at most, if that long, if the people really wanted their democracy. Gandhi's nonviolent direct action as it was practised in India gave me the hope that the American people might withhold even its negative consent from the conqueror (though Bertrand Russell, when he came to tea at our suite in Eliot House where his son John was one

of my roommates, said that he had given up the pacifism that
he had held till as late as 1938 because the Nazis and the Japanese were willing to destroy twenty or thirty percent of the
population, as opposed to the British scattered bombing in
India, and nonviolence would not work in the face of this).
But above all, from the time when I had studied international
relations and the League of Nations in high school through
all my studies of history, political science, and economics at
Harvard, everything combined to teach me that balance of
power was not the way to peace. The "war to end wars" only
sowed the seeds for future wars, the war "to make the world
safe for democracy" helped bring on totalitarianism. This new
war to destroy totalitarianism would only fasten on our country the very militarism that I feared while laying the ground-
work for future conflict.

My final decision was made on fairly clear grounds. I felt
that only good means could bring about good ends. I felt that
war would do more harm than good; for I felt that the loss of
individual lives and the injury to countless other individuals
would be a greater evil than the negative value of defeating
Hitler through force of arms. I believed that true love of
democracy and nonviolent resistance could more effectively
preserve democracy than could war.

This decision seemed to me in consonance with the ideals
of Judaism, as I understood them. The very existence of the
Jews down through the centuries as a people without state or
military protection in the midst of latently or actively hostile
peoples was in itself a testimony to the way of peace, and I
was proud of the fact that my last name means "man of
peace." I was aware of the special problems entailed in being
that *rara avis*—a Jewish C.O. When I visited my home before
I made my final decision, the rabbi of our Temple said to me,
"A Jew has no business being a conscientious objector," a
statement which I later learned was only a personal prejudice
since the Central Conference of American Rabbis recognized

Jewish C.O.'s. Again and again in the years that followed, I
was asked the question: "How can a Jew be a pacifist in the
face of the Nazi persecution of the Jews?" I knew of this persecution (though not of the extermination of millions), and I
identified myself as a Jew on official forms, if for no other
reason, because I wanted to identify myself with those perse-
cuted. But I did not think that our waging war against Germany could in any way reduce the Nazi terrorizing of the
Jews.

I had one highly vivid dream during this period which I
have always believed to be of significance. It occurred a short
while before Pearl Harbor. I dreamt that I was a soldier on the
Philippine Islands fighting the Filipinos. The fighting was going on over a sort of fence at very close range. I went out and
came back in. Then I announced to the lieutenant that I was
a conscientious objector and would not fight. Nevertheless,
he sent me out to the front line (actually only a very small
space in all). I saw a Filipino, raised my gun and took aim, but
a strong feeling against killing nim came over me, and I could
not shoot him. Then I heard the bullets whistling by me and
knew that in another second I myself would be killed. A
terribly real fear of death took possession of me, a fear much
stronger than any I have ever consciously experienced. Just
then I heard a bell ringing, and suddenly courage and the
strength of my beliefs returned to me. I was much moved and
said over to myself the famous passage from John Donne's
nineteenth Meditation, "No man is an island, entire of himself,
but we are a part of the mainland. Any man's death dimin-
isheth me. Therefore, never send to find for whom the bell
tolls. It tolls for thee." The fighting abruptly stopped, and we
went over and shook hands with the Filipinos, after which
some girl told me to go out to Harvard Square to buy food
for a celebration!

During this period I faced one by one the objections to
pacifism that I encountered. One of these was the theory of

choosing the "lesser evil"—war—as opposed to the greater evil
—the conquest of the world by the Nazis. This theory was in-
validated for me by my belief that war would not prevent but
exacerbate the very evils it was supposed to get rid of since it
used militarism, indoctrination, violence, and conquest as the
means to its professed ends. More of a challenge to me was
the best known antipacifist book of the period, Reinhold Niebuhr's *Moral Man and Immoral Society*. Along with the tendency of individual men to absolutize their own selves at the
expense of others, Niebuhr saw the very economic and political institutions of society as making impossible that sort of
peaceful international cooperation and nonviolent direct action that the pacifist hoped for. I did not share Niebuhr's
somewhat dark view of human nature, and I did not agree that
all political and economic institutions necessarily led to war
since I believed in the possibilities both of democracy and of
socialism. I do not remember how I dealt with the time-worn
hypothetical case in which someone attacked me or my family
personally. I know I was ready to sacrifice personally, but I
know too that the case added up to no real argument not only
because it was hypothetical but also because it was in no sense
analogous to the decision of a country as to whether to make
war or of an individual as to whether to take part in it. To
the accusation that I was allowing somebody else to defend
me, I replied that I was willing, indeed anxious, that my country should organize itself for nonviolent resistance to the Nazis
and was not looking to others to do what I would feel com-
pelled to do if they did not.

One of the most remarkable confrontations I had on this
subject was with the father of a sometime girl friend from my
home community. I knew he held me in the highest respect
and would, indeed, have welcomed me as a son-in-law. He
asked to talk with me and listened with real attentiveness to
what I said. But then he asked me if I did not feel that it was
selfish to hold a view that the majority did not hold. Although

I responded warmly to our conversation and to his parting gift of a copy of Ecclesiastes, I could not accept that definition of "selfishness." When I told the man at the Cambridge employment office that I was a C.O., the official asked me, "How long have you held that theory?" "It's not a theory," I replied archly, "it is a conviction." Yet I spun out theories so far that at one point I even tried to work out a system of mathematical probabilities for deciding whether or not to join the American Field Service and do ambulance work in Africa! Would the help I gave the wounded soldiers really be greater, I asked, than my contribution to the war through healing these soldiers so they might return to battle?

Finally, my alternatives seemed to boil down to the unhappy choice between doing nothing—that is, spending (as it turned out) three and a half years in Civilian Public Service camps for conscientious objectors largely performing "made work," work manufactured to keep the workers busy—and doing what seemed harmful in itself and in its results—taking part in a war that was likely to produce new conflicts and new wars. The former course seemed more realistic but not a particularly creative one at a time when I, like so many others, burned with a desire to do something positive for peace and social reform. I pictured myself at times as a man tied to a chair, to whom others said, "We will untie you from the chair if you will agree to kill your fellow man. Otherwise you must remain tied to this chair." I cannot dignify this with the appellation of a tragic choice, but it was certainly an anguished one for the year and a half before my final decision to become a conscientious objector—a choice that was of the greatest importance for my future life and thought.

[Chapter 3]

From Mysticism to Basic Trust

To make a decision means to accept the consequences, and in my case this meant, both literally and figuratively, changing the ground on which I stood. During the years in Civilian Public Service I encountered new people and situations that tried my pacifism and forced me to seek deeper roots. Out under the bright stars and clear skies of the Sierra Nevadas, where during the day I fought forest fires and for the rest of the time walked behind a tractor throwing rocks off the road with a shovel, I began to realize that I had not yet come to terms with the meaning of life for myself. Trying to give my life to the service of others before I had found either meaning or wholeness in my own life now seemed to me an evasion. Conflicts with my fellow campers and with the foremen plus my own reading and thinking made me move away from my ideas of socialism organized from the top to greater concern with cooperatives and community living in the daily relations between people. At the time I rejected Marxian socialism because it concentrated on class conflict rather than on the change in individuals from egocentricity to cooperation, which I now saw as the real key to socialism. I also came to the

strong conviction that I would have to change my own character before I could change others and became deeply concerned with becoming whole and integrated. I had to go forty
years through the wilderness, I felt, in order that I myself
might become a creative person and not just a channel for the
creativity of others.

In January 1944 I was selected as a member of a detached
service unit of thirty conscientious objectors in a state institution for the feeble-minded near Philadelphia. During my first
month at the institution I underwent a crisis of my ego which
centered on the importance of living my new beliefs. In Cali-
fornia I had already started brief periods of meditation, and
it was this which came to my aid now. I was particularly
stimulated to meditation by the writings of Gerald Heard, a
modern mystic who is mainly concerned with the "evolution
of consciousness" from ordinary fissured consciousness to
superconsciousness, an integral combination of the conscious
and unconscious which he identifies with the path of perfection of the saints. Through Heard and through our "Gemeinde" (a group of four C.O.'s in the unit who read and meditated together) I was introduced to the mystical and devotional literature of Christianity, Hinduism, and Buddhism and
to religiously oriented psychologists such as Jung and William
Sheldon.

I began regular periods of meditation of an hour at a time,
two or three times a day. These periods of meditation seemed
to give me the peace and strength I needed to meet the problems with which I was constantly confronted in my duties in
the wards. They also led me to a radical withdrawal from
even the most ordinary of activities. I discontinued the labor
education work that I had been doing in Philadelphia on my
days off, feeling that I must first go through the period of
"purgation" before I could be of help to others. I gave up
eating meat and in general restricted my diet as much as pos-

sible. I turned away entirely from any interest in girls and decided that my commitment to the life of the spirit necessitated a life of celibacy in some type of free monastic community. In my group and individual meditations, feelings of quiet and peace were gradually succeeded by unusual states of prayer and exaltation. At times my consciousness seemed to rise, enabling me to concentrate for hours at a time in wordless devotion. In three-day retreats held once every three months with C.O.'s from other units, I deepened the fellowship of silence, prayer, meditation, and devotional reading. But I cut myself off almost altogether from the regular life of my own unit. I would never play cards, dance, or even, if I could help it, converse with the other members. Instead, I tried to feel the presence of God at every moment by means of silence, inner concentration, and the constant repetition of phrases from Brother Lawrence or Hindu song-words (*mantrams*).

When I wrote my statement for the draft board, the only religion I was able to claim was the conviction that the meaning of my life lay in doing good for others and that I was not willing, therefore, to take part in a war that meant denying this purpose. Now my belief that good ends could only be reached through good means deepened from a political to a religious perspective in which the present was no longer seen as the means to the future but as the very reality out of which meaningful human existence and peaceful human relations were to be built. Pacifism for me became absolute and a way of life.

Gandhi remained important here, but even more important was the nineteenth century Hindu saint, or "avatar," Sri Ramakrishna, who worshipped the divine Mother in the prostitute, or his follower Brahmananda, whose mystic devotion tamed the savage jungle tiger. The Sermon on the Mount became more than a Christian social gospel: it was the narrow way of the mystic, and Jesus was the man who had realized union with the divine. The Bhagavad Gita was a poem of war, but from it I extracted *ahimsa*, or noninjury, plus the concern with stages of spiritual development, and the *apûrva*, or subtle causes and effects, which fortified my conviction that only good produces good. The world became one vast spiritual reality in which the refusal of the Buddha to receive insults, the flowing with the Tao of Lao-tzu, the compassion of Christ, the selfless love and humility of Saint Francis were so many wonderful exemplifications of an all-encompassing spiritual unity beside which the immediate goals of my social action days faded into obscurity. Gandhi seemed less meaningful than Sri Ramakrishna because the latter stood at the divine source from which Gandhi was further removed. Nehru seemed less meaningful than Saint Francis praying to be an instrument of God's peace.

> O Lord, make me an instrument of Thy peace.
> Where there is hatred, let me sow love
> Where there is injury, pardon
> Where there is doubt, faith
> Where there is despair, hope
> Where there is darkness, light
> Where there is sadness, joy.
>
> O Divine Master
> Grant not so much that I seek
> To be consoled, as to console
> To be understood, as to understand
> To be loved, as to love.
> For it is in giving that we receive,
> It is in pardoning that we are pardoned,
> It is in dying that we are born to Eternal Life.

Along with the image of Saint Francis came the image of the Quaker saint James Naylor, an early English Friend of the time of George Fox who was imprisoned and cruelly beaten for his religious views and who, according to legend, left us this testimoney as he lay dying on a roadside:

> There is a spirit which I feel that delights to do no evil, nor to revenge any wrong, but delights to endure all things, in hope to enjoy its own in the end. Its hope is to outlive all wrath and contention, and to weary out all exaltation and cruelty, or whatever is of a nature contrary to itself. It sees to the end of all temptations. As it bears no evil in itself, so it conceives none in thoughts to any other. If it be betrayed, it bears it, for its ground and spring is the mercies and forgiveness of God. Its crown is meekness, its life is everlasting love unfeigned; it takes its kingdom with entreaty and not with contention, and keeps it by lowliness of mind. In God alone it can rejoice, though none else regard it, or can own its life. It's conceived in sorrow, and brought forth without any to pity it, nor doth it murmur at grief and oppression. It never rejoiceth but through sufferings: for with the world's joy it is murdered. I found it alone, being forsaken. I have fellowship therein with them who lived in dens and desolate places in the earth, who through death obtained this resurrection and eternal holy life.

I found fellowship with Naylor and with Kenneth Boulding, the economist poet, whose twenty-six *Naylor Sonnets* [1] I committed to memory and meditated on during long hours as a night attendant. One of these sonnets fixed itself on my spirit as no mere memorizing could do when, after a long night's imprisonment in a foul-smelling ward for imbeciles, I emerged one morning at six to see the "eastern fire" rise in golden glory and "cleanse the foul night away."

> My Lord, Thou art in every breath I take,
> And every bite and sup taste firm of Thee.
> With buoyant mercy Thou enfoldest me,
> And holdest up my foot each step I make.
> Thy touch is all around me when I wake,

[1] Fellowship Publications, Nyack, N.Y.

Thy sound I hear, and by Thy light I see
The world is fresh with Thy divinity
And all Thy creatures flourish for Thy sake.
For I have looked upon a little child
And seen Forgiveness, and have seen the day
With eastern fire cleanse the foul night away;
So cleanest Thou this House I have defiled.
And if I should be merciful, I know
It is Thy mercy, Lord, in overflow.

For years each morning when I awoke this sonnet was with
me, and each evening when I went to sleep Saint Francis came
to me with his prayer. Whatever of depression and fear, filth
and horror has remained in my memory from my time with
the feeble-minded, I have taken with me from there something
infinitely precious and ever present: these images of man that
have been my daily companions in all the years since then.
But even when these images first took hold of me, the "savior"
in Ramakrishna's parable, who looks over the garden wall and
returns to tell others about it, was more appealing to me than
the "saint" who goes down into the garden and leaves the world
behind. And in Dostoievsky's great portrait of the Russian
staretz, or holy man, Father Zossima, I found an image of active love that gave me the positive side to the conviction
gleaned from Nicolas Berdyaev's *Dostoevsky* that a compulsory good, imposed upon people in the name of the general
welfare, is not good. In Father Zossima pacifism and mysticism
fused into one way of life—the way of humble love:

> At some thoughts one stands perplexed, especially at the
> sight of men's sin, and wonders whether one should use force
> or humble love. Always decide to use humble love. If you
> resolve on that once for all, you may subdue the whole
> world. Loving humility is marvelously strong, the strongest
> of all things and there is nothing else like it.

Father Zossima's humble love is no mere idealism. It is based
on the responsibility of each for all, the recognition that the

man who stands before you might not have been a sinner had you guarded your own image or given him the physical and spiritual help he needed. And this responsibility in turn is based upon a loving relation to all creation—a mysticism of reciprocity and active love.

Brothers, have no fear of men's sin. Love a man even in his sin, for that is the semblance of Divine Love and is the highest love on earth. Love all God's creation, the whole and every grain of sand in it. Love every leaf, every ray of God's light. Love the animals, love the plants, love everything. If you love everything, you will perceive the divine mystery in things. Once you perceive it, you will begin to comprehend it better every day. And you will come at last to love the whole world with an all-embracing love. . . . My brother asked the birds to forgive him; that sounds senseless, but it is right; for all is like an ocean, all is flowing and blending; a touch in one place sets up movement at the other end of the earth.

As my experiences of mysticism deepened, spiritual growth became for me the self-evident meaning, path, and goal of life. It is not a path that I ever voluntarily left. I was broken out of it. The strenuous and intense, sometimes ecstatic and sometimes terrifying road that led me from mysticism to basic trust, I can only indicate here through a few milestones on the way —fragments of statements and letters that give some glimpses of the stages through which I passed.

In May of 1944 my world-view still retained the personal concern for sincerity and for love that had drawn me to mysticism:

"The only thing in any of us really lovable is the sincerity and integrity which at once searches for God and is God," I wrote. "It is this which gives the desire for unity and understanding with others, the loneliness, the reaching out. The vision of God as intense, awful Being and actuality makes the truth not an impersonal, inanimate scheme of purposeful existence, but rather the opposite—the essence of complete and understanding love. Thus the universe, far from being cold and detached, is part of us and is made up in essence of that in us which is most feeling and sensitive to the happiness and suffering of the world. We cannot allow our attention to our own development to cut us off from the sufferings of others. On the contrary, it must fill us full of an ever growing sympathy and love for the whole world.

"To be able to feel—to bear in oneself the sufferings of the world—without becoming either insensitive or heart-broken—one must have a religious basis in the knowledge of the creative love of God which—despite the evil, the insensitivity, the pride and greed, the brutelike and impersonal qualities of men —pervades and lies at the core of the universe."

At the age of twenty I had boasted that I would not become conservative when I was forty and believe in God. Yet at the age of twenty-four I became a believing, if rather eclectic, mystic without any intellectual conflict at all. Along with my wrestling and thinking, my experience in meditation gave me an immediate conviction of the self-validating, intense, and heightened reality of mystical consciousness. On the other hand, I now found that the moral values that I once held so unproblematically not only needed a religious base but were meaningful only to the extent that they were permeated with the life of the spirit. Gerald Heard was the turning point in my progress from socialist humanism to mysticism. His synthesis of the latest findings of modern science bridged the gap from the pseudoscientific mechanism of my college days to an appreciation of the mystical element that I now discerned in all religions. He also helped me to channel my intuitions of the need for inner spiritual development into a definite way of life. I came to the belief that each of us contains in himself a spark of timeless and spaceless Being which being itself infinite and eternal, unites us with the Infinite and Eternal and with each other; we all contain the same spark, indeed, and that "spark" contains us and contains all the universe.

Thus through Heard I reached the point which I then considered basic to all the great religions, namely, that we must deny our little egos or selves in favor of that Self, Reality, or Being which is alone real and of absolute value. The sort of mysticism that I tried to impose upon myself, as a result, was a very lonely and self-denying one. I would go around repeating Heard's statement, "One to me is name and fame, one to me is praise and blame," and would try in every way to mortify my ego in situations many of which were already very mortifying in themselves or in my relationship to them. The "Credo" that I wrote during this period for a three-day silent retreat has a strongly Heardian cast:

I believe that man stands at the peak of our space-time creation; that he encompasses within himself all the past of our universe and all of its unconscious and yet to be unfolded future. I believe that man's evolution from the physical to the psychophysical finds its fulfillment in the expansion of consciousness, i.e. in spiritual growth. I believe that the individualization of man's consciousness, by putting him out of touch with the subconscious and with the real Center of spiritual power, has resulted in an egocentric and self-destroying civilization. Thus I believe that the greater need of mankind is the reintegration of the conscious and subconscious through a new mutation of consciousness. I believe that this expansion of consciousness must follow the pattern of the great saints of all religions who transcended their own individualities in an ever increasing at-onement with God. I believe that such an evolution and complete transformation is possible because man is in essence not a physical, nor even a psycho-physical creature, but a spiritual being, possessing infinite power, knowledge and love. Thus I believe that man's goal of union with God is fulfilled through and is synonymous with the realization of his true Self.

I believe that the space-time universe that we see is but the reflection of the one, infinite, unchanging, and eternal Being, and that despite the illusion of multiplicity, the real self of each of us is actually the one real Self of the universe. We must die to our own individual selves and to our limited space-time view of existence before we can know God as the Self within the self and as transcendent Being, eternal, infinite, and One without second.

I was particularly troubled in the year that followed by my inability to decide on either a way of life or a mystical tradition that I could make fully my own. I often visited the Swami of the Ramakrishna-Vivekananda Society in Philadelphia, who was generous with his time but could not help me in the growing tension I felt between various pulls: toward active love, toward the search for the truth, toward meditation and spiritual exercise, and my desire for a way to express my emotions in worship. What troubled me most was the lack of a tradition or symbol to which I could wholly give myself. My attempts to meditate on Sri Ramakrishna, on Christ, and on the Buddha did not resolve my conflict.

It was during this period that I became acquainted with Hasidism and Jewish mysticism. Dr. Simon Greenberg, then Rabbi of the Har Zion Congregation in Philadelphia, often had me to dinner at his home where we discussed problems of religion and metaphysics. He lent me an early translation of Martin Buber's *The Legend of the Baal-Shem*, and it was in this book that I first felt that I had found a mystical tradition which expressed fully my own emotions. I was also greatly attracted by Buber's classic, *I and Thou*, which I read at the same period, and I made long excerpts from it which I shared with my Gemeinde friends. Yet I regarded both Hasidism and *I and Thou* as representing a mystical way by no means incompatible with the Vedanta and Zen Buddhism, in which I continued to interest myself. None of the books that Rabbi Greenberg gave me on Judaism succeeded in interesting me apart from those on Hasidism and the Kabbala.

My greatest desire at this period was to be in a position where I could devote all my energies to the life of the spirit, turning away from everything active to contemplation and recollection. As a step in this direction I enthusiastically supported the formation of a special Retreat side-camp in North Carolina to which those C.P.S. men who wished to join together in the search for God might transfer. This project was only set up with the greatest difficulty, and the transfers could only be arranged as new men entered the various detached service units. I was the first to transfer out of our unit and found myself the second member of the Retreat to show up.

The Retreat itself did not get underway for a couple of months and then with only four campers. One of these (a high church Episcopalian) had come to the Retreat with the express purpose of finding disciples to join him in a monastic life vow the following Easter. In order to keep him from walking out and going to prison as he threatened to do, we gave him almost a completely free hand in directing the Retreat. He imposed upon the group a Christocentric and highly ritualistic Christianity in place of the silent meditation which we all had in mind. All of the prayers were in the name of Christ and for the sake of Christians, as a result of which I found some of my childhood reactions against Christianity returning. I sorely missed the periods of silent meditation which had been so essential to me at the institute for the feeble-minded, and I was deeply disturbed by the increasing efforts of our self-appointed leader to convert me to the belief in Christ as "the Only-Begotten Son of God, through faith in whose crucifixion and resurrection we are saved." He said that it was only pride and self-will that kept me from believing, and I was too conflicted at that time to be altogether sure that he was wrong. He shouted at me, stamped his feet in rage, and tried to force upon me a "holy obedience" to him to which I had never agreed.

About a month before this situation reached the explosion

point I entered into correspondence again with my Harvard friend John Russell, who had been assigned by the British navy to Washington. I communicated to him my new beliefs, and he replied with that moderation and rationality which had been typical of him even at Harvard. In September 1945 I wrote him a letter about my mysticism and its implications for society. The style of this letter was much less rarified than that of my "Credo"—enough so, at any rate, that he could find some connection between the writer and the socialist he had known at Harvard:

"I would call myself a short-term pessimist, but a long-term optimist. I am pessimistic, compared to most people, as to the possibility of constructing even a half-decent world with the questionable means which you propose—'a blend of reason and fear, respect and enlightened self-interest,' 'new taboos,' and changes in the schools.

"On the other hand I am a long-term optimist in believing, unlike you, that such intangible means as goodwill, love, self-lessness, will be of real value to society and to Good and happiness.

"I believe that there is an inner core of self which has sufficient perspective and sufficient sincerity that if given a chance it will eventually be a guide in distinguishing between better and worse in terms of what is truest to one's self. My belief in this inner perspective, my trust that at some basic point *all* people are capable of being sincere with themselves, and in that sense good, arises out of my own experience and intuition. If our truest self is in some way receptive to a larger spirit of reality, it may be that by concentration on that self, through prayer, meditation, and purity of heart, we may unscreen ourselves to the radiations of that Reality, which may in turn change our character, conduct, and consciousness, and truly lift us up.

"I cannot worship our civilization as such. Most of it only exists in the heads of scholars and aesthetes. The rest is carried largely as prejudice, custom, and blind habit. The good in it in order to become manifest must be created ever afresh, usually in opposition to the tenets of the civilization itself. The whole thing bogs down and becomes spiritless with the least excuse. Anyway I believe man called to a higher goal than this 'crate' which boxes in so much human misery, suffering, and futility. Like Ivan Karamazov, I would turn my ticket in if that were the best God could offer us. An intangible act of love seems to me more important than a dozen laws on the statute books, variously misapplied and distorted or ignored. Even a socialist state still pervaded by enlightened self-interest would probably see as much corruption, undoubtedly as much selfishness, as much grasping for power and exploitation of one by another, as the capitalist state.

"No matter how bad a person may seem or be, he is still affected by the outgoing love of another person, if only it be through the calming and stilling of his own discordant and divided energies and desires. The inner state of mind and feeling communicates itself so completely as to wholly determine the person's reaction to you, even though he does not know why he so reacts. I believe with the mystics that the truly spiritual man who is pure in heart does have a great power to affect and change the lives of others for good."

A series of events which I shall touch on in the next chapter led me to shed my world-view and my techniques for achieving mystical consciousness in favor of a simpler trust. In a letter of November 28, 1945, to the men who were coming down to join the Retreat camp, I wrote for the first time about this basic trust.

> I have felt with ever greater force the hand of God working through me and moulding me, not according to the pattern of my conscious mind, but rather according to the hidden plan of unfolding of my deep inner self. Thus it has been necessary for me to go through humanism, Marxism, Christian, Buddhist, and Hindu mysticism to realize and iden-

tify my inner spirit as that of the Hasidim—the Jewish mystics of Eastern Europe of two centuries ago—perhaps even as the spirit of my own Hasidic grandfather.

The ascendancy of my own conscious mind—even in directing my path of spiritual growth—has had to give way to a very real faith in the guidance of God in each moment, a desire that He should work His will through me, and a calm certainty that my sole need and duty is to live each moment as fully, relaxedly, and sensitively as possible. I came down to this Retreat to find the peace and free time in which to grow spiritually in fellowship with other seekers. I have found conflict rather than peace, conscious problems rather than higher mystical states. Yet I have grown through conflict and the confusion and pain which it caused, and I have found in my problems a surer guide to self-realization than my yoga exercises [breath control] or my attempts to empty the mind and contemplate the limitless in meditation.

Not without considerable suffering, my conscious point of view which interpreted the whole world according to the Perennial Philosophy, popularized by Huxley, gave way to the realization that I know nothing except that God will guide me and work through me if I let Him. I have come to see that one can and must find God as well in the world as in the depths of one's soul; that the body and senses must become a throne of the spirit rather than a neglected and forgotten partner. I have found that I have a good deal of what Rilke calls "unlived life" "of which one may die."

I have had deeply impressed upon me the truth of what Buber has said in the section on "The Life of the Hasidim" in *The Legends of the Baal-Shem:*

"This liberation does not happen through formulas of exorcism, nor through any kind of prescribed and peculiar action; such things would all grow from the foundation of otherness. 'With his every action a man can work at the figure of the Glory of God, so that it may step from its hidden place.' It is not the nature of the action which gives it its character, only its consecration."

My readings of the saints, my concern with the latest findings of modern physics and psychology, my breathing exercises, my Hindu mantrams and set meditations, my conscious intellectual structure of mysticism and metaphysical cosmology—all these things arose from a "foundation of otherness," and through successive crises have been discarded. When I left Philadelphia to come down to this Retreat, I was quite certain that I was going to lead the life of a celibate monk, either in a Vedantist monastery or in a semimonastic community of seekers. All that has been revised radically in the last few weeks, so that I now know that I shall live a life of service in the world and shall have a family—both central parts of the Hasidic tradition. However, the service I shall give will be what I call "integral social action"—remaining open to the will of God at each moment and sensitive to the needs of those around one; rather than the formal social action—cooperatives, socialism, labor unions—to which I gave my time and for which I prepared myself in college.

I believe that the love of God and my fellow man which I feel growing in my heart, the faith in God's guidance in the moment, and the deep inner peace and joy which that faith engenders will not leave me permanently, even when I go back into the world.

In contrast to so much of my spiritual growth which had linked one intellectual superstructure to another, I did not come to the idea of basic trust intellectually. I came to it or it came to me at a time when I found that all will, all power of self-determination had been taken from me and I was surrounded by what seemed an infinite blackness. In that situation which undermined the very ground of what I took to be my "I," I was sustained—not without some injury, not without crumblings inside, but nonetheless sustained. All I could do, but also all I needed to do, was to walk one step at a time and to discover what was asked of me moment by moment.

This basic trust came to me not in spite of but because of the destruction of all that had so carefully been built up. It was a shattering experience to be forced to recognize that what

I had taken to be the whole of reality was really a world-view in my mind—shared with some other people, to be sure, but lacking a real encounter with otherness. Yet the fact that my self was not destroyed along with what seemed to be its very foundation and security revealed to me the reality and meaning of basic trust. I know since then that we are given back to ourselves moment by moment, that we are given a ground. I have not adopted basic trust as a theological postulate or a religious discipline. I too can say with the Psalmist, "Though I walk through the valley of the shadow of death, I shall fear no evil, for You are with me." Yet I cannot know whether I would continue to trust if I were thrown into the subhuman existence of a concentration camp and finally exterminated like an insect.

I would not have reached this basic trust if I had not gone through the mystical, but also I would not have reached it had I simply remained in the mystical. That is what gave me an unusual affinity with Martin Buber. Later I discovered that many of the theologians who had taken over Buber's "I-Thou" philosophy could not really understand it because they were so resolutely antimystical. They did not understand the residue of immediacy and presentness that remains after you remove the metaphysical structure which claims that the mystic becomes one with the All or is so already.

No sure ground under his feet, contemporary man seeks for touchstones of reality around which to focus his experience, structure his values, guide his life. If he is open to his full potentiality, he finds not one but several touchstones. At times the iron filings of his life are pulled in different directions by magnets each of which claims to be *the* touchstone of reality. One of the most important double pulls experienced by the open man is that between the exploration of "inner space" through mystic meditation or psychedelics and the call to make real the space *between* man and man in the life of dialogue. This is not a question of "inner" verus "outer" since the interhuman, when it is genuine, demands that the inwardness and uniqueness of each partner be brought into the meeting. But it is a basic decision as to priorities. Is "all real living" higher, or expanded, consciousness or is it "meeting"? This double pull is one that I have experienced in my own life. The mystic inwardness that I have known I now wish only to bring into the full reality of the present—to make present in my response. I can no longer make it an end in itself.

I have sometimes been asked whether I would call basic trust a touchstone of reality and in particular whether I would speak of it as my own latest touchstone. All I can say is that this trust has lasted and I suspect will last—not as an intellectual position but as an attitude. But I do not see it as negating any of my earlier touchstones. On the contrary, basic trust has to do with the very meaning of touchstones. For touchstones of reality imply that we do not have to be "hung up" on the either-or of objective, universal meaning or a meaning that is merely subjective and cultural. To say that we can have some contact with reality without having to make the claim that it is *the* reality, to say that we can have touchstones of reality and even share them—that takes a certain trust along the way. If I have a witness to make, it is that the way opens for each person as it does. It is not a prescription. What I can point to in my own life—what we all can point to—is that from time to time we are given a ground on which to stand so that we can go forth to meet the next moment. Perhaps we do not need more than that. Touchstones of reality are not universal ideals shining above history and above our own lives. They are existential realities that remain meaningful only insofar as they are shared, witnessed for, and made living again in the present.

[Chapter 4]

The Shattering of Security

When I was an undergraduate at Harvard, Freud was a part of the intellectual atmosphere, but only in the most popular and general way. The course in psychology that I audited was largely behavioristic, suggesting that the consciousness itself was no more perhaps than an epiphenomenon of the basic physical reality. The only book of Freud's that I read was his study of Leonardo da Vinci. When my friends warned me that if I kept myself working under such great pressure I might have a nervous breakdown, I imagined this to be literally a disorder of the nerves without any connection with the emotional life of the person experiencing it.

Once during my year and a half at the institute for the feeble-minded I took up the invitation of a kind Quaker woman and stayed for a short period at her house. She passed on to me a suggestion of the psychologist Fritz Kunkel for a simple, "direct" way of releasing anger—to address a chair as my Aunt Lucy and tell it what I thought of it! When I found myself under increasing tension and with a persistent pain in the back of the neck, I tried to take my problems to the Swami of the Ramakrishna Order in Philadelphia. But this kind and gentle man did not want me to trouble his spirituality with the bad vibrations which I brought with me from a world that he had excluded. When I described what seemed to me to be something approaching "samadhi," or "superconsciousness," he said that the blood must have gone to my head!

It was in the spring of 1944 that I read for the first time Erich Fromm who has had a lasting influence on my thought even when I have found myself increasingly critical of him. Fromm's *Escape from Freedom* made such an impression on me that I quoted a central passage from it a year and a half later:

> Only if the different spheres of life have reached a fundamental integration is spontaneous activity possible. . . . In the spontaneous realization of the self, man unites himself anew with the world—with man, nature, and his self. Love is the foremost component of such spontaneity—love as the union of the individual with others on the basis of the preservation of the individual self. Work is the other component—work is creation in which man becomes one with nature in the act of creation. In all spontaneous activity the individual embraces the world. Ours is only that to which we are genuinely related by our creative activity, be it person or inanimate object.[1]

After Fromm's phrase "the preservation of the individual self" I added in parentheses, "which I take to mean individual integrity." The term "spontaneity" I undoubtedly understood at this point in terms of the "Modern Gnostic" liberation from the shackles of consciousness and inhibitions. But Fromm's sentence about the fundamental integration of the different spheres of life I transposed from the context of relationships to other people and to work to the inner world of the "real Self" about whose integration, or "individuation," I was concerned. This latter context I had taken over from Jung, whose

[1] From a "diagram-letter" of November, 1945, from which I shall quote at length below.

writings exercised as profound an influence on my thinking at that time as the various mystical texts that I read.

When the remarkable English Quaker Irené Pickard came to visit our unit of C.O.s at the "school" for the feeble-minded, she introduced me to T. S. Eliot's *Four Quartets* and to the writings and thought of C. G. Jung. Following her advice I began writing my dreams down every morning. I found that I not only remembered my dreams as I could not have before, but dreamed in a more and more Jungian manner, replete with "archetypes," or universal images, of the "collective unconscious" accompanied by great intensity of affect. The emptier my waking life in the wards of imbeciles or in the special diet kitchen, the richer and more charged my dreams: blue flowers and golden weddings, levitations and figures of the Great Mother, even at one point the sobbing of a nine-year-old child, whom I knew to be the child that had always been there deep within me. When I became concerned with occult happenings and extrasensory perception, I speculated as to whether they were not "really" events within the unconscious, as Jung would for the most part see them, instead of objective external happenings.

What has remained in me of the influence of Jung, even after I became all too alienated from him, is his emphasis upon dreams as genuine symbols of an ineffable reality that cannot be expressed in any other way, rather than merely as disguised signs of external reality, à la Freud. Also important to me is his concept of the "shadow"—that which disturbs us in others because they manifest openly what we have repressed and allowed to turn malignant in ourselves. Along with this there has remained the belief in the reality of an "archetypal" dimension of intensity that enters into our dreams and at times into our waking life. Certainly it was Jung who encouraged me in the contrast between my "small, petty, false outer self" and my "great, true, heroic inner self."

Except for the writing of the dreams and an occasional

encounter with an actual Jungian therapist, my Jungianism remained entirely theoretical. But Jung's theories of individuation and of symbols were an important part of my world-view. These "touchstones" were threatened when I came into active contact and conflict with the quasi-Freudian psychology that underlay a group psychodrama which eventually destroyed my world-view altogether. In an attempted novel, which I wrote soon after these events, I pictured this conflict between "touchstones" as an issue between Freud and Jung:

> One of the ideas which I picked up, in particular from Caroline, was that of the necessity of symbolic conflicts between people to work out their problems. When I arrived, Rachel told me of her symbolic fight with Caroline the night before in which Caroline stood for her father. Now the line between symbolic and actual fights became harder to draw. Caroline seemed to feel that she had to have conflicts with each member of the house quite apart from what they might symbolize of her own past. But she did not make clear the form these conflicts were to take.
>
> "People are real in themselves as well as being symbols of the past," she announced the evening of the following day.
>
> "That's encouraging," I observed. "It makes things so much more homey." Caroline did not fail to notice my dry humor.
>
> "Don't you believe in the reality of symbols even now?" she asked.
>
> "Of course, I do," I replied. "But I may not agree with you as to what they symbolize. I have often suspected that you think of symbols as Freud did—specific signs of occurrences of the past. I am inclined to agree with Jung. To me symbols refer to no specific objects, but rather indicate general emotions or states of being which can never be expressed directly."
>
> "Don't you think your childhood had any effect on what has been happening to you this week?"
>
> "A very great effect. But the fears I had when I was a child were no more specific than the fears I have now. If a person symbolizes something to me, he symbolizes something

that actually exists now at this moment. If I say that he is a symbol of some person I knew in the past, it's only because that person symbolized for me the same sort of thing as he does. The person in the past was a symbol too. He also stood for a complex of intangible feelings and perspectives. Those feelings remain inside me and are called up by this other person who resembles him. But it's the present that is important now and not the past."

On August 25, 1945, the United States exploded the atomic bomb over Hiroshima and Nagasaki, bringing the Second World War to an end and ushering in, in the most ominous way conceivable, the new atomic age of mankind. The prospect of eventual release from Civilian Public Service camps in six months or so, instead of relieving my tension and inner restlessness only heightened it. To escape from it and from the ever more oppressive conflict with my would-be converter, I took such opportunities as I could find to immerse myself in the life of a group to which I had become close in Chapel Hill—a number of artistically creative young people living together in a large house and promoting a type of group "psychodrama" under the leadership of the oldest among them—the Caroline of the excerpt from my uncompleted novel. This "Creative House," as we called it, anticipated by a quarter of a century what is beginning to happen everywhere today as people enter into "basic encounter" groups. Each member of the group worked out his problems in terms of the others. All the members of the house seemed engaged in constant self-analysis (mostly Freudian) and analysis of each other. Yet the really important things that happened seemed to occur of themselves as a part of a group dance in which each knew instinctively what part to take and, without cues of any sort, all moved simultaneously in consort with one another. The reality of these "synchronistic" happenings I cannot even now deny, such as the time after four hours' sleep when I woke up and re-entered the "dance" at exactly the moment when Caroline returned from an attempted suicide. Looking back I see this group as a manifestation of what I call "the Modern Gnostic," a daemonic temptation to reach for instant self-realization that Martin Buber aptly depicts as "the lust for overrunning reality," where everything becomes possibility, but actuality itself is crippled.

These friends in Chapel Hill were all involved in The Carolina Playmakers of the University of North Carolina. Caroline, the leader of the psychodrama, was a twenty-six-year-old young woman of unusual force. After her mother came to visit, she said to us, "I murdered my mother. But it was necessary. She was dead anyway." She also committed other symbolic murders and suicides—leaping out at people with a dagger, jumping from a second-story window of the house, walking in front of cars at night. When she encouraged her husband, a Harvard friend of mine, to try "free association" with me, a great deal more came out than either of us anticipated. I became aware that I had been suppressing my emotions to a dangerous degree and that what I took to be the saintly life was leading to ever greater hostility in relation to other people. This was the opening event in a whole series of connecting happenings that shifted my focus from my solitary mysticism to the "group dance."

Taking part in the interaction of this group when and as much as I could, I experienced my own atomic explosion. My Heard-Huxley world-view, which had seemed to encompass all of reality and answer all possible questions, was shattered by the experience of an upsurge of life-force and an encounter with evil with which it was powerless to cope. This breakthrough gave me back emotions with which I had lost touch, but it took away from me the ability to force myself any longer to regular practice of mystical meditation and to the constant effort to recollect the mind during the rest of my waking hours. The volcanic force of the events that broke me out of my mystical regimen can only be intimated here, not described.

Although I never accepted the psychology of "Caroline," the self-appointed leader of the "Creative House," the group psychodrama in which I found myself caught up during the fall of 1945 had a lasting effect on my view of the relationship between religion and psychology—through the undeniable effects of the events themselves. If the long-range effect was a confusion which I have not been able to sort out to this day, it is nonetheless to this period too that I owe the firm conviction that there is in each of us a real personality that exists in mutual relationship with what comes to meet it in the world. This conviction remained with me after the other aspects of my "psychology" fell away, but at that time I added it as one further element in a complex picture, rather than boldly remaking the picture as a whole. Thus in a thirteen-page single-space diagram-letter of November 1945, I wrote: "My greatest mistake was my failure to realize that half way between the inner Self—the Center which is God—and the outer small or false self is my real personality which has been emerging in the past month with ever greater force.

"The Small or False Self is a reflection of the true personality, made up of fragments of the real personality distorted by fear and greed. The God-man, in contrast, is an integral combination of thought, emotion, intuition, and physical (vital) harmony. He lives in the moment, has no separate or external purposes, receives direction from the Center. It is just as necessary for him to realize God in the world as in the depths of his self. Realizing God in oneself takes the form of the nondualistic identification of one's Self with the Self of the Universe, of God-immanent with God-transcendent. Realizing God in the world arrives at the same goal, but reaches that goal by way of the I-Thou relationship. When the relationship between I and Thou becomes great enough and barriers are dissolved, then I and Thou are forgotten in the relationship.

"Freud would describe these comments as attempts to resolve a clash between the superego—the sense of right and wrong which demands purity and complete dedication—and the id—the basic life instincts which demand expression of libido and sex energy through sex relationship and activity. Actually, it is a real synthesis of the two because in the harmonious relationship sex and external action both have their place. One achieves timelessness and spiritual consciousness only as the rhythms of one's life and actions become identical with the larger rhythms of the universe. It is not asceticism— the conscious putting aside of sex and pleasure—which constitutes nonattachment, but rather the removal of all those fears and greeds which produce tension and make real harmonious living in the moment impossible.

"At times one wrestles with the question as to whether to interpret the events of the breakthrough as insanity, steps toward integration, or true mystic revelation. For me they were all three. When a person with as much basic energy as I have nevertheless has a small and unintegrated self which blocks the free flow of that energy, tensions are built up which might produce insanity. However, the release of those tensions is also a necessary prelude to the integration of the self and the spontaneous activity which should follow that integration. Finally the integration is not an end in itself, but a means whereby one goes inward to the realization of God-within and outward to meet the Eternal Thou in others and in the world."

A dream that I had a few weeks before this "letter" expressed the conviction about returning to a dedicated life in the world in a much more immediate and vivid fashion. I dreamed that I was riding with several other of the fellows in the camp in the back of one of the Dodge trucks which the Park Service used to carry the men to and from work. We were standing up in the back of the truck, as we usually did, and looking out of the sides and over the top to the road ahead. We found ourselves going through the streets of a town, similar to some through which we occasionally passed on the way home. I looked back along the street and saw three men walking along together. They were all my age. The fellow in the middle was a very nice looking, clean-shaven boy. He was manacled to the hands of the other two fellows who carried pistols at their side. I felt great sympathy for the boy in the middle: it was a great shame that such a person should be in so unpleasant a position. Farther along the street the truck passed a group of little children, walking in rows of three abreast. As I looked closer at them, I discovered that they all had beards and that they were chained to each other in a type of chain gang. Deeply moved by their suffering, I fell on my knees and said the Lord's Prayer. Then an overwhelming conviction came to me that my way of life was to help relieve the suffering of mankind, even though such work might seem less exalted than the mystic path of contemplation.

The transition to this life in the world was at the same time something of a detour which set me back quite as much as it moved me forward. For all my use of Buber's terminology of meeting and the "I-Thou relationship," the predominant tendency of our Modern Gnostic psychodrama, into which I eventually fell myself, was one of "intuition" of what the other person did not know himself followed by attempts to break down his shell or "defenses" for the sake of his "liberation." All these breakthroughs, breakdowns, symbolic murders, and pseudo-liberations were real events, but as therapy, integration of the self, or mystical revelation, they were pure illusion—the "lust for overrunning reality." We even invented a gnostic theory of two classes of neurotics. "Neurotics B" could be helped by ordinary psychotherapy. "Neurotics A," in which we classified ourselves, had to follow the higher road of liberation and rebirth which no mere psychotherapist could undertake. We were perhaps suffering from what Jung has called "inflation" in which the personal unconscious is overrun by the archetypal images of the collective unconsicous and is puffed up by identifying itself with them. But we might also be viewed as a logical extension of Jung's own distinction between the ordinary therapy of Freud and Adler and the goal to which he could help bring the truly spiritual man—that individuation of the Self, i.e. integration of those conscious and unconscious components which rightly belong to the individual, that was his own touchstone of reality.

The mystical and the gnostic served as my touchstones of reality up till the shattering of my new life-stance with the dissolution of the knot of relationships that formed the "Creative House" and its sequel in Washington, Philadelphia, and New York. This dissolution was inevitable once the hostilities among its members came out into the open. Only later could I recognize the danger common to my Jungianism, my relationship to mysticism, and the group dance. This was the tendency, particularly strong in the whole gnostic psychodrama, to see other persons as functions of one's own becoming— one's spiritual perfection, one's self-realization, or one's individuation. The whole experience of the "group dance" had its dark face of evil and its radiant face of a breakthrough to greater emotional freedom. In retrospect these two faces so commingle as to foreshadow the Dialogue with the Absurd which I arrived at many years later.

[Chapter 5]

The Way Back into the World

I carried with me back into the world a deep confusion as one of my "touchstones of reality" broke up or gave way to another until finally socialism, pacifism, mysticism, and even the "group dance" had ceased to be life-ways for me. I was left with unanswerable questions as to what in all that I had experienced was real and what was self-deception, or even delusion, in which intensity and the release of repressed forces masqueraded as personal wholeness, and irresistible compulsion masqueraded as the "will of God." Intensity, I soon recognized, often seems to be wholeness because it helps us look away from those anxieties in ourselves that we are afraid to face. One of the persons in the "Creative House" about whom the pyschodrama centered and with whom I was most closely involved was Susan Lindsay, the daughter of the American poet Vachel Lindsay. This relationship was so intense and seemed so real to both of us that, despite the bitterest opposition on the part of Caroline, we got married. After only two months of marriage, Susan left me to marry my friend John Russell, who was a part of our new group.

Since my divorce from Susan I have had no word of either

her or John except the report by *Time* magazine of their marriage in 1946 and their divorce seven years later. Recently,
however, I came across a letter of Bertrand Russell's concerning them, a letter remarkably in the spirit of this autobiographical account:

[*I wrote the following soon after going to live in Richmond
in the house which I shared with my son and his family.*]

May 12th, 1950

I have been walking alone in the garden of Pembroke
Lodge, and it has produced a mood of almost unbearable
melancholy. The Government is doing great works, all bad.
Half the garden is incredibly lovely: a mass of azaleas and
bluebells and narcissus and blossoming may trees. This half
they have carefully fenced in with barbed wire (I crawled
through it), for fear the public should enjoy it. It was incredibly like Blake's Garden of Love, except that the "priests"
were bureaucrats.

I suffer also from entering into the lives of John and Susan.
They were born after 1914, and are therefore incapable of
happiness. Their three children are lovely: I love them and
they like me. But the parents live their separate lives, in separate prisons of nightmare and despair. Not on the surface;
on the surface they are happy. But beneath the surface John
lives in suspicious solitude, unable to believe that any one can
be trusted, and Susan is driven beyond endurance by sharp
stabs of sudden agony from contemplation of this dreadful
world. She finds relief in writing poetry, but he has no relief.
I see that their marriage will break up, and that neither will
ever find happiness or peace. At moments I can shut out this
terrifying intuitive knowledge, but I love them both too
much to keep on thinking about them on a level of mundane
common sense. If I had not the horrible Cassandra gift of
foreseeing tragedy, I could be happy here, on a surface level.
But as it is, I suffer. And what is wrong with them is wrong
with all the young throughout the world. My heart aches
for the lost generation—lost by the folly and greed of the

generation to which I belong. It is a heavy burden, but one must rise above it. Perhaps, by suffering to the limit, some word of comfort may be revealed.[1]

During the years since this sorry end of the "group dance," the confusion left by the collapse of what had seemed the surest of my touchstones became indelibly associated in my mind with a stanza from "The Chinese Nightingale," an otherwise light and joyful poem that Susan's father wrote not long before he committed suicide.

> Years upon years I but half remember,
> May and June and dead December,
> Dead December, then again June.
> Man is a torch, then ashes soon.
> Life is a loom weaving illusion.
> O who will end my dream's confusion?

My confidence that I could carry my freer, more spontaneous life back into the world proved unfounded. I found myself catapulted out of the shattered unity of the "Creative House" and of my marriage into a more terrible loneliness than I had ever known. In the fall of 1946 I wrote a short poem, "Trembling under Bright Lights," that came out of my immediate experience:

> Trembling under bright lights I stand
> And in abysmal silences reach over
> Strident voices to compendiums of
> Music, harmonies enclosing and releasing to terror,
> With the unsteady contraction of the epileptic's fist,
> Reflecting in its spasms
> The unbearable intensity
> Of visceral pain.
>
> On a ridge between two abysses I walk
> And through the darkness fearfully move on.
> Blind beyond utter blackness lies the way;

[1] *The Autobiography of Bertrand Russell, 1944-1967*, Volume III (London: George Allen and Unwin Ltd., 1969), p. 89.

On either side of me, grimaced with gray,
Lurk sharp and jangled horrors of the night
And the lost defeated loneness of the day.

Closing to comfortless darkness of death
Or opening to tearing, unmerciful pain,
I pray for enclosure and wait with each breath
Till the bright lights shall merge to effulgence again.

What I described many years later in *Problematic Rebel* as
"the problematic of modern man"—the bewildering intermix-
ture of personal freedom and psychological compulsion, inner
division, and the crisis of motives—I depicted more concretely
in "D. W.," an autobiographical vignette that I wrote in the
fall of 1946 after "Trembling under Bright Lights":

There are times in life when one is unbearably tense, with
all the nerves inside one vibrating tautly and angrily, threatening to burst into the noisy silences of sprung strings. If at
such times one would try to move slowly and absolutely
rhythmically or to play a piece on the piano with a wooden
and unvarying beat, the result might be surprising. The
rhythm, instead of releasing the tension into relaxation, might
shut it up and press it inward until one suddenly collapsed or
screamed. It is not really the rhythm that produces this result. We have all known people who move through life like
dancers, flowing with its waves and pulsing with its beats.
But with them the rhythm pulses from the center outward
toward the light, and in them the secret of life is revealed
as joy welling up from deep and ever-flowing springs. When,
on the other hand, the beat is from the outside in, pressing
in on unconscious fear and horror, the grim truth of life may
seem to be a vision of evil and blackness. St. John of the Cross
says, to be sure, that that vision of evil is merely the prelude
to the final beatific vision of good. Surely that is what he
meant by his "dark night of the soul." And according to
Huxley, the best means of facing in to the "dark night" is
silent meditation on life "sub specie aeternitatis."

But with winter coming on in the Smokies, it was a bit of

a problem to find a place to meditate where there was a
stove and where one was not too much distracted from things
Eternal by the uncompromising chill of the early November
morning. The important thing was to avoid distractions,
which was a little difficult since Paul, our local evangelist,
insisted on bringing his two dogs with him into the room
where we meditated. It took a while for the dogs to get the
idea—or perhaps they were waiting for the real thing. Once
one of them caught a bat and ate it right in the middle of
services. It was a very small dog and an even smaller bat.
But the incident aroused a little choking fear inside—something you could not quite understand, or perhaps did not
want to; something that went with the dark and the cold
outside. You might, of course, fall back on a comforting line
from *The Four Quartets:* "Below the boarhound and the boar
pursue their pattern as before but reconciled among the
stars." But you had to be among the stars to get the reconciliation. If the boarhound and the boar were rushing between
your legs while you were trying to get there, you were un-
likely to succeed.

And even if you did get rid of outside distractions and,
what is far more difficult, relaxed the body and concentrated
the mind, you would be likely to come up against that fear
which does not like rhythm. The more regular your breathing and the stiller your mind, the greater the fear. If you are
honest, you can put your finger on the trouble: it is nothing
other than the fear of losing in the great unvarying rhythm
of Eternity your individuality and all the little off-beats and
syncopations which make up our personal life. That is, indeed, the last great fear. Once you are over it—over it with
your whole being—there is no more fear, even as there is no
more "I." You get over it completely, however, only at the
very end of the path. Until then, your life is at best in and
out, back and forth across the boundary. If on the Eternal
side of the boundary the fear is gone, on the temporal it is
likely to seem even greater than it is; so that there is a danger
of an unconscious swing outward, away from the still and
centered life to the pleasing jangles of multiplicity. That

swing is a sort of inner fear or frustration, and it is something one cannot take care of by superimposing rhythm from without. In fact the more you press the rhythm inward on the fear, the more likely you are to reach the point where you collapse or scream.

There is actually no need to dramatize the matter, since what we have been discussing is only an exceptional instance of one of the most common of all sensations—that of frustration and restlessness before the passage of time. We are all familiar with the tedium of a monotonous and unpleasant job, and with the tyranny of the minutes which seem intent on slowing up their movements to the point where they have curdled the life inside us with the sickly fear that we shall never see the light beyond them. It is the sort of thing that grows on you. Each day you are just a little more defeated; each hour that scar grows just a little deeper till finally the very knowledge of having to work so many hours a day becomes unbearable. Your only hope then is not to admit into your mind those sickening moments of fear when time stands still or crushes you as in a vise.

Undoubtedly the best method of passing time is not to think about time, and one of the most natural methods of not thinking about time is to have something pleasant to think about. On this particular November morning, I was shovelling coal into a wheelbarrow in order to fill the bin in the Park Service office. The job itself was not monotonous, it even had some elements of interest, such as how to pick up with the big fork enough coal to fill the barrow and what to do about the fact that most of the coal left in the pile was crumbly and unusable. But there was also something not only pleasing but decidedly unusual to think about—a postcard from D. W., a person whom I had never met. What was really exciting about the post card was what it said. It informed me that not only was the letter which I had recently sent to my friend John [2] wonderful, but that I was wonderful and that he—D. W.—was very anxious to meet me.

[2] My letter of September 1945 to John Russell.

It was not unpleasant to find a disciple, and it was exciting to move from the slow progress of the life of purgation and discipline to the breathtaking release of the "prophet of the new world," the spiritual Uranium 235. When the pent-up energy burst into motion a few weeks later, it took the form of a series of concentric circles or group experiences. On the third circle outward we found ourselves in Washington. The transfer which we had made from individual tension to that of a group had provided only temporary relief, and the tension was now closing in on us with that spiritual blackness which inexorably follows going beyond one's spiritual means. We were on the whole a sorry mess of prophets, and I, in particular, was somewhat less than "wonderful." I called D. W. on the phone, and he volunteered to come over.

He was quite other than I had expected. It was hard to know whether he was a modern St. Francis, living a simple and God-centered life; or whether he had moved so far in the other direction—away from the rhythm and natural beat of life—that only his distance from the vanities of this world created the illusion of his being nearer the Eternal Verities.

He had come from a highly respectable family. He had gone to a distinguished Eastern prep school and the most traditional of Eastern colleges. After college he took a fling at a couple of law schools, but could not make the grade. Then he started on that gradual progress away from conformity and respectability that led him to become in the end more out of step with the ordinary life of the average man than any one I have met. When the war came, he became a pacifist and not only refused to go to war but refused to do any alternative service. He was sent to prison where he refused to obey the rules because of racial segregation. Then after about a year, he was sent to a psychiatric clinic. After a couple of weeks they told him he did not belong there and released him. He was then theoretically under the supervision of a parole board; but finding that still too much like conscription, he started going from one place to another and notifying his parole board after he moved. Eventually he even tore up his draft card and ceased to notify the parole board altogether. Then he took to picketing the White House to free his fellow C.O.'s who were still in prison.

"Do you ever run up against the law when you are picketing?" I asked.

"Oh sure," he said. "I have been picked up a couple of times."

"Didn't you get in trouble for not having a draft card?"

"Well, they might have given me five years," he said. "But the first time after they learned my name, they contacted some people who knew me and finally released me."

"What did they do the second time?" I inquired.

"The second time I did not even give them my name. After all, you can't force squirrels to give you their names, so why should I allow the government to coerce me into giving mine?"

There seemed to be no answer to make to that question, so I asked him what happened next.

"Some friends chanced to see me at the police station," he said, "and they got the police to let me off."

He worked as a bus boy for enough days to earn a little money for food. Then he stopped work and did whatever he pleased. He had no regular lodgings, but slept first at one friend's house and then another's.

But most amazing of all was his appearance. He was thin and boyish with a certain springing resiliency to him. You would never take him for over twenty-two or three, yet he was nearing thirty-five. His clear blue eyes shone with the simplicity of a child. Yet his forehead was wrinkled like that of an old man. His eyes spoke of spirituality and his forehead of suffering; but the flickering panes of muscles in his cheeks spoke of disintegration, tension, and deep unrest. He seemed shut in a prison of his own tensions, helpless to release himself, yet eager to find the word of life that would free to bloom the spiritual flower within. He had come to me for help, and I, equally helpless and deeply ashamed, could only look at him from behind cigarette smoke and utter a few wise sayings, on which he, in his own queer fashion, took notes.

He left my life as abruptly and unexpectedly as he had entered, and he seemed deeply arhythmic from first to last. Yet there is something about his eyes that speaks to me of realities which I have forgotten but would like to remember. And there is something about his wrinkled forehead which tells me of a suffering that I have known but find too painful to recall. And there is something about his youth which, despite the flickering panes in his cheeks, makes me ask whether I can simply dismiss him as neurotic and out of step with life. Perhaps there is that in him too beautiful and fine to tune itself to the unresolved dissonances of our life. I did not laugh long at his tragedy. He was a sensitive and beautiful instrument, and that instrument was broken—broken, I am afraid, beyond repair.

But what I want to know is whether this instrument broke because its player kept tightening the strings—always fighting life and never relaxing to it? Or did we, with our common sense and practical wisdom, harry and torment it until one day, perhaps unnoticed, it lost its harmony and jangled the air with the noisy silences of sprung strings?

Like my poem, "D. W." was a long way from the confident faith of the letter I wrote in November 1945 to my fellow Retreaters. But I did not lose sight of the way that had opened up for me, nor did I lose that basic trust that had come to me in the midst of so much upheaval and so much pain. The strongest conviction that I developed during my last weeks at camp was the belief that my way of life should be *in* the world but not *of* it. I returned to Martin Buber's *The Legend of the Baal-Shem* and his *I and Thou* during this period and found that they expressed in a way valid for my new experience the reasons for my rejection of solitary contemplation and for my turn to an activist mysticism in the world. I was convinced that I had found in Hasidism the right way of life for me, and I wished to give my life to reviving the Hasidic movement in America.

With this in mind I went to see Simon Greenberg who sent me to talk to Dr. Abraham Joshua Heschel, who had just come to the Jewish Theological Seminary in New York. Like Dr. Greenberg, Heschel emphasized the fact that Hasidism is a part of Judaism and cannot be understood apart from it. He felt that I could best help Hasidism by becoming either a rabbi or a writer and that in either case I should go through the Seminary (which trains rabbis for Conservative congregations and requires of its students a pledge concerning the observance of Jewish law). Since I did not know Hebrew, he said I would have to study it intensively for a couple of years. Dr. Greenberg offered me money from his temple fund to support me during my first six months of study, and I seriously considered doing as Heschel advised. But I was troubled by the fact that I had no feeling for the Jewish law and could not sincerely accept it nor did I feel, as Heschel assured me, that I could be confident of being able to accept the law even after two years of study. I decided, therefore, that it would be dishonest if I accepted Rabbi Greenberg's money. I was also troubled by the exclusivism that might result from my associating myself with the Seminary and becoming a rabbi. I felt very close to my Gentile friends and felt that if I were to find the truth it should be for them as well as for my Jewish friends. For these reasons I finally abandoned the idea, hoping instead to forge ahead to the place where I could find a truth that would be helpful to all seekers such as myself. Toward this end I entered graduate school.

From the beginning of my graduate work I found myself antagonistic toward research divorced from purpose and analytical thought divorced from emotion and intuition. The idea of scholarship which I held before myself was that of "integral thought"—an integral combination of thought, intuition, and emotion. For this reason I could not happily confine myself to philosophy abstracted from the concrete experience of literature and history, nor could I study literature as meaningful in itself without reference to its relation to life and to the search for meaning in life. Although I took my M.A. in English, the title of my M.A. thesis was "From Inquisitor to Saint: The Search for Faith in Ten Modern European Novels." The same motivation led me to do my doctoral work in an interdepartmental program that would allow me to combine a number of fields of interest—philosophy, religion, literature, history, and social thought—and that would give me the maximum possible freedom to integrate all my work around a central problem.

Before I "narrowed down" my fields at the University of Chicago to comparative history of religion, history of Judaism and Jewish mysticism, and European cultural history from the eighteenth to the twentieth centuries, including philosophy, I composed—not for the Committee on the History of Culture which gave me my fellowship but for the Committee on Social Thought about which I had heard earlier—an entirely impractical plan of study for the Ph.D. Rediscovering it after twenty years, I am amazed by the accuracy with which it charts the actual course which my thinking, teaching, and writing have followed from 1947 to the present. Still more striking to me is the fact that at that time, before I had immersed myself in Martin Buber's interpretations of biblical Judaism and found through them the way to biblical trust, I was already centrally concerned not with mysticism or theological faith, but with basic, or as I would now call it, existential trust:

> I believe that the focal need of our age is faith, defined not as a specific intellectual or religious belief but as a general attitude of trust—a feeling of being at home in the universe. The common man of today lives in growing fear and insecurity; for he does not really believe that the leaders of the nations will be able to find those means of unity which will stave off the destruction that each country is preparing for its neighbor. The leaders themselves are in the clutch of a fear and a distrust which are more powerful than all the

rational arguments which show the need of finding peaceful settlements of our international problems. Thus we are caught in a vicious circle. Unsatisfactory political, economic, and social conditions create insecurity which in turn prevents that cooperation and trust which might make possible the solution of those problems. The resulting spread of fear and destruction is forcing increasing numbers to turn from political and economic specifics to the question of their relationship to the universe itself. The universe has become to man like an oppressive and inhuman machine of fate. Those creative forces in man which might use the discoveries of science to build a new and joyous world are paralyzed by that fear which makes man feel helpless before the political and industrial juggernaut which he has himself built up.

I have decided, therefore, to make faith, defined as a basic trust in life, the central theme of my plan of study. . . . Faith thus defined ought to be studied not so much in terms of theology in its aspect of specific creed or philosophy in its aspect of verbal proofs of the existence of God as in terms of those original sources of religious faith—of trust in life— from which theology and metaphysics are usually derived— the Psalms, the Prophets, the life of Jesus, the "Way of Life" of Lao-tzu, the life and teachings of the Buddha, *The Gospel of Sri Ramakrishna*, the legends of the Baal-Shem, the Vedic Hymns and the Upanishads.

During the twenty years since in which I have studied and taught the comparative history of religion, openness and response to the unique basic attitude of each has been my principal guideline. Hinduism, early Buddhism, Zen, Taoism, biblical faith, Judaism, Hasidism, Christianity, the Quaker movement—these do not merge for me into a "perennial philosophy." Yet each has a truth which I cannot dismiss or ignore, a truth which I have made my own and which has become a part of my life-way.

There is nothing in all this incompatible with my central commitment as a Jew. There is no contemporary Jew, nor for that matter any contemporary man, who does not have to hear and respond to the word that comes to him from many cultures, life-styles, and religious ways. My approach to the issues that arise in contemporary religious thought, in the relation between religion and ethics, and in the social problems of our time is predominantly informed by my commitment to the biblical covenant and to Hasidism. Yet here too this in no way means an exclusion of other insights or a mere deduction from theological premises. My commitments themselves are of an existential, not a theological nature: they stem from the encounters and searchings of my life.

PART TWO

In
Dialogue with
the Religions

[Chapter 6]

Journey to the East

My "Journey to the East" has been a spiritual quest, like that of H. H. in Hermann Hesse's novel, and like H. H. I have lost my way repeatedly only to find it again. Did my mysticism confirm me through its glimpses of an aurora borealis of the spirit? Or did it unconfirm me through enticing gleams of a light that I could not remain open to and integrate into my life? In any case what it left me with was the conviction of having touched on a reality that I could neither set before my path as a guiding light nor resolutely dismiss as a will o' the wisp. When a member of our mystical "Gemeinde" who had joined a monastery of the Ramakrishna Order came after fifteen years to visit my Comparative Religion class at Sarah Lawrence College, he made no secret of his surprise that I taught Hinduism with such an open mind. But could he, who had once promised me that I would find my own "guru," recognize the way I was now taking as a spiritual path at all? Could even I claim that my Neo-Hasidism and my immersion in Martin Buber's thought amounted to a recognizable religious way or that my studies and teaching of comparative religion were more than a reminiscent dramatization of what had once been my total reality?

"Light on the Path" is the name of an occultist book which I still possess in my library. The touchstones of reality that I have brought back with me from my Journey to the East do offer me light on the path, or rather light on *my* path. For the only way I can now follow is my unique one which claims no universal sanction as a variant of the "perennial philosophy." If I am still "religious," it is not with a focus either on mystical enlightenment or on the rituals and creeds of any organized religion. The great religions, including the religions of the East, have continued to give me glimpses into the way of man at least as important as any that I have found in Western philosophy. But this is not because of a detached interest in philosophical anthropology, any more than it is because of an interest in religion as a spiritual sphere separate from the demands and realities of everyday life.

If I use my touchstones for the understanding of religion, I have used my dialogue with the religions in the first instance as a source for my touchstones. In this interplay the insights into the way of man that came to me during my "mystical" years of immersion in Hinduism, early Buddhism, Taoism, and Zen have continued to grow in the quarter of a century of study and teaching in comparative religions since that time. I prefer to label myself as a philosopher rather than as a scholar of religions, if a label be needed. But as a philosopher I have always claimed the right to draw the material for my philosophizing from whatever sphere seems suitable to the questions that concern me. Since these questions are always integrally related to the problematic wholeness of man, it is small wonder that I have continued to find in the scriptures of the great religions some of the sources of my insights.

In the chapters that follow I offer the reader not an objective, scholarly survey of the world's great religions, but the fruits of my own dialogue—and the roots as well in the form of the particular passages from the scriptures of these religions that I have meditated upon and made my own. My ethics and my theory of knowledge are rooted here as is my turning away from metaphysics and theology to an "ontology" of basic trust.

Nowhere is the approach of touchstones of reality more fruitful than in trying to understand religion. We do not comprehend religion if we imagine it to be a statement of creed or a feeling that rises within us or a theology or philosophy of religion that tells us about the nature and attributes of God. Religion has always been a way that man walks. In entering into dialogue with the religions, therefore, we are not looking for *the* truth, either in the sense of the Platonic truth—a metaphysical absolute—or in the sense of one religion being true and the rest false, or in the sense of a "perennial philosophy" in which we can say what is the "essence" of all religions and what is only the "accidental," cultural expression. Insofar as we can enter into dialogue with it, each religion will say something to us of its uniqueness and will say something to us about our life—our life as man but also as the particular men that we are. Religion helps man understand himself because religions are, in the first instance, touchstones of reality. But these touchstones of other men can only become touchstones for us in real dialogue in which we respond from where we are. We cannot *become* Mohammed or Lao-tzu or the Buddha or Jesus, but we can meet them and know them in that meeting. We cannot be an ancient Greek, but we can respond with "pity and terror" to the downfall of Oedipus or feel in the depths of our own lives Socrates' drinking the cup of hemlock.

What is common to all great religions is that each in its own way sees man as a problem to himself. Why is man a problem to himself? Because of the given of human existence. The awareness of self, of the passage of time, of change, in oneself, others, and the world, of the fact that one is mortal and will die, of the fact that one moves inexorably and irreversibly from youth to age, of possibility and the need for choice, of freedom and the checks on freedom by the limitation of our inner resources and the constraint of our natural and social environment, of one's dual existence in self-relationship and interpersonal relationship, in inner awareness and outer social role, of one's dual consciousness in waking and sleeping, in languor and intensity—all these in themselves make man's existence problematic for man. Through all of them there run discontinuities and confusions which force man to seek a reality amidst appearance, a stability amidst flux, an order amidst chaos, a meaning amidst paradoxes and incongruities. What is the self? What is time? What is reality? What is life and death? What is consciousness and what is the essence of the objective world? These questions have been an integral part of all human existence from the earliest times till today.

The Zen Buddhist asks, "When you are dead, and your body is cremated, and the ashes scattered, where are you?" "Then was not nonexistent nor existent," says the Hymn to "Creation" from the Rig-Veda, Hinduism's earliest scriptures, perhaps eighteen centuries before the Christian era. "Death was not then, nor was there aught immortal. . . . Who verily knows and who can here declare it, whence it was born and whence comes this creation? The gods are later than this world's production . . . whether he formed it all or did not form it, whose eye controls the world in highest heaven, he verily knows it, or perhaps he knows not." It is not such a long way from this hymn to Alice crying in *Through the Looking Glass* because Tweedledee tells her that she is only a part of the Red King's dream and would go out "like that" if he were to wake up. Alice says, "Why, I wouldn't be crying if I were just a part of his dream!" But Tweedledum says, "Do you think those are real tears?" And she cries anew.

HINDUISM

Hinduism's special contribution to our understanding of the problem of man, the problem of the fully human, is its profound insight into consciousness, into subjectivity, into the relation of those to inner energy, motivation, and concentration, to the nature, the meaning, and the effectiveness of human action. We cannot understand Hinduism without understanding that remarkable vision of social order, the caste system. The Hindus did not simply invent gods for the sake of sanctioning the four social-vocational castes. They had a profound sense of coherence between the divine order and the social order. The identity of the various nature gods with the divine order, the sense that man walked in that order, and the moral laws that went with that order—all these were present before what we think of as the earliest Hindu scriptures came into being. The Rig-Vedas begin at the end of that long tradition, with the gods, the cosmos, the social order all fully set. Only then did the *rishis*, the forest sages, discover the esoteric, mystical teaching hinted at in the Vedas—these ancient hymns of wonder. "To win a steed, to win a cow, have I not drunk of soma juice?"

The stage of wonder and of numinous awe of the hymns of the Rig-Veda is succeeded some centuries later by the Upanishads. The Upanishads are dialogues halfway between the earlier, more direct expression of religious experience in the Vedas and the later more systematic and philosophic formulations of the insights that grow out of this experience. The Upanishads are particularly concerned with the nature of the self and its relation to absolute reality. The self, however, is treated as self only in the sense of the subject of consciousness, the subject of experience, rather than as the self in personal relations with others. What is more, this consciousness is seen as universal rather than as individual.

In the beginning this was Self alone, in the shape of a person. He looking round saw nothing but his Self. He feared, and therefore any one who is lonely fears. He thought, "As there is nothing but myself, why should I fear?" Thence his fear passed away. For what should he have feared? Verily fear arises from a second only.

Another Upanishad says,

Verily, a husband is not dear, that you may love the husband; but that you may love the Self through the husband, therefore a husband is dear.

Verily, a wife is not dear, that you may love the wife; but that you may love the Self through the wife, therefore a wife is dear.

Verily, sons are not dear, that you may love the sons; but that you may love the Self through the sons, therefore sons are dear.

In each case the word "Self" is capitalized. It does not mean the individual self of the husband, of the wife, of the son, as if these were three separate selves. It means *the* Self, the one existing, indivisible Self.

In both of these quotations the relation of the self to other selves is either replaced by or reduced to self-relationship— the relation of the self to itself. The "self" that is left, as a result, is stripped of all essential characteristics of the ordinary self that we know in our day by day relationships, save consciousness. It no longer has personality, character, name, social relations, body, mind, individuality. It does not even have uniqueness, since the value and reality of the self lie in the Universal Self within and not in any unique personal stance in relation to the world. From this concern with essence, it follows that the true Self is independent of the body in which it dwells, and therefore the true Self is immortal. So in the Svetaketu Upanishad the father says to the son, "Know this. This body indeed withers and dies when the living Self has left it; the living Self dies not." Because we take the body to be the reality, when the body dies we assume that the self has died. But if we know that the self within, the subtle essence, is unchanging in the midst of change, we will know that *this* Self does not die because of the death of the body.

> "This is the world," men think, "there is no other"—thus he falls again and again under the sway of death.
> The knowing Self is not born, it dies not; it sprang from nothing, nothing sprang from it. The Ancient is unborn, eternal, everlasting; he is not killed, though the body is killed. If the killer thinks that he kills, if the killed thinks that he is killed, they do not understand; for this one does not kill, nor is that one killed.

We can understand this progress to absolute subjectivity in terms of our common experience in which the dreamer is more real than the dream, in which the continuity of the self is set in contrast to the flux of the world that the self witnesses, in which we are aware at times of the consciousness as detached from the senses, as when we concentrate so much on a certain matter that although our auditory senses are fully functioning, we do not hear what is going on around us. Though music is playing, we do not hear the music. Someone may even call our name, and we do not hear it. This is true with all the other senses too. A person can look and yet not see anything because he is intent on something else. If we can thus withdraw the consciousness from the senses, we can conceive of the mind remaining within itself without going out to the senses. If we follow this through, we discover that consciousness is not, as we often think, simply a matter of sensation—that, apart from sensation, consciousness exists itself as something pure, something *sui generis*, something in itself. So the mystic experiences it when he reaches a state that seems beyond time, beyond place, beyond awareness of itself—a state of pure consciousness, resting and dwelling in consciousness. Yet he knows that in some way this very consciousness also enters into the perception of the world to which he relates. Thus the very beginning point of the Hindu yoga of meditation is the withdrawal of consciousness from the senses into the mind, leading to inner illumination.

We also are aware of our self as detached from what we habitually associate with it—sense impressions, name, form, social relations. Somehow each of us has a sense of himself as transcending all these things, no matter how aware he may be at the same time of his self as constituted within all of these things. Finally, according to mystics the world over, man finds, by going within, an intensified consciousness that not only is ineffable and all-absorbing, including every other sensation, reflection, and concern, but also is a self-evident and self-guaranteeing reality of existence, compared to which our waking consciousness seems unreal. The dreamer dreams that his dream is real, but when waking he knows that it is only a dream compared to the waking consciousness. Similarly, when we attain this higher consciousness, our waking world seems to us, in comparison, a dream. Thus the world is unreal *only* in comparison with this higher reality.

The progress to an absolute essence of the self and the idealist emphasis on the witness as more real than what is witnessed is coupled in the Upanishads with an analysis of objective reality which reduces it from particular objects to the categories in which those objects are seen and then from these categories to undifferentiated essence, so that *nama-rupa*—the world of name and form—disappears into the Absolute. The world of particulars is seen to be nothing but waves on the ocean of reality. In the Svetaketu Upanishad, Svetaketu goes away to school and returns to his father when he is twenty-four, "having then studied all the Vedas—conceited, considering himself well-read, and stern." His father says to him, "Svetaketu . . . have you ever asked for that instruction by which we hear what cannot be heard, by which we perceive what cannot be perceived, by which we know what cannot be known?" Svetaketu has to confess that he did not learn this in school and asks his father to instruct him, which he does by a series of images. Put salt in water, his father says to him, and then taste the water. The water at the bottom tastes like salt, the water in the middle tastes like salt, and likewise the water at the top, yet one cannot see the salt. So the subtle essence in the world, so the subtle reality. And "Thou, O Svetaketu, art That." *Tat Twam asi*—you are that subtle essence. Take the seed of the mighty banyan tree, peel it down and down and down until one comes to the life within that one cannot see. So is that subtle essence, and "Thou, O Svetaketu, art that." "My dear," says the father, "as by one clod of clay all that is made of clay is known, the difference being only a name, arising from speech, but the truth being that all is clay; and as, my dear, by one nugget of gold all that is made of gold is known, the difference being only a name, arising from speech, but the truth being that all is gold . . . thus, my dear, is that instruction."

The father is saying that the particular category is only a name. The reality is the gold. Through this method the objective world is reduced to one essence and reality, just as the self is reduced to one essence and reality. In *Through the Looking Glass* the "Wood with no Name" is one of the eight squares through which Alice must pass before she can become Queen Alice. Alice comes on a fawn in the wood and asks it what its name is. The fawn says, "I can't remember, but I'll tell it to you when we get to the edge of the wood." Alice puts her arm around the neck of the fawn, and they walk together to the edge of the wood. Then the fawn comes to and says, "Why, I'm a fawn, and *you* are a little girl!" and scampers away in great fright. Thus the name gets in the way of the basic reality. A good deal of the philosophy of the yoga of discrimination or knowledge in Hinduism is built up in exactly this fashion: *neti, neti,* "not this, not this"—*This* is not reality and *this* is not reality. It is really a critique of the abstractions and categories whereby we try to get hold of the world. Only when we progressively back away from the categories and from the world of particulars, are we ready to arrive at that awareness of identity which is at the root of the mystical experience. The philosophy itself does not give one the experience, but it may be a necessary preparation for it—for the final leap—just as in Plato's *Republic* the dialectic of the philosopher leads him out of the cave up the hill to the top of the hill where he then makes the leap to the sun, which represents the direct knowledge of the Good, the True, and the Beautiful.

Having arrived at these two separate points, the absolute subjective essence within the self and the absolute objective essence of reality, then through a combination of direct mystical experience and philosophical contemplation stimulated by that experience, the two aspects of absolute subjectivity and absolute objectivity are identified. In a lightning flash there arises the central insight of the Upanishads and of the whole nondualistic Vedanta: *Brahman is Atman, tat twam asi*—Thou are That. *Brahman* is the name of the impersonal Absolute, the One without Second. It must in no way be identified either with God as we know Him in the Western tradition or with any particular Hindu deity or with *Brahma*, the masculine creator God in the Hindu trilogy which also includes Vishnu the preserver and Shiva the destroyer. Brahman is quite beyond our concepts. He can only be known as "not-two," though sometimes in more positive fashion he is spoken of as *Sat Chit Ananda Brahman*—Being, Consciousness, Bliss Absolute.

Atman is the name for self. It originates in the word for "breath." We know from a great many religions and languages the way in which the word for breath becomes the word for "spirit." So the statement that "Brahman is Atman" is the statement that this objective universal reality out there is identical with the Self discovered within. From this basic

insight, the whole system of Vedanta philosophy developed.
This whole religious approach begins with the intense need,
the wholly concentrated desire of man to find his true way.
"The good is one thing, the pleasant another," Death tells
Nachiketas in the Nachiketas Upanishad. Those men who seek
after pleasure will always be deluded. To say this is to say that
there is a life of appearances and a life of reality. It is to say, as
Socrates says to the Athenians, "Are you not ashamed that you
value the things that are *not* valuable, like money, fame, and
prestige, and you do not value the things that are truly valuable? You do not value your soul." Or in the words of Jesus,
"What doth it profit a man to gain the whole world if he lose
his soul?" "Only when man shall roll up the sky like a hide,"
says an Upanishad, "will there be an end of misery, unless this
truth has first been known." No greater contrast could be
found to the epicurean view which looks on pleasure as the
sole meaning and the only possible fulfillment of life. The
Gayatri mantram, perhaps the most famous Hindu prayer, begins, "From the unreal lead us to the real, from darkness to
light, from death to immortality."

The aim of Hinduism is not just enlightenment, *samadhi*,
but *moksha*, liberation, freedom from being reborn. This
liberation comes only when one gets rid of all the *karma* from
one's past lives and fulfills one's *dharma*. *Dharma* is the cosmic
order; it is the law which governs it; it is also your individual
destiny through all your lives within the order. *Karma* is what
you build up from your actions in each life; for these determine what befalls you and what you must rise above in your
next life. It is not enough to be a good, or moral, man. You
have to work through even that. But you cannot leap "beyond
good and evil." You have to follow the order to get beyond it.
Hinduism at its fullest is thus at one and the same time both
a cosmic religion and an acosmic one.

The most central Hindu scripture is the *Bhagavad-Gita*, the
"Song of the Lord." The Gita is a philosophy of action based

on the insight of the Upanishads, on the experience of count-less seekers, and, the Hindus say, on the grace of Krishna, who was held to be an incarnation of the divine. Perhaps the central statement in the Gita is, "He who sees the action that is in inaction, the inaction that is in action is wise indeed." The "action that is in inaction" is the effectiveness of the man who does not seem to act, who does not interfere in the world arbi-trarily, and yet acts out of the wholeness, the fullness, the con-centration of his being, out of the spiritual state that he has reached. The inaction that is in action is the ineffectiveness of the busy, active man—the typical Western political, social worker, or anyone, for that matter, who rushes around think-ing that if he does more and more things, he is accomplishing more and more. What is at stake here is not merely the accom-plishment of a goal, but the total meaning. One cannot realisti-cally speak of the goal and the way to the goal as separate en-tities. The Hindus speak of *apûrva*, a subtle cause. One's actions begin as gross and become subtle so that one is not aware of them. Yet they have their effect, whether for good or for evil. So to the Hindu the old argument about means and ends is radically transformed. Everything has its effect: if one uses a good means, it will have a good effect; if one uses a bad means, it will have a bad effect. The aim is not merely the pil-ing up of external structures, moreover, but is inner spiritual growth and enlightenment.

The Bhagavad-Gita begins with the moral and spiritual dilemma of Arjuna, caught in a difficult life-conflict of respon-sibilities and duties. On the one hand, Arjuna feels that it is a righteous war, and, on the other hand, he does not want to kill his kinsmen and his teachers. "What will happen to the castes and to the families, if I do?" he asks Krishna, the avatar, or incarnation of God, who is his charioteer. Krishna does not so much solve this ethical problem or dilemma as suspend it by dividing Arjuna into two parts: on the one hand, a spiritual essence which does not act and is untouched by action and, on the other hand, an acting being, whose actions are predetermined by cosmic destiny, by his own *karma*, and by the social position into which he is born.

The first argument that Krishna uses is that of the strict nondualist. "Dream not you do the deed of the killer," he says to Arjuna and quotes the words of the Upanishad, "No one slays and no one is slain." One might think that simply no ethical conclusion could be drawn from this "suspension of the ethical." But Krishna says, "Therefore fight." He has removed the obstacle to what Arjuna, his chariot already on the field of battle, was about to do when overcome by his scruples. If Krishna's first argument is acosmic, his second is cosmic. "Even if you should suppose this self subject to death and rebirth, grieve not for what is unavoidable. Death is certain for the born, rebirth for the dead." Though this argument does not deny the reality of killing, it makes it a matter of less moment than each person's individual destiny, or *Dharma*. From this standpoint, as in Plato's *Republic*, "justice" means that each person fulfills his individual task within the order. It does not apply to the *direct* relationship between man and man. Hence the moral concern for others, for what I ought to do in this situation which they and I share, is simply not present. The third level of argument is a form of predestination. Arjuna is granted a vision of Krishna's thousand-armed immortal self, and he sees all of his foes already mangled within the jaws of this numinous-monstrous being: "I am come as Time, destroyer of peoples. Therefore, strike, stay your hand, no matter. By me these men are slain already." True freedom is not found within the order of time but only beyond it. This too suspends the ethical in the sense of removing any real freedom of choice on Arjuna's part that would give his actions moral seriousness and make their consequences real.

All these arguments, little as they speak to the ethical conflict per se, clear the way for the overwhelming concern of the *Gita*—Arjuna's caste duty as a *kshatriya*, or warrior, to fight in a righteous war, and with it that *karma yoga*, or yoga of action, which lies at the heart of this central scripture of Hinduism.

One's reason, one's motivation, one's relation to an action determine its very nature, quality, and effectiveness. Karma yoga—the yoga of action—is action without attachment to the fruits of action. You live in the world and act, but you are not acting for the sake of the result. There are two ways by which one reaches karma yoga. One is coupled with the yoga of meditation, that is to say, here the senses attach themselves to the sense, the "gunas" to the "gunas." I am not the doer. I am only the witness. There is the knower who knows the field of action, but he is not identical with it. This is radically different from our Western point of view whereby we identify ourselves first and foremost with our actions. The other way to karma yoga is devotion. I do this, but I do it not for myself but for God. I give every thing that I do to God. Like Brother Lawrence in his monastery picking up straws for the love of God: "Lord, I cannot do this unless Thou help me." In either case, you cannot simply cease to act. You cannot abstain from action. This is no quietism; for even if you do not move at all, your mind is ceaselessly churning. The "gunas"—the qualities—are acting on one another.

If you want to help others, you can only do so out of your spiritual state of being. And yet you cannot cultivate that state of being in order to help others. If you do so, you will be thinking of the fruit of the action, and therefore your state of being will not be that out of which effective help can proceed. This is a paradox. But this is the only true, the only effective action, according to the Gita. Gandhi gave an incomparable demonstration of the way this could be put into practice in his *satyagraha*, his nonviolent direct action.

> He who is ever brooding over result often loses nerve in the performance of duty. He becomes impatient and then gives vent to anger and begins to do unworthy things; he jumps

from action to action, never remaining faithful to any. He who broods over results is like a man given to the objects of senses; he is ever-distracted, he says good-by to all scruples, everything is right in his estimation and he therefore resorts to means fair and foul to attain his end.[1]

Søren Kierkegaard in his beautiful book *Purity of Heart is to Will One Thing* says that one should be like a man taking aim and that one should concentrate upon the aim and not upon the goal. In Eugen Herrigel's *Zen and the Art of Archery* we find the identical point of view as the real secret of the Zen approach to archery: one does not try to attain something by looking at the target, the goal. One concentrates on "the means whereby"—to use the phrase of F. M. Alexander—and the means is no mere technique, but includes the very spirit of the doing.

The Hindu search for superconsciousness and for enlightenment raises the question of whether the essence of man, the true man, is to be found in consciousness or in the whole man, the whole person. Is it found by leaving the world that is given to us—the social world, the world of nature, the world of the senses? Or is it found by remaining in relation to the life of the senses and to other people? Is the goal of man enlightenment and individual spiritual salvation or is it a way of life which does not attain individual perfection yet affirms and redeems the human world? When inwardness and inner spiritual development are seen as the goal of life, external actions tend to become relativized. As a result, the problem of ethics is never a problem of "What ought I do in this situation?" but of "What is the spiritual stage I have reached and what is the right way for me to act in terms of this spiritual stage?"

Many religions confront us with the question as to whether the highest and most authentic existence is not that in which not only lust but the total post-Freudian attitude toward sex

[1] Quoted in Louis Fischer, *Gandhi: His Life and Message for the World* (New York: Signet Key Book, 1954).

as a wholesome and natural thing must not be overcome in favor of the use of this energy for spiritual enlightenment. Gandhi suggests that the highest stage is the stage of chastity. But one finds the same in Saint Paul who says, "I wish you could be chaste, even as I, but if you cannot contain, it is better to marry than to burn." All over the world, in fact, there are mystics who suggest that the highest way is the way that overcomes the "vulgar sexual act," that directs this energy to God. They believe that the goal is spiritual perfection which demands all of your energies—not just on the level they now are, but transformed and elevated through concentration and devotion—to become the basis of a whole new state of spiritual being. One cannot leave aside any part of one to do this.

On the other hand, there is here an implied dualism not only between spirit and flesh, but also between individual consciousness and the social world, which is considered, if not an evil world, at least a lesser world. The two of these factors work together to induce men to concentrate attention on the inner, on inward spiritual perfection, the realization of man's spiritual essence. This constitutes a great issue in the history of religions, one of those which exclude the possibility of any common "essence" that could be extracted from all religions. Does one hold that the true goal of spiritual existence is this sort of inner perfection in which one relates to the world either as a hindrance or as a stepping-stone to this perfection? Or does one believe that what is asked of one is a completion of the world which will forever leave oneself imperfect?

At first glance, the problem of chastity, or of sex, seems to be that of the choice between the "interpersonal" or the lack of it, whether salvation or the goal of life depends upon other people or means the exclusion of them. The derogation of sex is usually accompanied by the derogation of the social life in favor of going inward for the sake of some type of personal enlightenment or the search for spiritual perfection. Often however, it is precisely because of the confusion that over-comes men in the sphere of the interpersonal that they are driven away from sex altogether to a pursuit of an individual perfection that will cleanse them. Vachel Lindsay's "Life is a loom weaving illusion. Oh who will end my dream's confusion" very probably had its origin just here.

The suffering of existence comes because of the fact that we try to hold on to a world in which all things change, perish, and pass away. Again and again men discover in the course of human existence, as the preacher in Ecclesiastes has immortally expressed it, that "all is vanity"—there is nothing new under the sun: things go and they come, they move in cycles—and again and again this has led them to a sense of futility about human existence and to turning away from human existence to something which transcends it. Hasidism, as we shall see, holds that there is a third alternative to giving oneself over to the phantasmagoric play of the satisfaction of the senses and of lust, on the one hand, or leaving that behind and trying to move altogether into an individual sphere of chastity, on the other—namely serving God with the "evil" urge.

After a lecture of mine at Pendle Hill, a Quaker study cen-ter in Pennsylvania, my wife asked me, "What touchstone of reality do you still retain from Hinduism?" My answer was that it gives existence a depth-dimension which is always there for me even when I do not spell it out—a transpersonal con-sciousness the reality of which I recognize, though not as the only reality. Hinduism was at one time in my life a "live op-tion," in William James's phrase, a road that I could and did follow. I have taken a different path in the years since. Yet I believe that the options which we choose and later reject are almost as important for us as the options we ultimately choose and make our own. They remain with us, like an obligato to the melody of our lives.

EARLY BUDDHISM AND ZEN

Buddhism comes from Hinduism just as Christianity comes from Judaism, except that the Buddha himself organized the new religion as Jesus did not. The Buddha came from Nepal in the North of India and undoubtedly did not know of the esoteric tradition of the Upanishads. He had a whole other touchstone of reality. He was a prince of the Sakya clan who, according to the legend, was protected from the vicissitudes of life until, at the age of twenty-nine, he saw the signs foretold at his birth—a blind man, a sick man, a beggar, and a corpse. Recognizing the misery of the world, he left his wife and his son Rahula (fetter), leaped over the wall with his trusty horse, and went into the forest where for six years he practiced such asceticism that his belly cleaved to his backbone. Then he decided he was going to follow "the middle way" between extreme asceticism and the way of the world. Finally under the Bo tree he attained enlightenment. Mara the Tempter tried to get him to enter immediately into Nirvana—cessation of existence. But he resisted the temptation and returned to the world "to turn the wheel of the doctrine" and to found the order, the Brotherhood of monks.

The Buddha was a greater social revolutionary than Gandhi; for he rejected the Hindu caste system. For him a Brahmin was not a man who has a certain caste-mark on his forehead, but a man who is noble in character and action. The Arhat, or disciple, follows the noble Aryan way. He begins with the four noble truths that all existence is suffering, that suffering is caused by old age, birth and death, that these are caused in turn by our craving for existence, and the way to liberation from suffering is the Eightfold Path. The Buddha preserved from Hinduism the ideas of karma and reincarnation, but he did not hold existence to be illusion. On the contrary, it is all too real. We must find the way that will liberate us from this suffering by liberating us from our craving for existence. This way is the Eightfold Path: right views, right resolution, right speech, right action, right livelihood, right will, right mindfulness, and right meditation. Right mindfulness is not moral judgment but the simple awareness of what one is doing and feeling at every moment that gives us detachment from it: "Now I am walking. Now I am standing. Now I am feeling lust." The final stage is *dhyana*, right meditation. It is from this word that the Chinese Buddhists developed Ch'an Buddhism and the Japanese Zen. Right meditation has four stages from joy to equanimity. At the end of these four stages one has attained *nirvana*. Whereas Hinduism, if only with negatives, points to an Absolute, to Brahman, the One without Second, and says, "This is a reality compared to which this world is a delusion," one does not find in early Buddhism any positing of an absolute. Nirvana, so far as the Buddha describes it, is simply the backing away from the world in progressive stages until you no longer are there in it.

This point of view is given unforgettable expression by the Buddha in one of his early sermons called, "Questions Which Tend Not to Edification." Malunkyapputa came to a friend and said, "I am not going to stay in the Order unless I learn whether the world is eternal or it isn't eternal, unless I learn whether the soul exists after death or does not exist after death." When these statements came to the ear of the Buddha, he said to him:

> When did I say, Malunkyapputa, that if you joined the order, I would tell you whether the world is eternal or is not eternal, whether the soul exists after death or the soul does not exist after death.

And he said further, "These are of no practical value. They do not help religion. They do not help in the way." Thus the tendency to identify religion with finding out the answers to "ultimate questions"—Is there immortality? Does God exist? —is thrown aside in favor of a purely pragmatic view of action. The Buddha's concern is what counts now, what matters now, and the rest are "questions that tend not to edification." Why do you bother yourself with these things? This teaching stands in contrast with the Western, the Hindu, and even the later Buddhist fondness for metaphysics.

> It is, O Malunkyapputa, as if a man were wounded by an arrow thickly smeared with poison, and his friends and his companions and his relatives went to procure a physician, and he said, I will not let the physician draw out the arrow from out of my side until I find first what was the caste of the man who shot the arrow. Did he belong to the brahmin caste or to the kshatriya caste or to the vayisa or the sudra?

Meanwhile, of course, the man would have died. You too will die, the Buddha implies, if you waste your time with questions that are beyond the proper ken of man, using ken in the twofold sense of knowledge and of what is man's business.

In Buddhism one backs away from the world, and this backing away makes no statement and implies no assumption about the reality or unreality of the world. The emphasis here is not upon knowledge, therefore. It is not upon discovering what is the nature of the cosmos or the acosmos which includes or is identical with man. The emphasis here is anthropological, it is human. It makes no statement about reality, except one thing, and that is that it changes: "All things change, all things perish, all things pass away." If we try to hold on to any part of existence, we will suffer. We will suffer because the attempt to hold on goes against the fact of change. Our very enjoyment of this moment must mean our suffering and sadness in the next moment. It cannot but be so. If we were able to enjoy the moment, relate to it, and then let it go, that would be different. But something else happens. Not only do we have this momentary relation, but then we fix it: we record the fact that this was a pleasurable sensation or that that was painful. Thus, at a later time, we are drawn to this sensation or we shrink from it. As a result we are not able to accept the simplest and most elementary act of human existence—that all things change, perish, and pass away. Human life is a vain search for building security. We try fruitlessly to shore it up in every direction, like Kafka's mole who is never done fortifying his hole. Unable to accept her child's death, Kisogatomi went to the Buddha and pleaded, "Bring my child back to life." The Buddha replied, "Go and get me a mustard seed from a house in which no one has died, and I will bring your child back to life." With complete and simple good faith she went from house to house, carrying her child with her. Everybody gladly gave her a mustard seed, but when she asked, "Has any one died here," they answered, "Yes, a father has died here," or a sister, or a brother, a wife, or a child. Eventually she realized that death is a part of all human existence, and she was able to put her child aside.

The Buddhist may be characterized as a "stream uprunner" —one who applies his will, who is going to end his craving for existence, who is going to attain enlightenment, who is going to overcome death and rebirth. When have we ever seen a religion that laid out its way with such logical clarity: existence is suffering, suffering is caused by craving, the way to overcome craving is the eightfold path? We do not know that the Buddha himself followed the Eightfold Path in this way. This is the Buddha as a teacher, trying to help other men. The "compassionate Buddha" always remained close to the concrete situation, to the pragmatic problem at hand, "How can I help or how can we help ourselves escape from suffering?" He began with man, with anthropology, rather than with metaphysics or cosmology. This closeness to the concrete is renewed in sophisticated and paradoxical form in Zen—that form of Mahayana Buddhism which grew out of the most abstruse philosophies of "mind only," "the void," "suchness," and the interpenetration of all reality.

Buddhism is a great missionary religion that has lasted over twenty-five hundred years. At first, it spread southward into India where it remained for eighteen hundred years until the Muslims drove it out in the eleventh century of the common era. At the same time Pali, or Theravadin, Buddhism spread to Ceylon and from there to Indochina, where it is strong to this day. But in the course of the development of many schools of Buddhism after the death of the Buddha and the spread of Buddhism from India to China, Tibet, Japan, and Korea, there arose another image of man, another touchstone of reality, another way of discipleship—that of the *Bodhisattva* who takes the vow not to enter Nirvana until he has saved all sentient beings. This second type of discipleship is known as the *Mahayana*, or Great Vehicle, in opposition to the career of the Arhat who sought individual freedom from suffering and whose career was deprecatingly dubbed *Hinayana*, or the Little Vehicle. The Bodhisattva imitates the compassion of the Buddha. There also developed in Mahayana Buddhism the way of ordinary people who felt that they could not take on such a great task and aspired instead to enter the Buddha's Pure Land or Western Paradise by virtue of their perfect faith and the sufferings and sacrifice of the Bodhisattvas.

In the Mahayana Buddhist monasteries there developed a number of exceedingly abstruse philosophical schools, some of which undoubtedly influenced the Hindu Vedanta via the great nondualist philosopher and saint Sankara. The "Transcendent Wisdom" arrived at an almost complete reversal of early Buddhism as a result of which enlightenment in the sense of knowledge superseded enlightenment in the sense of liberation: there are no individuals to be liberated and to enter into Nirvana, since the notion of the existence of individual selves is itself an illusion. It is out of this soil, combined with the idealism of the Mind-Only school, and the breathtaking metaphysical negation of the school of the Void, that Zen Buddhism arose.

The goal of Zen Buddhism is different from that of early

Buddhism. It does not talk of reincarnation, and it is not trying to reach Nirvana. Instead it aims at *satori*—an abrupt, sudden enlightenment (according to the Rinzai school) very different from the gradual progress through four stages of *Dhyana* of the Eightfold Path. Satori comes through a great discipline of meditation which stands on the border of the inner and the outer. Therefore, it may come when a gong suddenly rings in the monastery or when a plate drops. Or it may come as in the story of the monk who takes the master's place when he is gone. When the master returns, he asks this disciple what he did. The disciple raises his finger in the way the master is accustomed to doing. The master, who is holding a knife he is using to cut vegetables in the garden, cuts the finger off. The disciple runs away screaming, but the master calls his name. The disciple turns around and looks, the master holds up the end of the finger that was cut off, and the disciple attains enlightenment.

Once a Zen master asked his disciples a question about the way, warning them that if none of them could answer he would have to cut the cat in two. None could answer, and the master carried out his threat. That afternoon a disciple who had been away came back. When he heard the story, he took a shoe off and put it on his head. The master said, "A pity you were not here before. We could have saved the poor cat." In another Zen story the master and a disciple are standing looking at the moon when a flock of wild geese fly in front of the moon. When the geese have flown by, the master asks, "Where are they now?" to which the disciple replies, "They are gone, Master." At this, the master gives the disciple a very painful tweak on the nose.

The next day when the master gets up to give his sermon to the disciples, this disciple comes up and rolls up the rug which symbolizes the end of the sermon. The master has no choice but to stop before he has started, but he calls the disciple to him and asks, "Why did you do that?" "Yesterday you were kind enough to give my nose a very painful twist," responds the disciple. "And what is wrong with you today?" asks the master. "Today my nose feels fine," the disciple retorts. This whole story points to what the Zen Buddhist calls "this moment" or "this day." It is a "now" which does not pass. Rather everything passes through it. One smells the cherry blossoms as one passes, but one does not try to hold on to the pleasant smell. Once two disciples were walking along, and they came to a young woman standing helplessly before a river. One of them picked her up and carried her across so that she would not get wet. The other disciple said nothing for a long while, but finally he could restrain himself no longer. "Brother," he protested. "You should not have done this. We are not supposed to have any contact with women." At this the man who had helped the woman exclaimed, "Are you still carrying her? I put her down a long time ago!"

My favorite Zen allegory of "this moment" is the one of the man who was chased over a cliff by a tiger who stood looking down at him hungrily while he clung for dear life to a vine growing at the edge of the cliff. Looking down, he saw another tiger beneath him with jaws open waiting for him to drop. Above where his hand could reach, two mice—one white and one black—went round and round the vine gnawing steadily at it; so that even if he did not lose his grip on the vine, it was only a question of time until the vine would break and he should fall. In front of him growing on the face of the cliff he saw a clump of wild strawberries. He reached out his free hand, took and ate them, and exclaimed, "How delicious!"

The most famous Zen method of concentration is the *koan* —a question that the disciple holds for years in a state of great tension. The *koan* is designed to force the disciple beyond ordinary intellection and with it those intellectual categories of one and many, same and not the same, that are the substance of human thought in general and of our Western Aristotelian logic in particular. "Where is the way?" the disciple asks the master. "No use inserting a wedge into empty space," the master replies. At this the disciple goes the master one better and says, "Space itself is the wedge," multiplying paradox by paradox. The master then strikes the disciple, who grabs hold of him and cries, "Do not strike me so! You may later strike others unreasonably."

Religion is often taken to be a movement away from mundane reality to the spirit floating above it. Zen Buddhism says no such movement is possible: there is only the one spirit-sense reality. It says, secondly, that it is our reason that has created the impression that there are these separate worlds of spirit and sense-intellect. This differs strikingly from Hinduism with its statement that this world is *maya,* or illusion, and that Brahman is reality. Instead, we have the remarkable statement that the "one" and the "ten thousand things" are identical, that "nirvana *is* samsara." It is our minds that bifurcate existence into body and spirit, the one and the many. We cannot overcome our existential dilemma by fleeing from the many to the one; for this very attempt to overcome dualism leads us to still another dualism—that of the one as opposed to the many. One must instead go right to the concrete particular which at the same time is the Buddha Nature. There is no process here of abstracting from concrete reality, of uncovering the essence and shucking off this world. There is no Hindu *nama-rupa*— no world of name and form which is to be understood as merely that and therefore illusion. On the contrary, the very particularity of things, their very name and form, is the only means through which one can attain enlightenment.

We are, as a result, confronted with opposite types of "nondualism." On the one hand, there is Hindu nondualism which says the many is unreal, the reality is the "not-two"—the One without Second. And on the other hand, there is Zen nondualism, which says both—the many and the one, or the "not-two"—are real; both are aspects of a reality which cannot exclude either the one or the many, either the senses or the spirit. The Zen Buddhist says that he overcomes the subject-object relation, that he gets "over there" and becomes the mountain that one sees. A Japanese Zen woman goes out and sees the morning-glory vine on the bucket she means to draw water from. She goes to the next farm for her water, and writes a *Haiku*, or seventeen-syllable poem: "Oh morning glory with bucket made captive, I beg for water." She and the morning glory are one; the distance is overcome, but in a very specific manner. It is not as if there were one essence or absolute that could be abstracted from the two apart from their particularity. The particularity is preserved.

> The two exist because of the One
> But hold not even to this One;
> When a mind is not disturbed,
> The Ten thousand things offer no offence.
> No offence offered, and no ten thousand things.

Zen Buddhism is perhaps the most intellectual form of anti-intellectualism that exists. It goes even beyond the "neti, neti" —the "not this, not this"—of the Hindu Vedanta. For it is absolutely opposed to the discrimination of the mind; it is absolutely against the intellection that cuts us off from the concrete world. If one is so intellectual that one gets all one's emotional satisfaction thereby, one cannot be a Zen Buddhist; for one will cling to the intellect and not be willing to go beyond it. Zen is just the everyday life—pulling up carrots in the garden, peeling potatoes in the kitchen.

> Walking is Zen, sitting is Zen,
> Whether talking or remaining silent, whether moving or
>   standing quiet, the essence itself is ever at ease.

One finds the "essence" just as much in the movement of the world as in the nonmovement. In that sense, Zen is like Taoism: it does not cling to one opposite or the other. Zen was much influenced by Taoism, in fact, with its sense of "the way" and of the coincidence of opposites.

Not knowing how near the truth is,
People seek it far away,—what a pity!

And straight runs the path of non-duality and non-trinity.
Abiding with the no-particular which is in particulars,
Whether going or returning, they remain for ever unmoved . . .
This very earth is the lotus land of purity,
And this body is the body of the Buddha.

Not only is there no illusion in this world, there is no escape from the world. The Buddha Nature, the particulars, and the no-particulars are all one reality.

It is impossible for us to meditate on any reality, religious or otherwise, without pointing to it. Through these pointers—words, symbols, myths, even rituals, we enable ourselves to return again and again to the insight or the contact we have achieved. But then the second step always follows: the tendency to regard the pointer as the reality and to lose what it is pointing toward. The Vedantists and the early Mahayana Buddhists were on the right track in trying to overcome the idea that things are divided up into myriads of discriminate things, but they did not go far enough. They turned it into an intellectual conception, and they said, "Reality is the 'not-two' " and fell into a world of intellectual discrimination between spirit and matter, the one and the many, the not-two and the ten thousand things. They could not get to the reality which is so concrete that it baffles all of our attempts to grasp it by any of these forms of mental categories. As a Zen text puts it, "They take the finger pointing to the moon for the moon itself."

The Zen Buddhist would say the same about Western attempts to identify the absolute, or God, with some particular image of God. A young man came up to me after a talk I gave on Jesus at a Southern university and said to me, "Have you

no faith in theology? How can you live without theology?"
I replied, "My faith is not in theology. My faith is in God."
He believed that only faith set down in propositions guarantees that the world is constructed so as to give one salvation
and happiness in the world to come. Such a belief opens itself
to any scriptural text only insofar as it can be fitted into a
ready-made theological category. Perhaps the most healthy
religion is the dialectic between the interpretation and the
religious reality. Most great theologians make a real effort to
go back again and again to the scripture and to the experience.
But we ought to be aware that their turning to the text often
takes place through the spectacles of their particular way of
looking, their favorite way of interpreting. This is not a criticism of having the categories, but of making the categories
reality, of forgetting that "the finger pointing at the moon"
is not the moon.

There is much in both Zen Buddhism and Taoism which
raises serious questions about the assumption of most of the
intellectual currents of the nineteenth and twentieth centuries
that *analysis* is the way to reach reality. If I take a thing apart
into its supposed parts, have I thereby grasped this thing?
Only if I assume that all things are really reducible to their
component parts. That often means, only if I have already
found what I believe to be the basic reality—such as a Marxist
dialectic or a form of economic determinism or Freud's or
Jung's theory of the libido or the analytical categories of the
linguistic philosopher.

The very different attitude of Zen is illustrated by the
following:

> It is the substance that you see before you—*begin to reason
> about it and you at once fall into error*. It is like the bound-
> less void which cannot be fathomed or measured. This
> universal mind alone is the Buddha and there is no distinction
> between the Buddha and sentient beings. . . . You have but
> to recognize that *real mind is expressed in these perceptions,*

but is not dependent on them on the one hand, nor separate from them on the other. You should not start reasoning from such perceptions, nor allow your thinking to stem from them, yet you should *refrain from seeking universal mind apart from them or abandoning them* in your pursuit of the Dharma. *Neither hold to them, abandon them, dwell in them, nor cleave to them,* but exist independently of all that is above, below, or around you, *for there is nowhere in which the Way cannot be followed.*[2]

Martin Buber in *I and Thou* has a remarkably similar passage in which he says,

> If you explore the life of things and of conditioned being you come to the unfathomable, if you deny the life of things and of conditioned being you stand before nothingness, if you hallow this life you meet the living God.

The way is right there before you, but you are going to miss it either if you say that perceptions are all illusion or if you take perceptions as the material for your analysis. Much of what is called "existential" philosophy in our day—Heidegger, Sartre, even Tillich—starts with existence but then goes on to analyze it into phenomenological categories. Unlike the Zen Buddhist it does not stay with the concrete, but quickly leaves it to go to one realm or another and thereby perhaps loses the really existential quality which does not yield itself to analysis.

Zen is practical and it does not deny the senses, and in this way, as we have seen, it is unlike the Vedanta. Like the Vedanta, it wishes to transcend the subject-object relationship, but it does not do so for the sake of some absolute reality entirely separate from the phenomenal world. To get the flavor of Zen, you have to grasp its paradoxical, concrete quality. Satori is not described in terms of any mystical rapture that would remove one from the world; in fact to understand Zen

[2] E. A. Burtt, ed., *The Teachings of the Compassionate Buddha* (New York: New American Library, Mentor Books, 1955), pp. 195–198, italics mine.

satori, one has to see it as just on the boundary line between the inner and the outer, so that when the satori comes it is like a lightning flash that brings these two together. One has to avoid, on the one hand, simple immersion in outer things, but equally one has to avoid a quietistic contemplation and submergence in the within, as one sees in the Hindu Yogin who, seated in his grass hut, withdraws his consiousness from his senses. There is no denial of the senses in Zen. When enlightenment has come, nothing is changed. The only thing that is changed is one's relation to it.

> Misty rain on Mount Lu,
> And waves surging in Che-chiang;
> When you have not yet been there,
> Many a regret surely you have;
> But once there and homeward you wend,
> How matter-of-fact things look!
> Misty rain on Mount Lu,
> And waves surging in Che-chiang.[3]

The way is not some other way, some mystical or occult path "out there" apart from the everyday world. It has to do just with the concrete here and now. Sometimes a therapist helps a schizophrenic patient involved in an inner world of fantasy by presenting himself to the patient again and again as simpler than he actually is—just as an everyday person— and that way over a number of years brings the patient to some contact with reality. We are all schizophrenics, the Zen Buddhist might suggest; we really do not see reality as it is. We think we do: we call the formulae of science "concrete," for example, forgetting that science, though useful, is precisely the most abstract way of apprehending nature or reality. We see everything in terms of space and time and number

[3] D. T. Suzuki, *Zen Essays*, I, p. 12, quoted in Daisetz Teitaro Suzuki, *Living by Zen* (Tokyo: the Sanseido Press, 1949), p. 7. *Living by Zen* is the best of Suzuki's books on Zen, in my opinion. Next to it is his *Manual of Zen Buddhism.*

and miss each thing's uniqueness. We miss the startling reality of "suchness" which is simply there. Between us and it is this veil of intellection of which we are unaware. Nor is this a question of the intellectual as opposed to the ordinary man. Every man, just by virtue of being human, is almost certain to have this veil between him and reality. Enlightenment means removing, overcoming this veil, and finding the reality that is simply there. When the great Zen scholar D. T. Suzuki came to Sarah Lawrence College once to speak to our Philosophy Seminar, there was a Hindu woman from my class in the History of Religions who joined us at supper beforehand. "Do you believe that God is in the sugar bowl?" Suzuki asked her. "Yes," she replied, and he rejoined, "So do we." "Do you believe that God is in you?" he pursued. "Yes," she again replied, and he again assented, "So do we." But then he asked her, "Do you believe the same God is in the sugar bowl and in you?" This time when she said Yes, he countered, "That is where we differ!" It is not the same God, even though it is not a different one. It is neither two nor one. The Buddha Nature is to be comprehended in and through birth-and-death, and birth-and-death must somehow harbor the Buddha Nature in it. Nirvana *is* samsara.

"All things are reducible to the One," says a typical Koan, "but to what will this One be reduced?" Evolution, to some people, is an explanation of how things got to be what they are, but if we do not remain content with that, where in turn does that lead us? Cause and effect, in the same way, may give us a sense of satisfaction. But if we press the question a step further and inquire, like Hume, into the reality underlying the connection between cause and effect, where does that leave us? "When you are dead, cremated, and the ashes scattered, where are you?" Where is the "I" which at this moment, in this consciousness, sees reality? The question is not, Where is this body, objectified and seen apart from you? You are still to see through your own eyes and ask yourself the question, How is it possible that the whole of reality is grasped through this "I" and yet that this "I" will cease to exist? This is a paradox of existence itself, one beyond which we cannot see.

"The bridge flows, the water remains standing," says a Zen Koan. If we were floating down the stream, the bridge would flow with us; the water would not flow at all. The water flows only when we are on the bank and have a stationary position relative to its flow. Heraclitus said, "No man can step twice into the same stream." From this he concluded, "All is flux." But a disciple of his said, "No man can step once into the same stream." The observation that all is flux is only possible when you have removed yourself from the stream. If you flow with the stream, you are not going to know that the stream flows. The very statement that "All is flux" is a static statement, for it presupposes a stationary observer and it presupposes getting hold of something, trying to hold on to it, and then, as a result, observing the next moment that it is gone. This, Henri Bergson tells us, is the beginning of the great error of all Western metaphysics. This metaphysics takes the stream of reality and freezes it into a solid block (idealism) or into myriads of tiny particles (empiricism), turns it into something static and discrete. It was the standpoint of the observer, the fact that man was becoming more aware of the subject-object split, that made him see that all is flux and that he could not step twice into the same stream. The "same" stream is the stream as we have fixed it with our categories—so high, the water flowing so fast, and so many thousands of pebbles in the stream bed. Thus the Zen Buddhist statement, "The bridge flows and the river remains standing," means a basic reversal of our customary perspective in relation to reality over against us—a reversal in the direction of the concrete and the particular, "the one *and* the ten thousand things."

However important it is that things be consistent when we are constructing bridges and roads, when we are dealing with ultimate realities, we encounter something that is necessarily paradoxical, something that pushes beyond the bounds that our categories can comprehend. For our categories are always within the given system. But if we are talking about ultimates, we are talking about what transcends, includes, or undergirds the system and is not included within it. There is no basic philosophy of religion that is not paradoxical, therefore, including the nondualist philosophy of the Vedanta, founded as it is on the paradox that we not only take *maya* to be reality but that it is indeed as real as creation, for creation itself is a paradoxical union of the utter Absolute with the world of the relative. But the Zen Buddhists retain their paradoxicality right down to the particular. It is a part of their life-style, their touchstone of reality.

TAOISM

Less intense and less paradoxical than Zen, but no less a mysticism of the concrete and the particular, is Taoism. The center of Taoism is the Tao—the way of life and the way of man in which man finds the "natural" course that flows with the stream rather than runs against it. Taoism accepts the opposites of *Yin* and *Yang*—feminine and masculine, dark and light, earth and heaven, receptive and active—without insisting on one or the other. It does not hold them in tension but swings easily from one to the other. Hence its action is *wu-wei*, the action of the whole being that has the appearance of nonaction because it does not intervene or interfere. This action seems most effortless just when it is most effective.

The word Tao roughly means "the way"—not just the way of man but the way that rounds heaven and earth. As Lao-tzu was leaving his kingdom for good at the age of eighty, the gate-keeper, according to legend, asked him if he would not write something down before he left. He wrote, as he stood there, the five hundred characters which constitute the *Tao-*

Te-Ching. Taoism resembles Hinduism and Greek religion in its intuition of cosmos and order, but in Taoism the order is not "up there" as in Hinduism, or on the surface, as in Buddhism, but within. All the similes are of the core, the womb, the heart of the matter. Nor is Lao-tzu's intuition of order articulated as is the Hindu *dharma*, the Greek *moira*, or the Confucian *li*—the sense of propriety, or of the way things should be done in men's relations to one another and to the state.

The *yin* and *yang* is also in Confucianism, but in Confucianism the active side is emphasized at the expense of the passive. Taoism gives equal place to the "feminine" virtues of receptivity and passivity. But Taoism does not insist even on these. It lets things flow between the opposites without making one or the other the basic reality. Neither is the Tao simply the unconscious or feeling, as Witter Bynner suggests in his introduction to *The Way of Life according to Lao-Tzu.* D. H. Lawrence, reacting against the domination of conscious, rational man, swung to the opposite extreme. Taoism, in contrast, does not place feeling above thought any more than it places thought above feeling. It does not need to overcorrect detached intellectuality by an emphasis on "gut-level" emotion. It knows that thought never occurs without feeling and that feeling never occurs without thought, even though we sometimes use our thoughts to mask our feelings and our feelings to mask our thoughts.

Lao-tzu's *Way of Life*, in the classic poetic translation of Witter Bynner, has proved to be of a lasting and ever new significance for me as no other Eastern scripture has. It does not contain the mystic secret of supreme enlightenment or *nirvana* or even *satori*. Rather, like that Confucian wisdom to which it otherwise seems so opposite, it represents a path that is not far from the common consciousness, a wisdom that gently informs and gently reproves just where our lives most stray from it. My own life, indeed, like that of most of the overcommitted men of affairs whom I know, has often seemed to me what I once wrote of K., the hero of Franz Kafka's novel *The Castle:* an illustration of the very opposite of everything that Lao-tzu taught about flowing with the Tao. But this is precisely why, along with its necessary Confucian counterpart of structure, propriety, and reciprocity, Taoism speaks so powerfully to our condition.

> Existence is beyond the power of words
> To define:
> Terms may be used
> But are none of them absolute.

In the Hindu Vedanta it is only Brahman, the One without Second, in the metaphysics of Plato and Aristotle it is only the Good or the Unmoved Mover that cannot be defined. The very nature of finite existence to these latter implies that it can be delimited into name and form, same and other, category and class. For Zen Buddhism and Taoism, in contrast, it is existence itself that is illimitable and ineffable. In Taoism both the core and the surface are essentially the same.

> If name be needed, wonder names them both:
> From wonder into wonder
> Existence opens.

Plato said that wonder is the beginning of philosophy, but the philosopher, as Martin Buber has said, neutralizes his wonder in doubt. From Descartes to the present even the beginning of philosophy is doubt and not wonder. Only here and there in Francis Thompson—"The angels keep their ancient places/ Turn but a stone and start a wing./ Tis ye, tis your estrangèd faces/ That miss the many-splendoured thing"— in William Blake's aphorisms—"How do you know but that every bird that wings its way through the air is a whole world of delight closed your senses five?"—in the philosophy of religion of Abraham Heschel, who sees each thing as pointing beyond itself and grounds all knowledge, art, and religion on "the awareness of the ineffable"—is any comparable insight found in the Western world. The one "name" which does not falsify existence, dividing it up and closing it off, is wonder: "From wonder into wonder existence opens." Taoism is an existential mysticism in which the concrete, precisely in its concreteness, reveals vista upon vista to the eye of the man who meets it in openness. "The senses" as Heraclitus said, are only "bad witnesses to those who have barbarian souls."

This means no disparagement of words. Only those words that attempt to fix and delimit, to close off and confine, are unreal, not those that point beyond themselves to a concrete reality that no concept can delineate.

> Real words are not vain,
> Vain words are not real;
> And since those who argue prove nothing
> A sensible man does not argue.

Words do not control reality, they serve it—for the man who uses them in flowing openness of reciprocity. "The oracle at Delphi neither reveals nor conceals," said Heraclitus. "It indicates." The sane man, in consequence, is the one who does not try to capture existence as a whole within the limited, and limitedly useful categories of analysis, whether scientific, psychoanalytic, or linguistic. Life reveals itself in its images if one opens oneself to the image in such depth that one allows it to speak—as every image does—of its source.

> The surest test if a man be sane
> Is if he accepts life whole, as it is,
> Without needing by measure or touch to understand
> The measureless untouchable source
> Of its images . . .

The man who cannot do this is literally insane, like the paranoiac whose whole endeavor is to create a world of which he is totally master, totally in control. When I discovered that one of my dearest friends, of whom I had lost track, had been for three years in a mental hospital, I believed at first, as did a mutual friend, that he was actually sane. But then he told me, in connection with his plan to sue the state for a million dollars, that he knew the name, address, and phone number of the governor, the lieutenant-governor, and everyone else who might be of importance for his scheme. "If one didn't know, one would think from his letters that he was sane," our mutual friend said to me. "They are perfectly rational." "What makes you think that rationality is a sign of sanity?" I responded. Even a philosophical "world-view" can easily become a form of insanity when it becomes so total that no otherness can ever find its way through its meshes.

The metaphysician discriminates between the real world and mere "appearance" or "phenomena," and he sets the goal of the true philosopher as ascending beyond the world of the senses to a face-to-face confrontation with absolute reality. Lao-tzu is content to allow the ultimate reality to speak to him in the only way in which it can speak to man—through its images. This ultimate reality for him is not some unmovable, self-sufficient absolute but the core, the womb of life, which constantly gives birth to the concrete realities which, changing and evanescent though they be, are as real as the Tao which flows through them. Although "the source" "appears dark emptiness," actually it:

> Brims with a quick force
> Farthest away
> And yet nearest at hand
> From oldest time unto this day,
> Charging its images with origin:
> What more need I know of the origin
> Than this?

We do not have to look beyond seeing for "the unseen" or beyond hearing for "the unheard." The true oneness "forever sends forth a succession of living things as mysterious/ As the unbegotten existence to which they return." Men have called these living things "empty phenomena/ Meaningless images,/ In a mirage/ With no face to meet,/ No back to follow." But that is because they insist on setting up a dualism between "mere appearance" and some entirely hidden, unmanifested Reality. The true meaning of "phenomenon," as Martin Heidegger has pointed out in our day, is precisely that it shows forth and manifests Being, and Being is not a static absolute but the very ground of existence in time. This cannot be known through philosophical reflection alone, however, but only through the way of life of the man who allows the Tao to flow through him and between him and all beings, rounding the way of earth and of heaven. "One who is anciently aware of existence/ Is master of every moment." There is no split for him between the eternal and the present, the origin and the immediate. His mastery is his openness in depth to what each moment tells him of origin. Flowing with life, he "Feels no break since time beyond time/ In the way life flows."

This is Lao-tzu's "sound man," the man who, holding the door of his tent wide to the firmament, can possess "the simple stature of a child, breathing nature," and just thereby "Become, notwithstanding,/ A man." Such a man is "at the core of life." He does not have "to run outside for better seeing." Abiding "at the center of his being," he understands the central teaching of Lao-tzu: "The way to do is to be." This does not mean passivity, for doing is still the emphasis. It means the action of the whole being in flowing interaction with everything it meets. In this flowing interaction the old paradox reemerges—that we find authentic existence, realize our true selves, manifest our true uniqueness not through aiming directly at it but through opening ourselves to and going out to meet what is not ourselves—immersing our selves in the stream of the Tao that is within, between, and beyond all creatures.

> A sound man by not advancing himself
> Stays the further ahead of himself
> By not confining himself to himself
> Sustains himself outside himself:
> By never being an end in himself
> He endlessly becomes himself.

We are so used to thinking of the spiritual life and/or self-realization as a goal, that we set out directly to become a new person. Instead of allowing our becoming to take place naturally and spontaneously as a byproduct of the way we meet life, we make ourselves an end in ourselves and thus distort and pervert the very means that we use.

Remaining at the center of one's being does not mean turning away from one's fellowman, as in so many other mysticisms, but responding to him from that very core. "A sound man's heart is not shut within itself/ But is open to other people's hearts." It means too recognizing that men do not possess fixed character—good or evil, honest or dishonest—but that the way in which I approach them, the way in which I allow the Tao to flow between myself and them frees them to possibilities of goodness, trust and openness, just as my mistrust and categorizing makes it difficult for them to break out of habitual modes of dishonesty and mistrust.

> I find good people good,
> And I find bad people good
> If I am good enough;
> I trust men of their word,
> And I trust liars
> If I am true enough;
> I feel the heart-beats of others
> Above my own
> If I am enough of a father,
> Enough of a son.

"Bad people" and "liars" are not bad and dishonest the way a table is a table or a chair a chair. Approached with openness and trust, they may be able to respond in kind. Approached with hatred and distrust, they will be confirmed in the mold in which their earlier interactions have already fixed them.

We can only help people if we are not *determined* to help them.

> It is said, 'there's a way where there's a will';
> But let life ripen and then fall.
> Will is not the way at all.

Lao-tzu perhaps needs the counterbalancing of Confucius, with his emphasis upon structure, and conscious intention, and the recognition that since men do not reveal their feelings, the only safe guide is not to do to others what you would not want done to yourself. In some moments of life it is structure that counts and at others flowing. "The way of life" is a swinging interaction of the two in which structure is both created and informed by flowing, flowing both preserved and facilitated by structure. Lao-tzu, nonetheless, has the deeper insight into that willing of the whole being which, in its openness and response, means spontaneity as opposed to that willfulness that tries to impose itself upon others. The man with the kind heart does not think of what his action will do for him; whereas the man with a just mind is always keenly conscious of "what's in it for me." Still worse is the man of conventional conduct, who will be the soul of courtesy and politeness as long as his notion of propriety is complied with, but who reveals the clenched fist underneath the smooth veneer as soon as he is not complied with. Such a man, even when he does not lay bare the violence that underlies his insistence upon harmony and decorum, "law and order," injures everyone he deals with. He forces on them a division into a submissive part and a rebellious part and denies to them the possibility of spontaneous and whole response. Lao-tzu's "sound man," in contrast, trusts in openness and reciprocity, stays in the lead of men without their knowing it, is content to appear a fool in comparison to the average man who is "so crisp and confident," but just thereby exercises the one real influence that can help the other find the way of life in his own way:

If I keep from meddling with people, they take care of themselves,
If I keep from commanding people, they behave themselves,
If I keep from preaching at people, they improve themselves,
If I keep from imposing on people, they become themselves.

"Those who tell do not know,/ Those who know do not tell." Lao-tzu's mystical teaching never leaves the ground of the concrete, the everyday—the simple problem which could have been solved before it became complicated, the "natural" way whose naturalism is not that of definition and manipulation but of openness and response. "Men knowing the way of life/ Do without acting,/ Effect without enforcing." "Deny the way of life and you are dead." "Men who have hardened are 'kin of death,'" but "men who stay gentle are 'kin of life.'" Those who are kin of life are not warlike. "A man with a will to kill will never prevail," says Lao-tzu. He will never prevail in history. Our history books are mostly made up of the story of men with the will to kill, from Alexander the Great and Ceasar down to Napoleon and Hitler. But there is another, hidden history, the history of the gentle who are "kin of life." This does not mean lying down and letting everybody walk on you. It means being like the water: finding your own level. There is a sense in Lao-tzu of a source that is there for us to use if we do not go against the stream, if we do not fight it. Only thus do we "double our strength to be strong." [4]

[4] The passages from Lao-tzu's teaching which I have quoted as the springboard for my interpretation are from *The Way of Life according to Lao-tzu*, trans. with an Introduction by Witter Bynner (New York: Capricorn Books, 1962), #1, 81, 21, 14, 10, 47, 7, 49, 55, 57, 56, 63, 76, 81 respectively.

More quickly than any of the other great religions, Taoism degenerated into systems of augury and magic. Yet Lao-tzu's way of life is part of the wisdom of the human race, a profound and enduring touchstone of reality.

[Chapter 7]

The Biblical Covenant:
Exile, Contending, and Trust

My great teacher Joachim Wach defined religion as a total response of the total being to what is experienced as ultimate reality. "Total response" because in religion, as distinct from scientific inquiry and aesthetic emotion, the whole being is responding and the whole being is involved in the response. Religion as we know it has always expressed itself in doctrinal forms as myth, creed, theology, metaphysics. It has expressed itself in practical forms as rituals, masses, and prayer—communal and individual. It has expressed itself in social forms as brotherhood, churches, and sects. It is impossible, indeed, to understand any actual religion except in terms of these three expressions and their interrelation.

But for all that, one cannot reduce religion merely to these expressions and interrelations, for their matrix is the religious reality that is expressed, and what is expressed is not in itself directly expressible. One of the great errors in the approach of many people to religion is to see it as a form of philosophy or metaphysics which is going to prove that God exists or describe his nature and attributes. This is to reduce God to an object, a part of the universe, to make him subservient to our logic, and in any case has to do with the detached observer rather than with the involvement of one's total being. Religion is a way that one walks. Religion is a commitment. Religion is one's basic response *whether* or not he calls himself religious and *whether* or not he affirms the existence of God. Some of our "labyrinthine ways," whether we are fleeing "the Hound of Heaven" or not, are so far underground that we ourselves are not aware of them when we come up again. Yet they too are important parts of our touchstones.

A large general contrast that one could make with some justification between Hinduism and Buddhism and the so-called Western religions—Zoroastrianism, Judaism, Christianity, Islam—is that the latter have a central concept of revelation whereas the former speaks in terms of illumination or "enlightenment." The reason for this difference is a profound one; for they differ basically in two respects—one is in their view of the ultimate nature of reality, of the relation of God, man, and the world. The tendency in much, although not all, Hinduism and Buddhism is to see this as one reality, as one basic Absolute, and this means that at the profoundest level God, the world, and man are not separate. Everything is God, if by "God" you no longer mean a God "out there," but *Brahman,* ultimate reality, the One without Second. In such a situation, revelation is not needed. What is needed is enlightenment, illumination; that is, the discovery of the absolute reality that is already here. The movement toward this Absolute is often seen under the aspect of *samadhi* or *satori*—a mystical or spiritual consciousness, "enlightenment." If we attain a certain state of spiritual consciousness, of spiritual being, then what already *is* the basic reality will be open to us so that nothing changes except us, except our relation to it. The veil is torn asunder, the illusion is pierced. Name and form and time and place, change and individuation are all seen as either illusion or as dependent reality. The essence of them all is the Absolute which is also the Absolute in us.

In the Hindu Upanishads, as we have seen, we find a progression from gods who were attached to nature, to gods who were behind nature, to the creative power (*prakriti*) that runs throughout nature, finally to the conception of an Absolute beyond change, yet somehow lying within, or underlying, or being the reality behind all name and form and change, behind all that we know of objective nature. There is also an inward progress in which what is taken to be the self, the personal self—this body, this name, the person, personality—is unmasked as not being the real self. The real self is found deeper in consciousness itself. From individual consciousness we come to that deep consciousness which is somehow the all-consciousness, the underlying consciousness in every self. It is not as if each of us has a different consciousness. We discover that the consciousness in each of us is identical with that in the other. Since this is so, we cannot talk of revelation since there is nothing to reveal. There is only something to uncover, something to discover, something to move toward, and we discover it primarily by moving inward, by sinking into this spiritual consciousness, by the type of spiritual exercises that enable us to withdraw the senses, to concentrate, to smooth the waves of the mind, to enable the spiritual energy to arise until finally illumination is secured.

The basic view of the Western religions is that God, world, and man are separate, although related. God, world, and man are not reducible to one reality; yet they stand in relation to each other. The way whereby man comes to know the divine, therefore, cannot be the mere opening up, unfolding, illumination. A gap has to be bridged, otherness has to be transcended. Revelation means not only that we go forth to meet the divine, but that in some sense the divine comes to meet us. Divine reality can approach us, can address us, can accost us, can demand of us, and our response becomes then the beginning of our way, the beginning of religious reality. This is why these are primarily history religions. This does not mean they reject nature. Far from it. The Hebrew Bible is full of the glory of God in nature—nature declaring the glory of God. Yet it is primarily through history that God speaks to man because history is none other than the concrete significance of this time, this place, this situation. In this time, place, and situation, in this concrete context, revelation comes not as some universal, which is always there for me to apprehend at each moment but does not itself move to meet me, but as the Eternal entering into time, as man meeting the Eternal in a moment of time, in a moment of history, whether it is the personal history of the individual or the history of a group of people.

The very beginning of understanding the problem of revelation is understanding that God is not reducible to the world and man or the world alone and man alone, any more than man can be reduced to the world or the world to man. This paradoxical view of God as in relation to man and yet apart from him is the very meaning of the term "creation"—not that God was some carpenter who at one time made an immense bird cage in which all of us now dwell, but that, transcending cause and effect, transcending space and time, not taking place as a cause in time, but creating, as it were, the very order of cause and time; creating anew at every moment, sustaining at every moment, Transcendence enters into relation with the world—sets it free and remains in relation with it. It is not a question of whether God *is* a person, in the sense of being like a man. It is the question of whether reality is seen as a meeting with transcendent reality *within* which meeting nature and the cosmos arise. Or whether it is the other way around: whether the cosmos becomes the all-inclusive in which man and God are set.

The Hindu notion of creation as "the play of the gods," or *lila*, has been rightly interpreted by Alan Watts and others as "sitting lightly to the world," though this attitude only truly comes to those who have gone through and beyond the order and attained enlightenment. The history religions, in contrast—Judaism, Christianity, and Islam—speak not of divine sport, *lila*, but of divine destiny—in the sense that God himself has a stake in creation, in history. History here is not the cyclical history that we see in the notion of the *kalpas* and *yugas* of Hinduism and the Great Year of ancient Greek religion. Rather it is linear, a line that stretches from creation to redemption, even though neither the beginning nor the end can be understood as a moment in time. Instead of an event being merely a part of a cycle or spiral, every event has its own uniqueness and its own meaning. As Martin Buber puts it, "Meaning is open and accessible in the lived concrete." We do not have to put away the world of the senses, or nature, or time, or history to find this meaning.

There is a basic trust in Hinduism, Buddhism, and Taoism—a trust which says that this world is not a place in which we are hopelessly lost. But there is a special emphasis on trust in the Hebrew Bible—a trust or faithfulness, *emunah*—that does not necessarily have a faith content. This trust does not mean security. The "happy man" in Psalm 1 is not assured of immortality in the world to come or of many sheep, goats, and camels in this life. He is compared to a tree planted by streams of water that brings forth fruit in its season. He has found a true existence that the sinner, however wealthy and prosperous, does not have. That is why the latter is compared to "chaff blown by the wind": dry and rootless, he loses his way; he has no way.

Thus at the center of the faith of biblical Judaism stands not belief, in the ordinary sense of the term, but trust—a trust that no exile from the presence of God is permanent, that each man and each generation is able to come into contact with reality. In the life of individual man, as of generations of men, it is the movement of time—the facts of change and death—

which most threatens this trust. Every great religion, culture, and philosophy has observed that "all is flux" and that man himself is a part of this flux. The conclusions that have been drawn from this fact, however, are as different as the world views of those who have drawn the conclusions. The response of biblical man has not taken the form of a cyclical order of time or an unchanging absolute, like the Greek, nor of the dismissal of time and change as *maya*, or illusion, like the Hindu, nor of the notion that one may flow with time, like the Taoist. He stands face to face with the changing creation and receives each new moment as an address of God—the revelation that comes to him through the unique present.

To stand before eternity is to be aware of one's own mortality:

> For a thousand years in thy sight
> are but as yesterday when it is past, . . .
> men . . . are like a dream, like grass . . .
> in the morning it flourishes and is renewed;
> in the evening it fades and withers. . . .
>   our years come to an end like a sigh. . . .
> yet their span is but toil and trouble;
>   they are soon gone, and we fly away. (Psalm 90:4–10)

This is the universal human condition—a condition which has tempted some men to see existence as unreal or as an ephemeral reflection of reality and others to "eat, drink, and be merry, for tomorrow we die." The psalmist, in contrast, prays that he may withstand this reality and heighten it, that he may make his existence real by meeting each new moment with the wholeness of his being:

> So teach us to number our days
> That we may get a heart of wisdom (Psalm 90:12)

In the beautiful poem of Ecclesiastes from the later Wisdom literature, time has become the cycle that goes round and round and will not reach a meaning. Even when at the end of the poem we are told to remember the Creator in the days of our youth, there is still no suggestion that we shall find meaning here, in the actual flow of time, but only somewhere above. But in the Psalms and in the Book of Job there is a wrestling for meaning despite the passage of time.

It is not only man's mortality, however, but the suffering of the innocent and the prosperity of the wicked that leads to the tempering of trust in Job and in the Psalms. The reaffirmation of trust takes place out of an immediate sense of exile. When God no longer prepares a table for the good man in the presence of his enemies; when the good man sees not the recompense of the wicked, but their prosperity and their arrogance, his trust is shaken. He cannot bear the fact that the presence of God is emptied out of the world, that the sinners who cannot stand in the judgment are nonetheless confirmed by the congregation, and divine and social reality are split asunder. The world is not built in such a way that the natural and moral order correspond. Neither the author of the Book of Job nor of Psalms 73 and 82 can say with the earlier Psalmist, "I am old and I have been young, and never yet have I seen the righteous begging for bread." It is not true. The righteous suffer and the wicked prosper. It is out of this situation that Job cries out and contends with a strength perhaps unequalled in any of the world's religious scriptures.

The basic paradox of the Hebrew Bible is the dialogue between eternal God and mortal man, between the imageless Absolute and man who is created in God's "image." If that dialogue is to take place, it must take place not in eternity but in the present—in the unique situation of a limited man who was born yesterday and will die tomorrow. Jacob wrestles with the angel, and Job wrestles with God to receive the blessing of this dialogue on which the very meaning of their existence depends. Job holds fast to his trust in the real God whom he meets in the dreadful fate that has befallen him, and he holds fast to the facts of his innocence and his suffering. At the heart of the Book of Job stands neither "blind faith" nor denial of God, but trusting and contending, recognizing his dependence on God yet standing firm on the ground of his created freedom.

Job wanted a dialogue with God, but when this dialogue comes it dismays him by forcing him to recognize that the partner with whom he speaks is the Creator who at each moment creates the ground of existence and transcends it.

> "Where were you when I laid the foundation of the earth?
> Tell me, if you have understanding . . .
> when the morning stars sang together,
> and all the sons of God shouted for joy?" (38:37)

The reality of creation is the reality of the otherness that man cannot remove into his rational comprehension of the world. We seek to "anthropomorphize" creation—to rationalize reality to fit the moral conceptions of man. Despite our power to "comprehend" the world, it has a reality independent of us. The real God is not the God whom man removes into the sphere of his own spirit and thought, but the creator who speaks to man through creatures that exist for their own sake and not just for human purposes.[1]

What Job asks for he does receive: not an explanation as to why he suffers, but at least this God who has become far from him comes to him, speaks to him out of the whirlwind and says, "Now I will speak and you reply." Then Job says, "Before I had heard of you with the hearing of the ear, but now my eye sees you." When Job earlier makes the statement, "I know that my redeemer lives," he couples it with the statement, "And I will see him, even out of my flesh"—when my skin is stripped away by disease—I will see him, "my eyes and not another." This is what does happen to Job at the

[1] For a fuller interpretation of Job and biblical faith see Maurice Friedman, *Problematic Rebel: Melville, Dostoievsky, Kafka, Camus* (Chicago: The University of Chicago Press and Phoenix Paperbacks, 1970), pp. 3–22.

end. Had Job *not* contended, had he followed the advice of his friends and accepted his suffering humbly as his due or God's will, he would not have known the terrible and blessed experience of God coming to meet him as he went forth to meet God.

The meaning of the biblical dialogue is not what we get from God—whether it be "peace of mind," "peace of soul," "successful living," or "positive thinking"—but our walking with God on this earth. The trust at the heart of this walking with God is tried and man is exiled by the facts of the passage of time, sickness and death and by the very social order that man builds. There is the possibility of renewing this trust, but only if we can bring the exile into the dialogue with God, not if we turn away from the exile or overlook it. What happened to Job can and does happen, in more or less concentrated form, to any man. Instead of turning Job's situation into the abstract metaphysical problem of evil, we should encounter it as a touchstone of reality. For the real question—the question that lies at the inmost core of our very existence—is not Why? but How? How can we live in a world in which Auschwitz and Hiroshima happen? How can we find the resources once more to go out to a meeting with anyone or anything?

In moving to so-called Western religion, we have not left the paradox which transcends Aristotle's law of contradiction, *i.e.* that a thing is either A or not-A. If we speak of God creating the world and yet remaining in relationship with it, we have already gone beyond this law. Even if we speak of two people talking with each other, we imply an interhuman reality incomprehensible in terms of Aristotle's logic. If they were entirely other than each other, they could not talk, and if they were the same, they would not need to talk. Nor is it the sameness in each other that speaks but one whole person to another, really other, whole person. Starting with trust as grounded in this paradoxical combination of separateness and relationship—arrows going apart and arrows coming together —we must recognize exile as inevitable.

In biblical Judaism trust and exile are inseparably coupled with rebellion. The story of Adam and Eve is not, as Nietzsche thought, "slavish Semitic obedience." On the contrary, the very meaning of the story is that man becomes man in rebelling against God, in ceasing to be a child and eating of the fruit of the tree of the knowledge of good and evil. Similarly the most famous statement of trust in the Book of Job—"He may slay me. I await it."—is followed by the statement, "But I will argue my ways to his face. This is my comfort, that a hypocrite cannot come before him." To bring each new situation into the dialogue with God means both faithfulness and contending. There can be no question here of "blind faith." When Kierkegaard made the story of Abraham's temptation to sacrifice Isaac the very paradigm of unquestioning obedience, he disregarded the story that appears just two chapters earlier in Genesis. Abraham not only pleads for the people of Sodom lest the innocent be destroyed with the guilty, but he contends with the Lord and demands that he be faithful to his own way of justice: "I who am dust and ashes have taken it upon myself to argue with the Lord. Will the Lord of justice not do justice?"

In Kierkegaard's interpretation of Abraham's "temptation" to sacrifice Isaac, moral responsibility disappears in favor of a "teleological suspension of the ethical" and an "absolute duty to the Absolute." In the actual story, however, Abraham does not sacrifice Isaac, but is only brought to that readiness that enables him to renew his *covenant* with God by bringing into it his relation to this unexpected son of his old age. The special covenant between God and Israel is the demand placed on Israel that it become "a kingdom of priests and a holy nation" (Exodus) through bringing every aspect of its existence—personal, social, economic, political, international— into its dialogue with God. Here social responsibility is not only the responsibility of one man to another, but the responsibility of a people as a people for its corporate existence. The prophets, accordingly, call the people to account not just as individuals who have strayed from the paths of righteousness, but as the Israel that has turned aside from the task for which it was "chosen"—the task of becoming a true people that realizes justice, righteousness, and loving kindness in genuine communal life and makes real the kingship of God in the social sphere as well as in the cultic and the specifically religious.

The covenant exists only in the mutuality of the address from God and the people's turning toward God. This covenant is no legal contract that can be made once for all; for it does not concern a part of the people's existence, but the whole. Therefore, with Israel as with Abraham, the covenant must be renewed again and again in each new existential and historical situation. The God who speaks to the people, correspondingly, is not a cosmic God who guarantees a universal moral order, but the God of the Ten Commandments whose "Thou shalt" is apprehended by the individual person and by the group only in the unique, concrete situation—the ever renewed demand of the ever new present. It is only modern man who has converted these commands into the impersonal "one must" of the social norm. The "ought" implicit in the command can be derived only from the responsibility of the person to what claims him in the particular situation in which he finds himself. One does not *apply* the Ten Commandments to the situation: one *rehears* them as utterly unique, present commands. Only through this "rehearing" do injunctions such as not to kill, to steal, and to bear false witness take on concrete meaning. You cannot "deal lovingly with your neighbor as one equal to yourself" as a general principle, but only in a mutual relationship in the concrete, particular situation.

Far from being opposites, "Love your neighbor as yourself" and "an eye for an eye and a tooth for a tooth" are the

direct and indirect statement of the same principle. "An eye
for an eye and a tooth for a tooth" is *not* the expression of
a vengeful God, but a primitive statement of basic social democracy in which no man is held of greater worth than another, because each is created in the image of God. Such
equality of man and man existed nowhere outside of Israel in
the ancient world. Throughout all history, indeed, the natural
inequality of man has justified razing a whole city to revenge
the murder of one privileged man; countless other men have
been exterminated with impunity because they were slaves or
serfs or members of an "inferior race." "An eye for an eye" is
not a religious rite, but a social law based on a fundamental
conception of social justice. No society has ever got furtner
than this principle in its actual administration of justice (despite all the talk about a higher "law of love"), and many still
are not up to it.

What keeps "an eye for an eye" from deteriorating into an
abstract principle that ignores the uniqueness of each man and
each situation is, "Deal lovingly with your neighbor as one
equal to yourself." Justice, which regulates the indirect relations of men, and love, which channels the direct, do not oppose, but complement each other. The Ten Commandments
proceed from the relationship to the God whom the people
met in history ("I am the Lord your God who brought you
out of the land of Egypt, out of the house of bondage") and
on this basis point to the demands of the covenant in the meeting between man and man. In Exodus, the same book of the
Bible in which the Ten Commandments first appear, this
recognition of the equality of one's fellow man before God is
extended to all men on that simple human basis of reciprocity
that underlies the Golden Rule—seeing oneself in the situation
of the other: "You shall not wrong a stranger or oppress him,
for you were strangers in the land of Egypt."(22:21) "You
know the heart of a stranger, for you were strangers in the
land of Egypt."(23:9) The man confronting you may be

weak and powerless, but even so he remains in dialogue with God and God will hear his cry: "You shall not afflict any widow or orphan . . . I will surely hear their cry."(22:22–23) "If ever you take your neighbor's garment in pledge, you shall restore it to him before the sun goes down; for that is his only covering, it is his mantle for his body; in what else shall he sleep? And if he cries to me, I will hear, for I am compassionate."(22:26–27) The compassion of God to man is also the compassion that man must exercise to his fellow man, even to his enemy: "If you meet your enemy's ox or his ass going astray, you shall bring it back to him. If you see the ass of one who hates you lying under its burden, you shall refrain from leaving him with it, you shall help him to lift it up."(23:3–5)

The *doing* of the Torah grows first out of the *hearing* in the dialogue with God, the social responsibility out of the covenantal relationship. "You shall be holy; for I the Lord your God am holy."(Leviticus 19) "The wages of a hired servant shall not remain with you all night until the morning. You shall not curse the deaf or put a stumbling block before the blind, but you shall fear your God: I am the Lord."(Lev. 19:13–14) The "fear of the Lord" is not the fear of punishment, but the awe before the Creator and his creation, before the otherness of the other man who cannot be treated as a mere extension of my own subjectivity. "The fear of the Lord" is not only "the beginning of wisdom," as the Book of Job says; it is also the beginning of the love of God and the love of man. "You must not hate your brother in your heart . . . you shall not take vengeance . . . you shall love your neighbor as yourself: I am the Lord."(Lev. 19:17–18)

To love your neighbor as yourself does not mean selflessness nor does it mean identification or empathy with your neighbor. It means, rather, meeting him as a unique person of value in himself and experiencing the relationship from his side as well as from your own. This means that the command, "Deal lovingly with your neighbor as one equal to yourself" is never an external command that I transfer from my relation to God to my relation to man. Rather it is precisely in meeting man that I meet God, and in the moment when I have to do with you there is no other way to this meeting. "The stranger who sojourns with you shall be to you as the native among you, and you shall love him as yourself; for you were strangers in the land of Egypt: I am the Lord your God."(Lev. 19:33–34)

The Torah is not, as has been thought from Saint Paul to Freud, a series of harsh laws, impossible of fulfillment, setting a standard of perfection that none can live up to and thereby condemning all alike to be sinners.

> This commandment which I command you this day is not too hard for you, neither is it far off. It is not in heaven, that you should say, "Who will go up for us to heaven and bring it to us, that we may hear it and do it?" . . . But the word is very near you; it is in your mouth and in your heart, so that you can do it. (Deut. 30:11–14)

It is the sufficient amount that is asked of one each day. This way of hearing and responding in the concrete present is the way of authentic existence for the individual and the people: "See, I have set before you this day life and good, death and evil. Therefore choose life."(Deut. 30:15) No external sanction or social contract is needed here as a basis for moral action and social responsibility. They are of intrinsic value as the path that man walks with God in history.

The prophetic protest is always essentially a call to turn back to God with one's whole existence. This turning (*teshuvah*) means shouldering anew the task of the covenant— the task of making real the kingship of God through becoming a true people in every aspect of communal and individual life. When the people follow a neighboring kingdom in sacrificing their first-born children to the god Moloch, the prophet Micah tells them that something very much less and very much more is demanded of them, namely, their whole existence: "to do justice, and to love kindness and to walk humbly with your God." (Micah 6:7–8) In the Book of Amos similarly, it is not "religion," but true community that is asked of men. The demand that Amos places on the nations in the name of God is the demand of the "covenant of brotherhood." It is out of this context that the vision of the Messiah arises, the "anointed one" through whom God will be with us (Immanuel) since through his leadership the true king will lead the people, or the remnant who have remained faithful, to make real the kingship of God. His reign will be characterized by peace, justice, and righteousness; in other words, by leading the people back to the task of the covenant. "With righteousness he shall judge the poor, and decide with equity for the meek of the earth." (Isaiah 11:4) The "suffering servant" of Deutero-Isaiah is no king but a prophet, but he, too, is seen as continuing the work of the covenant: "I have kept you and given you as a covenant to the people, to establish the land, to apportion the desolate heritage; saying to the prisoners, 'Come forth,' to those who are in darkness, 'Appear.' " (Isaiah 49:8–9) Even the anonymous suffering and death of this man for which the people despise and reject him, believing him smitten by God (Chap. 53), must be understood within the context of social responsibility. The man who remains an integral part of his community, while at the same time remaining faithful to the covenant from which the community has turned away, suffers much more than the lonely mystic who cuts himself off from responsibility for the community in which he dwells. By standing his ground and bearing this terrible suffering, the "servant" carries social responsibility into the depths of tragedy where political success and effectiveness give way before the direct communal reality that works in the hidden groundsprings of history.

The covenant is not theology. It has to do with history, with man, with real situations. In one historical situation Amos emphasizes *zedakah* righteousness; in another Hosea emphasizes *hesed* loving kindness: "I will heal your backslidings, I will love you freely"; in still another Isaiah emphasizes *kedoshah* holiness. The word of demand and the word of comfort are both real covenantal words. It is not a question of what sort of God each prophet believed in but of the situation into which God speaks. That is why every Bible that translates the Tetragrammaton, the ineffable and unpronounceable name of God, as Jehovah or Yahweh, including the *Jerusalem Bible*, completely misses the imageless God who is not known in himself but only in his relation to man in history. This God does not say, "I am that I am," but as Buber translates it, "I shall be there *as* I shall be there."

[Chapter 8]

Hasidism and Contemporary Man

Hasidism is the popular mystical movement of East European Jewry in the eighteenth and nineteenth centuries. The Hebrew word *hasid* means "pious." It is derived from the noun *hesed*, meaning loving kindness, mercy, or grace. The Hasidic movement arose in Poland in the eighteenth century, and, despite bitter persecution at the hands of traditional Rabbinism, spread rapidly among the Jews of eastern Europe until it included almost half of them in its ranks. Hasidism is really a continuation in many senses of biblical and rabbinical Judaism. While it is not a historical continuation of Christianity, many people have been startled by the resemblances between Hasidism and early Christianity, in particular between the founder of Hasidism—the Baal Shem Tov, or Good Master of the Name of God—and Jesus. Both spoke to the common, the ordinary folk; both represented something of a revolt against an overemphasis on learning; both tried to renew the spirit from within the tradition rather than destroying, cutting off, and radically changing the tradition.

The Hasidim founded real communities, each with its own *rebbe*. The *rebbe*, the leader of the community, was also called the *zaddik*, the righteous or justified man. "The world stands because of the *zaddik*," says the Talmud, and in Jewish legend this has grown into the myth of the thirty-six hidden *zaddikim* of each generation—the *lamedvovnikim*—without whom the world could not stand. Each one of these *zaddikim* had his own unique teaching that he gave to his community. Originally as it was passed down from generation to generation, the leadership devolved not so much on those who could receive a doctrine but on those who could embody a way of life. So the first effect of the *zaddik* was to bring the people to immediacy in relationship to God. Later, when hereditary dynasties of Hasidim arose and the *rebbes* lived in great palaces and were surrounded by awe and superstition, the *zaddik* became almost a mediator between the people and God—the very opposite of his original function.

Hasidism, like Zen Buddhism, grew out of the most abstruse speculation—first the medieval Kabbala of the Zohar ("The Book of Splendor") and later the Lurian Kabbala that arose after the Jews were exiled from Spain in 1492. If you go today to Israel and go up the mountains opposite the Sea of Galilee, winding round and round you finally reach, near the top, Zfat, or Safed, where the Lurian Kabbala arose. There men strove to bring the Messiah down. At one point in 1544 they all stood on the rooftops expecting that at that hour the Messiah would come. There developed in the Lurian Kabbala a marvelous gnostic doctrine in which the fall was not, as in the Zohar, a gradual emanation of ten *Sephiroth*. It was instead an event, a happening, in which heavenly vessels were so full of grace that they burst and the sparks of divine light fell downward to earth and were surrounded by shells of darkness. The *tikkun*, or restoration, meant accordingly freeing these sparks from their shells so that they could rise upward to their divine source. This could be done through men's *kavanot*—magical, mystical intentions with which one prayed and acted. It was believed that man could help bring the Messiah down through the part in the restoration that his *kavanot* made possible. This led to the pseudo-messianic movement of Sabbatai Zvi, which ended disastrously when Sabbatai Zvi was forcibly converted to Islam. Out of all this ferment and the Chmielnieski Cossack massacres of hundreds of thousands of Jews in village after village in Eastern Europe was kindled the movement founded by Israel ben Eliezer (1700–1760), the Baal Shem Tov. The Baal Shem said, "I have come to teach you a new way, and it is not fasting and penance but joy in God, in Israel, and in the Torah."

Hasidism is a mysticism which does not hold chastity to be the highest virtue. On the contrary, it sees marriage as the highest form of life. It is a mysticism which does not turn away from community, or put aside the life of the senses. Community is to be hallowed, the life of the senses celebrated and sanctified. Hasidism supplemented *kavanot* with *kavana:* it stressed the consecration and direction of the whole person as well as special mystical techniques.

My mother comes from two distinguished lines of Lubavitcher (Habad) Hasidim, yet neither in my home nor in the Reform Temple to which I belonged in Tulsa did I even hear of Hasidism until I was twenty-four years old. Although their father remained a pious Hasid to his death, my mother's cousins in an Israeli kibbutz retain no interest in Hasidism except as a childhood memory. Nor does this memory give them any sympathetic understanding of my 1960 neighbors in Jerusalem, the Polish Hasidim, resplendent on Shabbat in *streimal* (fox-fur hats), caftans, beards, and earlocks. My cousins' criticism of those Israeli Hasidim who through their opposition or their separatism seem to obstruct the growth and progress of the state is shared by most of the Israelis whom I have met.

The American counterpart of the Mea Shearim district of Jerusalem is the Williamsburg district of Brooklyn. I spent Shabbat at the home of a Williamsburg Hasid some years ago and stood from ten till two in the morning in a tiny *shtuebl* packed with over a hundred disciples of the Satmor Rebbe, good-naturedly fighting and shoving for the *shirayim*, food that the Rebbe gives from his thirteen-course meal. I was deeply impressed, particularly at one point when, after wishing the Rebbe would pass me a drumstick and then thinking that, dressed as I was, I was the last person he would thus honor, some one handed me a drumstick and said, "The Rebbe sent this for you!" Nevertheless, I took away with me the sense of a childlike devotion of the Hasidim to the Rebbe quite foreign to the individualized consciousness of the modern Jew. When I next visited Williamsburg to witness the dancing on Simhas Torah, I naively went into the synagogue of the Klausenberger Rebbe with a non-Jewish friend to inquire as to the time of their services. I was confronted by a young man with a bright red beard who, instead of answering my question, asked me, "Are you a Jew?" "Yes," I replied. "Do you speak Yiddish?" "No," I said. "You are a Jew and you don't speak Yiddish!" he snorted contemptuously. Then he turned to my friend, whose bowtie and cap marked him as a smart Greenwich Villager, and, pointing to him as a Hasid of the time of the Maccabees might have pointed to a swine that had been brought into the Temple, exclaimed indignantly, "And you brought *him* into the Synagogue!" My friend shrank out of the door, and I began to wonder whether my years of devotion to Hasidism had been misplaced.

Many American Jews have not even heard of Hasidism. Some of those who have are *Mitnagdim* from Eastern Europe, opponents of Hasidism who attack its superstition and its crudeness and who know it only in the often degenerate form in which it has come down to us. Others are intellectuals who know Hasidism either as an interesting form of Eastern European Jewish culture—a part of Jewish folk history to be studied for its anthropological interest—or recognize it as a strain in certain current approaches to Judaism which, objectionable in themselves, are rendered all the more so through the recrudescence of material from the unenlightened past that the modern rational Jew has made such splendid progress in shaking off.

An excellent and quite typical example of this latter attitude is a "re-examination" of Hasidism which sees "the contemporary revival of interest in Hasidism" as engendering a "romantic idealization oftentimes to the point of extravagance" and which blames this "neo-mystical orientation" on "the influence of Martin Buber's literary work in this field during the past half century." I have myself contributed to this "neo-mysticism" by translating and editing four of Buber's Hasidic books. The author of the article has the antidote for the neo-Hasidic sickness at hand: "An examination of the elements of irrationality and fantasy in Hasidic doctrine may have a sobering effect upon those who have been overly influenced by the current romanticist conception of Hasidism." After depicting the ignorant and superstitious intellectual climate in which Hasidism grew and spread, he proceeds to an attack on the nonsensical claims for supernatural powers advanced on behalf of the Baal Shem Tov both by the "Besht" himself and his followers. One of the sources he lists for his material on the Besht is the stories in Buber's *The Legend of the Baal-Shem*, the first of my own translations of Buber's Hasidic works. Nothing could have been more obvious, one would have thought, than that these legends make no claim to historical accuracy. Yet he takes them as reliable historical documents on which to base his criticism of the Besht. After reviewing the attacks on Hasidism by the *Mitnagdim* and the *Maskilim* of the time of the Besht, he comes out with the remarkable conclusion that, whatever Hasidism may have contributed to the Jewish people of the eighteenth century by way of warmth, enthusiasm, joy, and sense of fellowship, Hasidism is an anachronism in our day. "The deep chasm that separates us intellectually from Hasidism," the radical difference in their universe of discourse and ours make any attempt to revive

Hasidism "as a religious philosophy and movement for our contemporaries" a "confusion of nostalgia and sentimentalism with the imperatives and requirements of a modern man's faith." If there are among our contemporaries some "whose religious backgrounds and mental framework enable them to believe in and practice the Hasidic way of life," then these are men who may be dwelling physically in 20th century America, "but they are living intellectually in 18th century Poland." [1]

The "logic" of this testimony in the name of "rational" modern man amounts to saying that because there are some elements in Beshtian Hasidism that appear quite foreign to the contemporary American, therefore the movement as a whole has nothing to say to us. By the same logic one would have to dismiss the Bible as utterly irrelevant for modern man since there is ample evidence in it of beliefs concerning the supernatural, the demonic, and the miraculous that modern man must consider the products of ignorance and superstition or of an outmoded world-view. Thanks to this "re-examination," nonetheless, we are now in a position to define our problem more exactly. That Hasidism could be revived as a really modern movement is difficult, if not impossible, to imagine, despite the successes of the Lubavitcher Hasidim. That it can be revived as an element in a modern religious philosophy is not only imaginable but undeniably actual in a number of important contemporary philosophies of Judaism—those of Martin Buber, Abraham J. Heschel, M. Maisels, Elie Wiesel, and even, to a lesser extent, Leo Baeck, the great representative of liberal Judaism.[2] Our question, therefore, must be whether Hasidism potentially has some greater and more direct role to

[1] Israel J. Kazis, "Hasidism Re-examined," *The Reconstructionist,* Vol. XXIII, No. 8 (May 31, 1957), pp. 7–13.

[2] Cf. Leo Baeck, *This People Israel,* trans. by Albert Friedlander (New York: Holt, Rinehart & Winston, 1964). Dr. Maisels has told me that Hasidism, particularly that of Nachman of Brazlav, is like a pigment running throughout Maisels' *Thought and Truth.*

play in the modern Jewish and non-Jewish world than that of an element in the thought of various Jewish philosophers.

The first Hasidic book that I read was an early attempt at the translation of *The Legend of the Baal-Shem.* This was the first Jewish book that had had any impact on me since I was a child, the first that spoke to me as a mature, thinking man. As I look back on this impact, it was that of the Baal Shem Tov as an image of man—an image of *Jewish* man but also an image of *man* that superseded—without displacing—Saint Francis, the Buddha, Sri Ramakrishna, and Jesus in my allegiance. This image was, to be sure, a romanticized one in Buber's highly poetic retelling. Yet it was essentially the same man who spoke to me through these legends as later spoke to me through *The Tales of the Hasidim,* "The Baal Shem Tov's Instruction in Intercourse with God," and the accounts of the life and teaching of the Baal Shem to which I had access through English and German sources. This was the man who pointed out that Isaac and Jacob had to find their own unique relationship to God and could not base their searching on that of Abraham alone, the man who knew his relationship to God as the meaning and goal of his strivings compared to which no future life was of importance. The Besht did not emphasize mystical exercises, such as I had been concerned with, but wholehearted turning to God. He preferred a passionate opponent to a lukewarm adherent. "For the passionate opponent may come over and bring all his passion with him. But from a lukewarm adherent there is nothing more to be hoped." He turned away from asceticism and mortification of the flesh to the joyful recognition that each man is a son of the King. But he did not mistake the son for the King. His last words were, "Let not the foot of pride come near me!"

In Hasidism I found an image of an active love and fervent devotion no longer coupled with self-denial or metaphysical theorizing about unity with the divine. After my immersion in the individualistic and world-denying forms of mysticism that

I had found in Hinduism, Buddhism, and Christianity, Hasidism spoke to me in compelling accents of a wholehearted service of God that did not mean turning away from my fellow men and from the world. All that was asked was to do everything one did with one's whole strength—not the denial of self and the extirpation of the passions but the fulfillment of self and the direction of passion in a communal mysticism of humility, love, prayer, and joy. After my concern for techniques of spiritual perfection, I now learned that fulfillment and redemption do "not take place through formulae or through any kind of prescribed and special action," but through the *kavana* that one brings to one's every act. "It is not the matter of the action, but only its dedication that is decisive." A new image of man offered itself to me, that of the zaddik—the humble man, the loving man, the helper:

> Mixing with all and untouched by all, devoted to the multitude and collected in his uniqueness, fulfilling on the rocky summits of solitude the bond with the infinite and in the valley of life the bond with the earthly. . . . He knows that all is in God and greets His messengers as trusted friends.[3]

In the end the most important heritage that Hasidism has bequeathed us is not its doctrine and teachings but its image of man—the image of the Besht, the Maggid of Mezritch, Levi Yitzhak of Berditchev, Nachman of Brazlav, Shneur Zalman of Ladi, the "Yehudi" of Pzhysha, and a host of other zaddikim, each with a unique relationship to God and to his particular community.

Now that I am no longer a "mystic," I must ask in what sense, if at all, Hasidism is mysticism. The new generation of scholars of Hasidism, such as J. B. Weiss and Rivka Shatz-Ufenheimer, point to the distinction that must be made between the active mysticism of the Besht and other more qui-

---

[3] Martin Buber, *The Legend of the Baal-Shem*, trans. by Maurice Friedman (New York: Schocken Books, paperback edition, 1969), pp. 49 f.

etistic forms of Hasidism. The latter are similar to many phenomena with which we are already familiar from the mystical movements of other religions. The mysticism of the Besht, on the other hand, is unique, and because of its very uniqueness we may question whether it is properly designated by the general, vague, and usually misleading category of "mysticism."

This difficulty did not present itself to me when I first read *The Legend of the Baal-Shem*, for in this early work Buber gives equal emphasis, along with *avoda* (service), *kavana* (intention), and *shiflut* (humility), to *hitlahavut*—the ecstatic devotion and cleaving to God of the Hasidim. If it was in clear contrast to the equanimity of the Buddha and the nondualistic superconsciouness of the Vedanta, *hitlahavut* was sufficiently similar to the devotional mysticism of Saint Francis and of the Sufi mystics not to appear troubling. On the other hand, in Buber's later interpretation of Hasidism, *hitlahavut* drops out of sight in favor of the concrete, unexalted task of "hallowing the everyday." In his introduction to "The Baal Shem Tov's Instruction in Intercourse with God," Buber ends by identifying the mysticism of the Besht with religion as such, that is, with the dialogue between God and man.

> The Baal-Shem will probably be extolled as the founder of a *realistic and active mysticism*, i.e., a mysticism for which the world is not an illusion from which man must turn away in order to reach true being, but the reality between God and him in which *reciprocity* manifests itself, the subject of the message of creation to him, the subject of his *answering service of creation*, destined to be redeemed through *the meeting of divine and human need;* a mysticism, hence, without the intermixture of principles and without the weakening of the *lived multiplicity* of all for the sake of a unity of all that is to be experienced. . . . A "mysticism" that may be called such because it preserves the *immediacy of the relation,* guards the *concreteness* of the absolute and demands the *involvement of the whole being;* one can, to be sure, also

call it *religion* for just the same reason. Its true English name is perhaps: *presentness.*[4]

There is indeed, as Buber points out elsewhere, a theistic mysticism in which God remains the personal Thou. This phenomenon we know already from the Hindu Bhakti, Christian devotional mysticism, and Sufi mysticism. But if Hasidism, in addition, is the only mysticism that has become *ethos*, "the only mysticism in which time is hallowed" and the timeless moment of inner illumination meets the historical line of revelation,[5] in what sense does this mysticism of the concrete and the everyday differ from religion in general or from the religion of the Bible?

It is not possible to define mysticism in terms of some doctrinal content or philosophy, such as the overcoming of the subject-object duality in favor of unity or identity with the Absolute. The attempts of modern interpreters of mysticism, such as Evelyn Underhill, Aldous Huxley, W. T. Stace, and Gerald Heard, to define mysticism in this way will always be misguided. But neither can one define mysticism simply as immediacy in relationship to God, or presentness, since this is true of biblical religion too, and biblical religion is not mystical. I should define mysticism, rather, as immediacy and presentness *plus* presence—a strong sense of the immanence of God not as doctrine but as immersion in a directly experienced reality of divine presence. Mysticism includes not only personal contact with God but also the presence of the spirit of God. This is the *Brahama vihara*, or living in Brahman, of Hinduism, the flowing with the Tao of Taoism, the sudden illumination of the thousand and one things of Zen Buddhism, the testimony of Paul that in God "we live and move and have

[4] Martin Buber, *Hasidism and Modern Man*, ed. & trans. with an Introduction by Maurice Friedman (New York: Harper Torchbooks, 1966), p. 180 f., italics mine.

[5] Martin Buber, *The Origin and Meaning of Hasidism*, ed. & trans. with an Introduction by Maurice Friedman (New York: Harper Torchbooks, 1966), pp. 198 f., 239.

our being." Put in terms of modern Jewish philosophy of religion, mysticism includes both Martin Buber's dialogue with the "eternal Thou" and Abraham Heschel's "awareness of the ineffable." Our existence is not only God's address and our answering response; it is also discovering ourselves in the presence of God, knowing ourselves as known by God. Mysticism is not only "the lived concrete": it is also joy and praise, wonder and awe.

Hasidism has spoken most strongly to me through *The Tales of the Hasidim*—the "legendary anecdotes" that bear true witness in stammering tongue to the life of the Hasidim as Martin Buber has presented it to us. If I am asked about the uniqueness of Hasidic mysticism, I do not give a definition: I tell a tale. I can best witness, I believe, to the way in which Hasidism speaks to my condition and to the condition of contemporary man through the tales themselves. One can find motifs in Hasidism which add up to a teaching—a way of man, a way of life. But these motifs are very closely interrelated, and they are not so much parts of a system as they are wisdom. For example, Hasidism emphasizes the uniqueness of man without stressing self-realization. "When I get to heaven," said Rabbi Zusya, "they will not ask me: 'Why were you not Moses?' but 'Why were you not Zusya?'" We are called to become what we in our created uniqueness can become—not just to fulfill our social duty or realize our talent or potentialities, but to become the unique person we are called to be. This is not an already existing uniqueness that we can fulfill through "self-expression" or "self-realization." We have to realize our uniqueness in response to the world. A part of this response, for Zusya, was the fact that Moses was there for him—not as a model to imitate but as an image of man that arose in dialogue, a "touchstone of reality" that entered into his own becoming. Why did you not become what only you could become? does not mean, Why were you not *different*

from others, but Why did you not fulfill the creative task you
have become aware of as yours alone?

> Rabbi Pinhas said: "When a man embarks on something
> great, in the spirit of truth, he need not be afraid that another
> may imitate him. But if he does not do it in the spirit of
> truth, but plans to do it in a way no one could imitate,
> then he drags the great down to the lowest level—and every-
> one can do the same."[6]

There is a great tendency in our culture to exalt the different
and to confuse the different with the unique. The "different"
is merely a term of comparison. The unique is something
valued in and for itself. This is very important; for the search
for originality, which is so strong in our day, usually takes
the form of a different twist or a new wrinkle. What we ought
to be concerned about is our faithful response. If we respond
really faithfully, this will bring out our own uniqueness.

This also means, of course, that I must stand my ground
and witness for that unique creation which I am. When the
servant forgot to give Mendel a spoon, Rabbi Elimelech said:
"Look, Mendel, you must learn to ask for a spoon and if need
be, for a plate too!" This is related to the contending with
God which is essential to biblical faith. "Every man should
have two pockets to use as the occasion demands," said Rabbi
Bunam, "in one of which are the words, 'For my sake the
world was created' and in the other the words, 'I am earth
and ashes.'" This balance—neither affirming yourself absolutely nor denying yourself absolutely but recognizing
that you are given a created ground on which to stand
and from which to move to meet the world—is the true
humility of Hasidism. "If God so desires, let him take our
life," said the rabbi of Ger, "but he must leave us that with
which we love him—he must leave us our heart." Usually

[6] Martin Buber, *Tales of the Hasidim. The Early Masters,* trans. by Olga
Marx (New York: Schocken Books, paperback edition, 1961), p. 135–
"Originality."

it is not God who takes away our heart but we ourselves—by living in such a way that there are no free moments in which our heart might open itself to the address of the world and respond. "A human being who has not a single hour for his own every day," said Rabbi Moshe Leib, "is no human being." This is for me the most painful of all the Hasidic sayings; for I encounter it again and again as a judgment on my way of life and on that of most of my contemporaries! The fact that we ourselves have chosen our form of slavery does not make it any less slavery.

To realize one's uniqueness rules out every form of imitation, even of Abraham, Isaac, and Jacob. "Each one of us in his own way shall devise something new in the light of the teachings and of service," said the maggid (preacher) of Zlotchov, "and do what has not yet been done." When a son who inherited his father's congregation was reproached by his disciples with conducting himself differently from his father, he retorted: "I do just as my father did. He did not imitate and I do not imitate." The relationship between man and man was central to Hasidism, but only in spontaneous address and response and not in that invidious comparison and contrast that leads men to call one man "superior" to another. When someone praised one man to Rabbi Mendel of Kotzk at the expense of another, Rabbi Mendel said: "If I am I because I am I, and you are you because you are you, then I am I and you are you. But if I am I because you are you, and you are you because I am I, then I am not I, and you are not you." When Rabbi Abraham was asked why people feel so crowded despite the fact that the sages say that everything, man included, has his place, he replied: "Because each wants to occupy the place of the other." Uniqueness does not preclude dialogue. On the contrary, it is precisely through each standing his own ground and yet moving to meet the other that genuine dialogue from ground to ground takes place. For a person for whom there is no dialogue, even the ground of

life itself crumbles away. After the death of Rabbi Moshe of
Kobryn, a friend said: "If there had been someone to whom
he could have talked, he would still be alive."

When asked for one general way to the service of God, the
Seer of Lublin replied:

> It is impossible to tell men what way they should take.
> For one way to serve God is through the teaching, another
> through prayer, another through fasting, and still another
> through eating. Everyone should carefully observe what
> way his heart draws him to, and then choose this way with
> all his strength.[7]

Hasidism is like Hinduism in not having any one way that
man should walk. But the way for the Hasid is not a matter of
his caste duty or even his *dharma* or *karma* but of his personal
uniqueness, his "I" in the deepest sense of that term. To speak
of the heart drawing us does not mean the facile impulse of the
moment. Our "I" is not our image of ourselves but the deepest
stirring within ourselves. That stirring, in its response, becomes our way.

That is why the "evil" urge is so important to Hasidism. In
the Book of Genesis this word for "urge" appears as "imaginings." Before the Flood, the Lord gives, "For the imaginings
of man's heart are evil from his youth onward," as his reason
for destroying the world by flood. Yet after the Flood, this
same reason is given for never again destroying the world by
flood. For these same "imaginings," although evil from youth
on, *can* be directed to God. Similarly, the Talmud says man
must love God with *both* urges, the good and the "evil."
Without the evil urge no man could have a business or raise
a family. That means the "evil" urge is not evil in itself. It
is evil only when it is not given direction. It is evil only when
it is not given the personal meaning of our unique response to
the situation. It is needed for our service. The person who

[7] *The Early Masters*, p. 313—"The Way."

succeeds in being "good" by repressing the "evil" urge is not serving God with all his heart, mind, and might. The "evil" urge is the passion, the power which is given us to serve God. We cannot extirpate it or do away with it. When it seems to make us fail, it does so because we have tried to impose upon ourselves and our environment what we are determined to be. The "evil" urge is that something more in us that taps us on the shoulder and recalls us to ourselves. Often we have so lost touch with ourselves that we do not know what way our heart draws us to. It is then that precisely the "evil" urge which seems to wish to lead us astray comes to our rescue. By its very tempting of us, it tells us that we have left ourselves out of our own projects, that our deepest passion has not been given direction, that our decisions have not been made with our whole being. "He who still harbors an evil urge is at great advantage," said one Hasidic rabbi, "for he can serve God with it. He can gather all his passion and warmth and pour them into the service of God. . . . What counts is to restrain the blaze in the hour of desire and let it flow into the hours of prayer and service." This does not mean the repression of desire but giving it meaningful direction.

The "evil" urge was thus potentially good to the Hasidim, yet they had no illusions about its being an easy matter to give the "evil" urge direction. The Maggid of Mezritch was recognized as the successor to the Baal Shem because he answered the question of how man can break pride by saying that no one can break it: "We must struggle with it all the days of our life." Similarly the rabbi of Rishyn said to a young man who wanted help in breaking his evil impulse: "You will break your back and your hip, yet you will not break an impulse. But if you pray and learn and work in all seriousness, the evil in your impulses will vanish of itself." Sometimes the result is more of a draw, as when Rabbi Moshe of Kobryn compared the service of God to walking over a freshly ploughed field in which furrows alternate with ridges: "Now you go up, now you go down, now the Evil Urge gets a hold on you, now you get a hold on him. Just you see to it that it is you who deal the last blow!"

You cannot get a hold on the evil urge through self-mortification, however. The maggid of Koznitz said to a man who wore nothing but a sack and fasted from one sabbath to the next, "The Evil Urge is tricking you into that sack. He who pretends to fast . . . but secretly eats a little something every day, is spiritually better off than you, for he is only deceiving others, while you are deceiving yourself." When another Hasid, known for the harsh penances he imposed on himself, came to visit the maggid of Zlotchov, the latter said to him: "Yudel, you are wearing a hair shirt against your flesh. If you were not given to sudden anger, you would not need it, and since you are given to sudden anger, it will not help you." Worse and more harmful than the sin a man plunges into when he gives way to the evil urge is the despondency which overtakes him by way of his sinning. Once he sees himself as a sinner, then the evil urge really has him in its power. Instead of sinning and then saying, "But I won't sin again," like the cheerful sinner of whom the Seer of Lublin was so fond, he gives way to the image of himself as a sinner and loses what resources he might have had to direct the evil urge in the service of God.

The power of the evil urge is the power of desire—desire for something that turns out to be nothing. The Evil Urge goes around the world with his fist closed, and everyone thinks that in that fist is just what he wants most in the world and follows after it. But the Evil Urge opens his fist, and it is empty. Once some disciples of Rabbi Pinhas ceased talking in embarrassment when he entered the House of Study. When he asked them what they were talking about, they said: "Rabbi, we were saying how afraid we are that the Evil Urge will pursue us." "Don't worry," he replied. "You have not gotten high enough for it to pursue you. For the time being, you are still pursuing it." This is how it is with most of us.

We can feel for the man who came to ask the Seer of Lublin to help him against alien thoughts which intruded on him while he prayed. Even after the rabbi had told him what to do, the man went on asking questions until finally the rabbi said:

> I don't know why you keep complaining to me of alien thoughts. To him who has holy thoughts, an impure thought comes at times, and such a thought is called "alien." But you —you have just your own usual thoughts. To whom do you want to ascribe them?[8]

How does man serve God with the "evil" urge? Not through turning away from everyday life in the world but through bringing right dedication—*kavana*—to everything one does, through responding with one's whole being to the unique claim of unique situations. This means bringing all of one's passion into meaningful relationship with the people one meets and the situations one encounters. "What are all *kavanot* [special mystical and magical intentions]," exclaimed the Baal Shem, "compared with one really heart-felt grief!" "Every lock has the key that is fitted to it and opens it," said the maggid of Mezritch:

> But there are strong thieves who know how to open without keys. They break the lock. So every mystery in the world can be unriddled by the particular kind of meditation fitted to it. But God loves the thief who breaks the lock open: I mean *the man who breaks his heart for God.*[9]

In Hasidism it is not the doctrine that is important but the way of life, the image of man. Rabbi Leib, son of Sara, said he went to see the maggid of Mezritch not to hear him say Torah but to watch the way in which he laced and unlaced his felt boots. The caption of this tale is "Not to Say Torah but to Be Torah." Words are of importance when they mani-

[8] *The Early Masters,* p. 316—"Alien Thoughts."
[9] *Ibid.,* p. 104—"The Strong Thief," italics added.

fest life, not when they take its place. This applies most clearly of all to prayer. The Baal Shem once refused to enter a synagogue because it was crowded from floor to ceiling and wall to wall with prayers that had been uttered without real devotion. Even the right mood is of no avail if the motivation is wrong: the man who prays in sorrow because of the bleakness which burdens his spirit does not know the real fear of God, and the man who prays in joy because of the radiance of his spirit does not know the love of God. His "fear is the burden of sadness, and his love is nothing but empty joy." Honest grief, in contrast, is that of a man who knows what he lacks, while the truly joyful man is like someone whose house has burned down and who begins to build anew out of the deep need of his soul: "Over every stone that is laid, his heart rejoices."

Once the maggid of Mezritch let a sigh escape when, as a young man, he was poor and his baby was too weak even to cry. Instantly a voice said, "You have lost your share in the world to come." "Good," exclaimed the maggid. "Now I can begin to serve in good earnest!" *Kavana* does not mean that what is important is "purity of heart" but that one must bring oneself with all one's possibility of response into every action. This is the Hasidic image of man: "Only he who brings himself to the Lord as an offering may be called man." This bringing oneself is no once-for-all commitment but an ever renewed finding of direction, a responding to the call in each new hour. After the death of Rabbi Moshe of Kobryn, a disciple replied to the question, "What was most important to your teacher?" with the answer, "Whatever he happened to be doing at the moment."

From *kavana* we can understand the unique approach of Hasidism to love and to helping one's fellow man. The Hasidim rejected emphatically the image of the helper who stands above the person he wants to help and reaches down a helping hand. "If you want to raise a man from mud and filth," said

Rabbi Shelomo of Karlin, "you must go all the way down yourself, down into mud and filth. Then take hold of him with strong hands and pull him and yourself out into the light." This does not mean that you imitate his sins, but you must open yourself to the reality of the evil into which he has fallen and not try to bestow charity from above while keeping your soul free from any thing that might disturb it. Rabbi Moshe Leib of Sasov learned to love when he went to an inn and heard one drunken peasant ask another, "Do you love me?" "Certainly I love you," replied the second. "I love you like a brother." But the first shook his head and insisted, "You don't love me. You don't know what I lack. You don't know what I need." The second peasant fell into sullen silence, but Rabbi Moshe Leib understood: "To know the need of men and to bear the burden of their sorrow, that is the true love of men." This love only exists in mutual relationship, in that dialogue in which one experiences the other's side of the relationship, knows the other from within. Each person needs to be loved not in his universal humanity or divinity but in his uniqueness, including what he lacks.

Rabbi Moshe Leib not only understood this; he lived it. He shared so earnestly in the spiritual and physical sufferings of others that their suffering became his own. When someone once expressed his astonishment at this capacity to share in another's troubles, he replied, "What do you mean 'share'? It is my own sorrow; how can I help but suffer it?" The Yehudi, the "holy Jew," was asked why the stork is called devout or loving *(hasidah)* in the Talmud because he gives so much love to his mate and his young, but is classed in the Scriptures with the unclean birds. The Yehudi answered: "Because he gives love only to his own." We must love the other—the stranger, the enemy—even as we love our family. In both cases our love must be an openness and response to the unique person that we meet. Mixed with this insistence on concreteness is a good measure of Hasidic realism and humor, as in the story that the rabbi of Zans used to tell about himself:

> In my youth when I was fired with the love of God, I thought I would convert the whole world to God. But soon I discovered that it would be quite enough to convert the people who lived in my town, and I tried for a long time, but did not succeed. Then I realized that my program was still much too ambitious, and I concentrated on the persons in my own household. But I could not convert them either. Finally it dawned on me: I must work upon myself, so that I may give true service to God. But I did not accomplish even this.[10]

The title of this tale is "Resignation," resignation without any admixture of bitterness, despair, disillusionment, defeat. No other tale expresses so precisely my own history!

The Hasidic demand that we discover and perform our own created task, that we channel the passion of the "evil" urge into the realization of our personal uniqueness, that we act and love with *kavana*, or inner intention, implies the strongest possible rejection of all those ways whereby we divide our lives into airtight compartments and escape becoming whole. Becoming whole does not mean "spiritual" wholeness or the wholeness of the individuated Self within the unconscious (to use the language of Jung). It means that personal wholeness the necessary corollary of which is the wholeness of our lives. When one disciple of Rabbi Bunam asked another, "To what purpose was man created?" the latter replied, "So that he might perfect his soul." "No, indeed," said the former. "He was created so that he might lift up the heavens!" Our true wholeness is not the perfection of our "immortal soul" but the fulfillment of our created task. Only the latter brings our personal uniqueness into being in integral relation with the creation over against which we are set. Our existence does not

---

[10] Martin Buber, *Tales of the Hasidim. The Later Masters*, trans. by Olga Marx (New York: Schocken Books paperback edition, 1961), p. 214.

take place *within* ourselves but in *relationship* to what is *not* ourselves. To make our goal spiritual perfection, consequently, means a foreshortening of our personal existence.

The rabbi of Kotzk explained the biblical injunction, "Ye shall be holy unto me," as the demand not for perfection but for authentic humanity: "You shall be holy unto me, but as men. You shall be humanly holy unto me." We are not asked to be saints or supermen but to be holy in the measure and manner of man, in the measure and manner of our personal resources. This is a seemingly easier demand than perfection but in fact it is harder; for it asks you to do what you really can do rather than despair over what you cannot. We take our ideas and ideals with grim seriousness, says Martin Buber, but we do not allow them to have a binding claim upon our everyday lives. "No amount of hypocritical piety has ever reached this concentrated degree of inauthenticity!" Our wretchedness is due to the fact that we do not open our lives to the holy, Buber adds and concludes: "A life that is not open to the holy is not only unworthy of spirit, it is unworthy of life." This is not a question of being punished for being "unworthy." It is a matter of the meaning of life itself.

To open our lives to the holy does not mean to rise above our situation. It means to bring our situation into dialogue with God. The openness to the holy does not mean leaving the everyday for a higher spiritual sphere but "hallowing the everyday" through a genuine openness to what meets you. "Whoever says that the words of the Torah are one thing and the words of the world another," said Rabbi Pinhas of Koretz, "must be regarded as a man who denies God." C. H. Dodd, the biblical scholar, said, "Many people seem to think that everything that happened in the Bible happened on Sunday." If there ought be no dualism of "sacred" words and "secular" words, neither ought there be a dualism between words and silence. When the Yehudi discovered that a young man had taken a vow of silence for three years except for the

Torah and prayer, he called the young man to him and asked him why it was that he did not see a single word of his in the world of truth. When the young man justified his silence by talking of the "vanity of speech," the Yehudi warned him that he who only learns and prays is murdering the world of his own soul. "What do you mean by the 'vanity of speech'?" continued the Yehudi, almost in the language of Lao-tzu. "Whatever you have to say can be vanity or it can be truth."

The rabbi of Rizhyn imposed upon a confirmed sinner a terrible penance: "From now until you die, you shall not utter a single word of prayer with empty lips; but you shall preserve the fulness of every word." The sinner himself had brought the rabbi the list of his sins to have penance imposed on him. The rabbi's response not only demanded a sincere inner repentance but a wholehearted turning of his existence. Only thus could a man who was used to living moment by moment in inner division bring the whole of his intention and the whole of his life into prayer. "What does it amount to that they expound the Torah!" cried Rabbi Leib, son of Sara. "A man should see to it that all his actions are a Torah and that he himself becomes so entirely a Torah that one can learn from his habits and his motions and his motionless clinging to God."

"Man is like a tree," said Rabbi Uri of Strelisk. "If you stand in front of a tree and watch it incessantly to see how it grows and to see how much it is growing, you will see nothing at all. But tend to it at all times, prune the runners and keep the vermin from it and, all in good time, it will come into its growth." "It is the same with man," he added. "All that is necessary is for him to overcome his obstacles and he will thrive and grow. But it is not right to examine him every hour to see how much has been added to his growth." If there is any single evil in our culture which overtops all others, it is this one of examining and measuring people all the time to see how far along they have come in school, in training, in business and professional life, in maturity, in self-realization, in comparison with their brothers and sisters, their classmates, their colleagues and fellow workers, or their neighbors. Even our "spiritual life" comes fully equipped, like Benjamin Franklin's chart of virtues, with measuring rods to show whether we have learned "receptive listening," realized our potential, grown in Christian humility and the love of God, or advanced in mystical contemplation or saintly perfection! The more we try to discover how far along we are and what progress we have made, the more we will get in our own way. The only true growth is that which comes through spontaneity, through a response so great and wholehearted that we forget to be concerned about ourselves. A great violinist may negotiate for what he is to be paid for a concert, but each time he draws the bow over the strings, he does not think of how much money he is making! Rabbi Hayyim of Krosno became so absorbed in watching a rope-dancer that his disciples asked him what it was that riveted his gaze to this foolish performance.

> "This man," he said, "is risking his life, and I cannot say why. But I am quite sure that while he is walking the rope, he is not thinking of the fact that he is earning a hundred gulden by what he is doing, for if he did, he would fall."[11]

Although Hasidism grows out of a theosophy—knowledge about God—and a very detailed one, the Hasidim tended to lay greater stress on simple devotion to God. In order to persevere in the Hasidic way of life, one does not need a special grace or faith in a set creed. But one does need trust—existential trust, trust in God, trust that God addresses us in the happenings of everyday life and that we can make our lives real by responding to that address. For the Hasidim, as for biblical man, God's hiding was as real as his revealing himself, and when God hid himself it was difficult to maintain one's

[11] *The Early Masters,* p. 174—"The Rope Dancer."

trust. The favorite disciple of Rabbi Pinhas complained to him that it was very difficult in adversity to retain perfect faith in the belief that God provides for every human being. "It actually seems as if God were hiding his face from such an unhappy being," he exclaimed. "It ceases to be a hiding," replied Rabbi Pinhas, "if you know it is hiding." Shneur Zalman, the rav of Northern White Russia and the founder of the Habad, or Lubavitcher, Hasidism to which my mother's family belonged, once asked a disciple, "Moshe, what do we mean when we say 'God'?" The disciple was silent. After the rav had asked him a second and third time without response, he demanded the reason for his silence. "Because I do not know," replied the youth. "Do you think I know?" said the rav. "But I must say it, for it is so, and therefore I must say it: He is definitely there, and except for Him nothing is definitely there—and this is He." The rav could not define God, or describe his attributes, or even assert his existence in the abstract. But he could and did point in his dialogue with his disciple to meeting God in our actual existence in all its particularity. A similar dialogue took place between Rabbi Bunam and his disciple Rabbi Hanokh. For a year the latter had wanted to talk with Bunam every time he went into his house but did not feel he was man enough. Once though, when he was walking across a field and weeping, he knew that he must run to his rabbi without delay. Bunam asked him, "Why are you weeping?" "I am after all alive in this world," he confessed, "a being created with all the senses and all the limbs, but I do not know what it is I was created for and what I am good for in this world." His master did not reply by showing him the meaning of his life or confirming his value in the world but by revealing that this torment was one that he too could neither resolve nor dismiss: "Little fool," said Bunam, "That's the same question I have carried around with me all my life. You will come and eat the evening meal with me."

Revelation, to the Hasidim, did not mean the incursion of the supernatural, but openness to the wonder of the everyday —"the enormous lights and miracles" with which the world is filled. Once a naturalist came from a great distance to see the Baal Shem and said: "My investigations show that in the course of nature the Red Sea had to divide at the very hour the children of Israel passed through it. Now what about that famous miracle!" "Don't you know that God created nature?" answered the Baal Shem. "And he created it so, that at the hour the children of Israel passed through the Red Sea, it had to divide. That is the great and famous miracle!" "Miracle" is simply the wonder of the unique that points us back to the wonder of the everyday. If you fell through the ice and were saved at the last second from drowning, your knowledge of all the laws of heat and friction that might account for the ice melting at just that rate, would not diminish by one jot the sense of wonder you would feel.

The rabbi of Kobryn taught:

> God says to man, as he said to Moses: "Put off thy shoes from thy feet"—put off the habitual which encloses your foot, and you will know that the place on which you are now standing is holy ground. For there is no rung of human life on which we cannot find the holiness of God everywhere and at all times.[12]

The true opposite of "the habitual" is not the extraordinary or the unusual but the fresh, the open, the ever-new of the man who hallows the everyday. When Rabbi Bunam was asked why the first of the Ten Commandments speaks of God bringing us out of the land of Egypt rather than of God creating heaven and earth, he expounded: " 'Heaven and earth!' Then man might have said: 'Heaven—that is too much for me.' So God said to man: 'I am the one who fished you out of the mud. Now you come here and listen to me!' "

12 *The Later Masters*, p. 170—"Everywhere."

It is only as persons that we can enter with our whole being into the dialogue with God that takes place in the heart of the everyday. To enter this dialogue means to hear and respond to God's "Torah," his guidance and direction in each hour of our lives. But it does not mean to freeze the Torah into a fixed, objective, universal law that demands only our external obedience and not our unique response to a unique situation. The rabbi of Kotzk heard his disciples discussing why it is written: "Take heed unto yourselves, lest ye forget the covenant of the Lord your God, which He made with you, and make you a graven image, even in the likeness of any thing which the Lord thy God hath bidden thee," and not, as they would have expected, "which the Lord thy God hath forbidden thee." The zaddik declared: "The Torah warns us not to make a graven image of any thing the Lord our God has bidden us." Even divine Law and divinely sanctioned morality may become an idol which hides from us the face of God. By the same token, we cannot limit the address of the Torah to the Scriptures; for the word of the Creator speaks forth from the creation and the creatures each day anew. We can learn not only from what God has created but from what man has made, the rabbi of Sadagora declared to his disciples.

"What can we learn from a train?" one hasid asked dubiously.
"That because of one second one can miss everything."
"And from the telegraph?"
"That every word is counted and charged."
"And the telephone?"
"That what we say here is heard there."[13]

In the fifth chapter of his classic little book *The Way of Man according to the Teachings of the Hasidim*, Martin Buber retells Rabbi Bunam's story of Reb Eisik, son of Reb Yekel, who lived in Cracow but who dreamt three times that

[13] *The Later Masters*, p. 70—"Of Modern Inventions."

there was a treasure buried beneath a bridge in Prague and finally set out and walked the whole enormous distance to Prague. He found the bridge but was afraid to approach it because of the soldiers who guarded it until the captain of the guard noticed him and asked him kindly what it was he wanted. When he had told the captain his dream, the latter exclaimed, "And so to please the dream, you poor fellow wore out your shoes to come here!" If he had had faith in dreams, continued the captain, he would have had to go to Cracow when once a dream told him to go there and dig for treasure under the stove in the room of a Jew—Eisik, son of Yekel. When Rabbi Eisik heard this, he bowed, traveled home, dug up the treasure from under the stove, and built with it a house of prayer. The moral of this story, says Buber, is that the fulfillment of existence is only possible "here where one stands," in the environment which I feel to be natural, in the situation which has been assigned me as my fate, in the things that happen to me and claim me day after day. If we had power over the ends of the world and knew the secrets of the upper world, they would not give us that fulfillment of existence which a quiet, devoted relationship to nearby life can give us.

There is another aspect to this tale which Buber does not bring out, but which his life and my own and that of most modern men show to be essential. Perhaps if we had not gone to "Prague," we should not have discovered that the treasure was hidden beneath our own hearth. There is meaning in our searching, even when it takes us far afield, if it enables us to come back home to the unique task which awaits us. A young person raised in Judaism or Christianity is often barred from any genuine relationship to these religions by the fact that they are associated in his mind with the parents against whom he must rebel, with a social system the injustice of which is manifest, and often in addition with a shoddy way of presenting the religion that seems more concerned with group belonging or social snobbery than with anything genuinely religious. Such a person might find liberation in the teachings of Hinduism, Buddhism, or Zen Buddhism which he encounters unencumbered by relatives and institutions. After these have liberated him, he may be able to go back to find the treasure under his own hearth. When one does come back, it is with a new relationship such as only the fact of distancing makes possible. This was my own experience in relation to Judaism. Brought up in a liberal Judaism of a very thin variety, I could never have returned to Judaism and established a new and deeper relationship with it had I not gone through Hinduism, Buddhism, Zen, Taoism, and Christian mysticism. Nor have I lost these other touchstones. They are part of the way in which I came to Hasidism and relate to it. Even if young people do not find their way back—and my own way to Hasidism was far more a way forward than a way back—they are still those who set out from Cracow. Whatever treasure they really find, however far it may be from home, is still bound to those original roots. These roots are embedded in the ground on which they stand and from which they respond to the new touchstones that call to them.

If man, to Hasidism, is a partner of the Creator, a co-creator who helps complete the creation by lifting the fallen sparks in the circle of existence allotted to him, he is by the same token a co-redeemer. The rabbi of Kotzk surprised a number of learned visitors with the question, "Where is the dwelling of God?" "What a question!" they laughed. "Is not the whole world full of his glory!" But he answered: "God dwells wherever man lets him in." Rabbi Nachman of Bratzlav, the great grandson of the Baal Shem, pictured human existence in terms of an *Angst* as strong as any that Kierkegaard ever depicted:

> Let everyone cry out to God and lift his heart up to
> him as if he were hanging by a hair, and a tempest were
> raging to the very heart of heaven, and he were at a loss

for what to do, and there were hardly time to cry out. It is a time when no counsel indeed can help a man and he has no refuge save to remain in his loneliness and lift his eyes and his heart up to God and cry out to him. And this should be done at all times, for in the world man is in great danger.[14]

But this very *Angst*, this very loneliness becomes redemptive, as Buber suggests by entitling the following saying of Rabbi Nachman "The Kingdom of God":

> Those who do not walk in loneliness will be bewildered when the Messiah comes and they are called; but we shall be like a man who has been asleep and whose spirit is tranquil and composed.[15]

The first saying is entitled "Prayer." Those who walk in loneliness do not wall themselves in in "demonic shut-in-ness," as Kierkegaard would say. They cry out to God. Even when they do not know how to pray, the silence beneath their words cries out:

> "We know very well how we ought to pray; and still we cry for help in the need of the moment. The soul wishes us to cry out in spiritual need, but we are not able to express what the soul means. And so we pray that God may accept our call for help, but also that he, who knows that which is hidden, may hear the silent cry of the soul."[16]

In the end redemption is neither the action of man alone nor of God alone but the completion of the dialogue between them. As Martin Buber said in the last sentence of *I and Thou*, "The event that from the side of the world is called turning is called from God's side redemption." If man's turning and God's redemption are two sides of one event, then the opposition that is so common between man's action and God's grace

14 Martin Buber, *The Tales of Rabbi Nachman*, trans. by Maurice Friedman (New York: Horizon Books, 1969; Avon Books–Discussion Books, 1970), p. 36.

15 *Ibid.*, p. 40.

16 *The Later Masters*, p. 145—"The Secret Prayer."

is a false one. This is not a matter of abstract theology, however, but of wholly concrete situations in which at times men have the resources to begin the turning and at other times not. Nowhere has this lability of the human situation vis à vis God been put more vividly than in a tale entitled "Turning and Redemption":

> The rabbi of Rizhyn laid the fingers of his right hand on the table after the morning meal, and said: "God says to Israel: 'Return unto me . . . and I will return unto you.' " Then he turned his right hand palm up and said: "But we children of Israel reply: 'Turn Thou us unto Thee, O Lord, and we shall be turned; renew our days as of old.' For our exile is heavy on us and we have not the strength to return to you of ourselves." And then he turned his hand palm down again and said: "But the Holy One, blessed be he, says: 'First you must return unto me.' " Four times the rabbi of Rizhyn turned his hand, palm up and palm down. But in the end he said: "The children of Israel are right, though, because it is true that the waves of anguish close over them, and they cannot govern their hearts and turn to God."[17]

This is not a statement about man's "sinful nature" and his dependence upon divine grace. It is a dialogue between man and God taking place in a concrete historical situation, the situation of exile when the resources to be "humanly holy" by serving God with the "evil" urge were at their lowest ebb, and the silent need of the soul cried out to God from beneath the waves of anguish. The love between man and God, like the love between man and man, is not a matter of merit or unearned grace but of the "between": If one loves less, then the other should love more for the sake of the relationship itself. It is in this spirit that we must understand one of the most moving of the Hasidic tales—one that at first glance gives the mistaken appearance of being close to the Pauline dualism

[17] *The Later Masters*, pp. 66 f.

between grace and law. This tale is entitled "The Judgment
of the Messiah":

A young man who lived in the days of the Great Maggid
had quitted his father-in-law's house to go to the maggid.
They had fetched him back and he had pledged on a hand-
clasp that he would stay at home. Yet shortly thereafter he
was gone. Now his father-in-law got the rav of the town to
declare that this broken promise was cause for divorce. The
young man was thus deprived of all means of subsistence.
Soon he fell ill and died.

When the zaddik had finished his story, he added. "And
now, my good men, when the Messiah comes, the young
man will hale his father-in-law before his court of justice.
The father-in-law will quote the rav of the town, and the
rav will quote a passage from the commentary on the Shulhan
Arukh [the "Table of the Laws" codified by Joseph Karo
in the sixteenth century]. Then the Messiah will ask the
young man why after giving his hand on it that he would
remain at home he broke his promise just the same, and the
young man will say, 'I just had to go to the rabbi!' In the
end the Messiah will pronounce judgment. To the father-
in-law he will say: 'You took the rav's word as your
authority and so you are justified.' And to the rav he will
say: 'You took the law as your authority and so you are
justified.'

"And then he will add: 'But I have come for those who
are not justified.' " [18]

The contemporary Jew stands in a stream of general culture
which presents to him other, more "spiritual" and less "anthropomorphic," forms of religion than Judaism. After a lecture that I gave on Hasidism to a Jewish audience, I was astonished at the complaint that Hasidism was "mechanistic"
and had no room for "love." When I had translated "mechanistic" into "materialistic" in my own mind, I understood
that the woman who had asked the question was approaching

[18] *The Later Masters*, p. 57.

Hasidism from the very un-Jewish but all too familiar dualism between the spiritual and the material according to which the concern with the everyday automatically signals the exclusion of the truly "spiritual." This widespread and insidious dualism recurs on a higher level in a statement by the Jew Mishe Gordon in *Doctor Zhivago*, the famous novel of the Russian-Jewish poet Boris Pasternak. Speaking of the rejection of Christianity by the Jews, Gordon says: "This glorious holiday from mediocrity, from the dreary, boring construction of everyday life was first achieved on their soil, proclaimed in their language, belonged to their race! And they actually saw and heard it and let it go!" [19] The knowledge that in Hasidism Judaism has produced a mysticism that "restores to the element of earth those whom preoccupation with thought had removed from it" while raising "to the heights of heaven . . . those who are burdened with the weight of earth" [20] could effect a decisive change in the attitude of those Jewish "seekers" who unconsciously share in the general depreciation of Judaism in Western culture as an inferior form of religion lacking in spirituality.

The same applies to the myriad of Jews who, like the novelist Irwin Shaw, author of *The Young Lions*, have accepted from the general culture the distorted understanding of the God of the "Old Testament" as a harsh and wrathful God in contrast to the loving and merciful God of the New. Hasidism not only stresses the love and mercy of God; it shows that to be a Hasid, a loyal follower of God, means to love one's fellow men and even one's enemies. It is a living embodiment of the dictum to "deal lovingly with thy neighbor as one like thyself." As such it demonstrates, as no amount of pointing to Leviticus can, that this injunction was taken over by Jesus from the Judaism in which he himself stood.

[19] *Doctor Zhivago*, trans. by Max Hayward & Manya Harari (London: Collins and Harvill Press, 1958), p. 117.
[20] *Tales of the Hasidim. The Early Masters*, Introduction, p. 11.

The love of Hasidism is not a spiritualized love but a love of the whole person. By the same token, it is not a purely forgiving love but one that places a real demand upon the other —the demand of the relationship itself. The "hallowing of the everyday" means making the concrete relations of one's life essential, and real relationship includes both mutuality and passion. Mutuality means that love does not simply flow forth from the loving man to others; rather it moves back and forth within the dialogue between them as the fullest expression of that dialogue. Passion means that one does not suppress one's humanity before bringing oneself into relation with others, but on the contrary directs one's "evil" urge into that relationship in such a way that, without losing its force, it ceases to be evil. It is in this sense that Hasidism represents a sanctification of the profane in which every natural urge is waiting to be hallowed and the profane itself just a name for what has not yet become open to the holy.

This concrete and realistic approach to the "evil urge" is vividly illustrated by a story of the Baal Shem's called "The Limits of Advice." When the disciples of the Baal Shem asked him how to know whether a celebrated scholar whom they proposed to visit was a true zaddik, he answered:

> Ask him to advise you what to do to keep unholy thoughts from disturbing you in your prayers and studies. If he gives you advice, then you will know that he belongs to those who are of no account. For this is the service of men in the world to the very hour of their death; to struggle time after time with the extraneous, and time after time to uplift and fit it into the nature of the Divine Name.[21]

So often the religious is conceived of as putting aside the extraneous and the profane and turning to the holy and the pure. But here the extraneous is precisely that which has something to ask of us. Once a group of Hasidim started to

[21] *Ibid.*, p. 66.

pray in one place and then went to another, at which the first place cried out: "What is wrong with me that you went to another place? And if I am evil, is it not up to you to redeem me?" The rav of White Russia once asked his son, "With what do you pray?" To which the son replied, "I pray with the verse, 'May every high place become low.'" Then the son asked his father, "With what do you pray?" The rav answered: "I pray with the floor and with the bench."

Jesus offered his disciples a counsel of perfection—"But I say unto you that he who looks at a woman to lust after her in his heart has already committed adultery." Paul, in contrast saw not only temptation but sin as inevitable—"Of myself (in my flesh) I can do no good thing." "The evil that I would not do I do." In between the teaching that man can overcome temptation altogether and become "pure in heart" and that which sees man as naturally sinful is the teaching, already present in the Bible and the Talmud but given strongest emphasis and exemplification in Hasidism, that the daily renewal of creation also means the daily renewal of temptation and with it the strength and the grace to direct that temptation into the service of God through an essential and meaningful relation with the world.

If the Hasidic hallowing of the everyday is of importance in contrast with Christianity, it is of still greater importance in contrast with gnosticism. Common to the ancient Christian and non-Christian Gnostics and to the more recent gnostical movements in Judaism associated with the pseudo-messiahs Sabbatai Zvi and Jacob Frank, is the substitution of the doctrine that within the commnity of the "elect" everything already *is* holy for the task of hallowing an as yet unhallowed creation. While antinomian gnosticism rejects creation in general as radically evil and incapable of being hallowed, it holds that its members, particularly the so-called perfect or elect, are so holy that they not only are allowed to sin but positively should do so in order to raise sin too to holiness. Revolting against the distinction between good and evil, the radical Sabbatians and the Frankists believed that they could redeem evil by performing it as if it were not evil, that is, by preserving an inner intention of purity in contrast to the deed. This illusion, divested of the weird and exotic costume of the Sabbatian and Frankist orgies, has a decidedly modern ring.

> Instead of making reality the starting point of life, reality that is full of cruel contradictions but just thereby calling forth true greatness, namely the quiet work of overcoming the contradictions, one surrenders to illusion, intoxicates oneself in it, subjugates life to it. In the same measure in which one does this, the core of his existence becomes burning and unfruitful at once, he becomes at once completely agitated and crippled in his motive power.[22]

This demonic "lust for overrunning reality" is not simply a product of unbelief but a crisis within men's souls, a crisis of temptation, freedom, and dishonesty in which "the realms are overturned, everything encroaches on everything else, and possibility is more powerful than reality." Whether or not liberal Judaism has Sabbatian roots, as some have held, there can be no doubt of the seriousness of this temptation for those contemporary Jews who stand within that part of the Jewish tradition that has thrown over the traditional safeguards of the Halakah with its guidance of even the smallest aspects of daily life. The fascination with the demonic in modern literature, the tendency of many to turn psychoanalysis or "psychodrama" into a cult of self-realization, the illustory belief that personal fulfillment can come through "release" of one's deep inward energies, and the more specific forms of modern gnosticism, such as the analytic psychology of Carl Jung, which advocates taking part in evil as the road to the integration of the self—all these show the peculiarly modern relevance of this "crisis of temptation and dishonesty." This crisis

[22] Buber, *The Origin and Meaning of Hasidism*, pp. 65 f.

accosts the contemporary Jew not only as a member of a Jewish group that has more or less freed itself from the Jewish law but also as a sharer and bearer of contemporary culture. "Behind the demonic mask one imagines that the countenance of divine freedom is to be discovered; one does not let oneself be deluded by the temptations, but one also does not drive them out." [23]

Hasidism offers a teaching that rejects both the radical separation of good and evil and the confusion of the two. But this teaching can only become ours if it is lifted out of the realm of spiritual inspiration and realized concretely in our interhuman relationships.

Particularly significant for the current constellation of religious philosophy and metaphysics in the Western world of thought is the Hasidic doctrine of *tzintzum*—the metaphor of God's self-limitation in the act of creation that Hasidism takes over from the Lurian Kabbala. The highest reality of the Divine, as Hasidism reinterprets *tzimtzum*, is not Meister Eckhart's impersonal Godhead but the Absolute who makes himself into a Person in order to bring man into relationship with him. "On account of his great love," says the Maggid of Mezritch, God limits his illuminating power in order that, like a father with his son, he may bring man stage by stage to where he may receive the revelation of the limitless original God." [24] God's relation to man and to creation is a voluntary contraction which in no way limits his absoluteness. Father John M. Oesterreicher, the editor of the series of Catholic "Judaeo-Christian Studies" *The Bridge*, sees the Hasidic doctrine of *tzimtzum* as an inferior conception which derogates from God's glory—a depreciation based upon a substantive and static misreading of the concept. Seen in its true dynamic and interactive character, *tzimtzum* stands as one of the great-

[23] *Ibid.*, p. 77.
[24] Buber, *The Origin and Meaning of Hasidism*, "God and the Soul," pp. 190–198.

est reformulations of the biblical understanding of creation. It shows God as at once separate from the world and man and yet in relationship to them, and in such a way that neither the separateness nor the togetherness can be shown as either temporally or logically prior. Creation, in this view, is the radical fact which establishes and reestablishes the world and behind which we cannot look to any primal state before creation or godhead before God. In our own existence we can neither begin with our separate existence as persons and then deduce our relations to others nor begin with our relations with others and then deduce our uniqueness as separate persons. Rather we must begin with both at once. In our relation to God, similarly, we cannot go back behind creation to some more basic fact. Yet this is just what not only the mystics but also the theologians and the metaphysicians constantly attempt to do. Through a logical analysis of the relationship between man and God, they separate out the two factors of separateness and relatedness and then make one or the other of them prior. Paul Tillich rightly attacks the theists for making God a person beside other persons. But what he offers instead is no more satisfactory—a "Ground of Being" that satisfies our logic's desire for a reality undergirding man's relation with God and that at the same time forgives and accepts as only a personal God could do! Alfred North Whitehead and Charles Hartshorne, on the other hand, say that since God cannot logically be both absolute and in relation, they prefer to sacrifice the Absolute in favor of an imperfectly actual God who attains his completion only through dialectical interaction with the world. The Hasidic understanding of the relation of God and the world does not have to fall into these logical either-or's. It can bear paradox because it sticks to the concrete given of our existence in which the seemingly irreconcilable opposites produced by our analytical thought exist together as one whole.

The significance of Hasidism for contemporary man and

for the contemporary Jew in particular is not limited to philosophy of religion. The nonmodern way of life and the near total adherence to Halakah of the Hasidism of today point up the gulf that divides them from contemporary Western man and the impossibility of a simple transplantation of Hasidism as a movement to the soil of modern Israeli or American culture. Nonetheless, Hasidism, in my opinion, has a contribution of the greatest significance to make to the contemporary Jew. It calls him to a realization of the covenant through which the Jews became and have remained a people—a reminder that to become a "holy people" means not just becoming a collection of well-meaning individuals but a never ending realization of righteousness, justice, and loving kindness in true community. In the Israeli kibbutz this community exists without the relationship to a divine center which in Hasidism built community out of a wholly personal mode of faith. In the Jewish communities of the diaspora, on the other hand, this center exists without the community—since a modern temple with all its multifarious activities is a cultural and social center, to be sure, but not a real community where people live and work together. Among the Hasidim of Israel and of Williamsburg there seems to be both center and community, yet the task of hallowing the everyday has fallen into abeyance in favor of a special sphere in which the holy is protected from the contamination of the profane. The Hasidism of the Besht may point the way to a true covenant community which does not now exist.

Martin Buber's own conversion to Hasidism came, he tells us, when as a young man he read the saying of the Baal Shem's, "He takes unto himself the quality of fervor. He arises from sleep with fervor, for he is hallowed and becomes another man and is worthy to create." [25] For all the moral idealism of contemporary Judaism there is little in it that could call out the highest allegiance and devotion of Jewish youth. The

[25] Buber, *Hasidism and Modern Man,* p. 58 f.

quality that is lacking in American Judaism, as in American religion in general, is fervor. One of the statements that is quoted in "Hasidism Re-examined" as characteristic of the extravagance of our current romantic neo-Hasidism is Buber's assertion in the Preface to *The Legend of the Baal-Shem*, "No renewal of Judaism is possible that does not bear in itself the elements of Hasidism." Whether or not the mature Buber himself would have stood behind this statement of his youth, *I* would—at least as far as the element of fervor is concerned. The unprecedented success of organized Jewish religion in America threatens to leave it a movement in search of a meaning unless it is caught up within a genuine movement of the soul. As Abraham Heschel has said, "Jewish belonging has taken the place of Jewish living." We do not need a "religious revival" in the sense of Billy Graham, nor certainly any turning away from study or from the full and, where possible, improved, use of our powers of reason. But we do need genuine fervor if the quantitatively greatest body of Judaism in the world is not also to be the thinnest and most meaningless.

Community and the overcoming of dualism, too, are elements of Hasidism without which no renewal of Judaism is possible. Can we make them ours—in our way? This is the challenge of Hasidism to the contemporary Jew. If we meet that challenge, a new stage of modern Judaism may be reached —a fusion of the fervor, community, and wholeness of Hasidism with the liberalism of the Western Jew and the communal and national consciousness of the Israeli. If we do not, the Jew and the non-Jew alike will still have the image of man that the Baal Shem has bequeathed us—ours to relate to as we can and will.

[Chapter 9]

Jesus: Image of Man
or Image of God?

Biblical Judaism is the mother of both rabbinical Judaism and orthodox Christianity and, by the same token, the grandmother or great grandmother of modern Judaism and modern Christianity. Despite the continuity of the name and people, it should not surprise us, therefore, that there is much in present-day Judaism that is farther from biblical Judaism than the teachings of Jesus who stood within the living tradition of biblical and early rabbinic Judaism.

My first significant encounter with Jesus was through my Christian pacifist friends, my second through Christian mysticism, my third through the study of the comparative records of the Synoptic Gospels (Matthew, Mark, and Luke) in the discussion groups run by the "Sharman" method.[1] Finally, I returned to encounter Jesus again from the standpoint of biblical, normative, and Hasidic Judaism as I had come to under-

[1] Cf. Henry Sharman, *The Records of the Life of Jesus* (New York: Harper & Bros., 1937), and *Jesus as Teacher* (New York: Harper & Bros., Student's revised edition, 1944).

stand them. In all of these encounters the Sermon on the Mount (Matthew 5–7) has had an important place. This is not because I imagine that Jesus gave this sermon as such. The evidence, on the contrary, is that it is made up of many fragments, and I am inclined to credit the Sharman approach which suggests that Luke's "Blessed are you poor" is more probably the form in which Jesus would have addressed the simple fisher folk he was supposed to have been talking to in Galilee than Matthew's "Blessed are the poor in spirit." For all this I have come back to the Sermon on the Mount again and again because it forms a whole, because it is central to so much of Christianity, and because it raises such basic problems.

One of the most basic is the use of the phrase "the kingdom of heaven." This is often taken by Christians to refer, as a matter of course, to heaven in the Christian sense. I am more inclined to believe, both from the usage of the day and the context in which it is used, that it refers to *Malchut Shamayim,* a common synonym for God. Certainly the emphasis in later Christianity upon this world's being a forecourt for the sake of gaining admission to heaven is hardly borne out by Jesus' emphasis upon the present. "Take no thought for the morrow, for the morrow shall take thought for itself . . . /Sufficient unto the day is the evil thereof." To be sure, this passage is prefaced by a contrast between laying up treasures on earth where thieves break in and rust destroys, but the meaning of this passage is made unmistakable when Jesus adds, immediately afterward, "No man can serve God and mammon. If the eye be single, the whole body is full of light." Jesus' emphasis is clearly upon loving God with all one's heart, soul, mind, and might, and such love means an unconditional trust which does not suffer the present moment to be used as a mere means to a future end. Jesus does not disparage the need for food, clothing, and shelter. Rather he says, "Your heavenly father knows you need these things," and adds, "Seek you first the Kingdom of God and all these things shall be added unto you."

The Kingdom of God, or the Kingdom of Heaven, is not thought of here as an afterlife but as finding authentic existence in the present through bringing one's life into dialogue with God. "You are the salt of the earth," says Jesus. "If the salt hath lost its savor, wherewith shall it be salted?" Man is the being who gives special meaning to the earth, yet if he has lost that authentic humanity which makes him man, nothing else—neither prosperity nor power nor prestige—can make up for this lack. For Jesus the Kingdom of Heaven is in us, and it is also among us.

Jesus begins the Sermon on the Mount with a series of paradoxes, on the basis of which some have assumed a dualism between the material and the spiritual. But little or nothing in all of the Synoptic Gospels confirms this interpretation. Rather, as Jesus says, "narrow is the way, and strait is the gate": the road to authentic existence is a difficult one—and yet so easy since it means a trust which leaves to God the "morrow" as do the lilies of the field. This trust is a continuation of the biblical *emunah*, that unconditional trust in the relationship with God that characterizes Psalm 23 ("Though I walk through the valley of the shadow of death, I shall fear no evil") and Psalm 91 ("He shall not suffer thy foot to stumble"). It is this latter verse that Satan quotes to Jesus as the second of the temptations in the wilderness. He takes him to the top of the Temple and invites him to throw himself down as proof that it is he of whom this was said. Jesus' reply, "Thou shalt not tempt God," is not only a quote from Deuteronomy, referring to the people's tempting Moses to strike the rock with his staff and produce water; it is also thoroughly biblical in spirit. *Emunah* is not a magic security, a guarantee that God will *have* to protect his favored one. It is a trust that remains constant even when we walk, as we must, through the valley of the shadow of death.

What are we to make of the series of contrasts in "The Sermon on the Mount"? "You have heard it said . . . But I say unto you." Most of them are from the direction of outer action to inner intention, but one of them at least (that concerning divorce) is in the opposite direction. The emphasis on *kavana*, or inner intention, was nothing new in Judaism, either in the Pentateuch or in the Prophets or in the Pharisees. What appears new is the valuing of purity of intention above purity of action. "Who shall stand on God's holy hill?" asks Psalm 24. "He who has clean hands and a pure heart"—not one or the other but both. Does Jesus in fact mean what Paul later taught in *Romans*—a dualism between the outer action "that killeth" and the inner spirit "that quickeneth"? "You have heard it said that ye shall not commit adultery," says Jesus. "But I say unto you that he who looks at a woman to lust after her has already committed adultery with her in his heart." What are we to make of this statement? If it be taken as the realism that "as a man thinketh, so he is," we can only call it a fair extension of what the commandment already implies. If we take it as a call to kill all lust within the soul, it becomes a counsel of perfection appropriate to the Christian saint but not to the Jewish image of man as forever tempted anew by the "evil urge" whose passion he must direct into the service of God. If we take it to mean that adultery is all right just so long as it is not committed with an impure heart, we fall into an antinomian gnosticism that is clearly far from Jesus' intention. If we take it to apply to the Christian image of man in general, we run head on against a strain in Christianity which sees man as given over to "original sin," associated by Saint Augustine with lust. In Romans Paul urges the average man to compromise since "it is better to marry than to burn" whereas in Ephesians he urges husbands to love their wives as their own bodies, as Christ loved and cleansed the Church.

How in the midst of all this are we to get back to what Jesus himself meant? I do not know. It has always seemed to me that Jesus never spoke against sex or marriage as such, but rather asked his disciples for total allegiance in response to the unusual demands of the hour. This is that "ethic of perfection" to which Albert Schweitzer points as associated with the expectation of a speedy coming of the kingdom. Nor can I see Jesus' statement as so much opposing as supplementing the commandment he cites. The Jewish position, in any case, occupies a middle point—one in which purity of heart can never be attained entirely since temptation and the "evil urge" remain real, yet one in which the "evil urge" never becomes an "original sin" that necessitates man's sinfulness unless and until he is redeemed by unmerited grace.

Whatever the difference between the everyday ethic of the Pharisee and Jesus' ethic of perfection, and whatever his notions about his own messiahship, Jesus did not call on his disciples to have faith in him but in God. Paul also knew trust in God—the first Epistle to the Corinthians is a great statement of it—but it is a trust that is always "through Jesus Christ our Lord." Due to his profound experience of inner division and the still more profound conversion experience that delivered him from it, it is in this form only that Paul knows the love of God, and it is in this form only that he sees others as knowing it. The immediacy between God and man is now broken by original sin, and it may only be restored by faith in Christ. "Wherefore, as by one man sin entered into the world, and death by sin; and so death passed upon all men, for that all have sinned." (Romans 5:12) The "law" is no longer the Torah which guides man in his dialogue with God but a part of a fearful dialectic in which man's consciousness of the law makes him "exceedingly sinful" so that only unmerited grace can redeem him. This means, for those who remain faithful to the God of Jesus but do not belong to the "household of faith" in Christ, the abolition of that immediacy between God and man which had been the essence of the covenant and the kingship of God. The law was added to the promise to Abraham, says Paul in Galatians, because of transgressions, till the offspring should come to whom the promise had been made—

Christ; "and it was ordained by angels through an inter-
mediary" (like the Gnostic archons). "The scripture con-
signed all things to sin, that what was promised to faith in
Jesus Christ might be given to those who believe. . . . the law
was our custodian until Christ came, that we might be justified
by faith." (Galatians 3:17–24). " 'I am the door' it now runs,"
(John 10:9) writes Buber in his contrast between the *trust*
(*emunah*) of Jesus and the *faith* with a knowledge content
(*pistis*) of John and Paul. "It avails nothing, as Jesus thought,
to knock where one stands (before the 'narrow door'); it
avails nothing, as the Pharisee thought, to step into the open
door; entrance is only for those who believe in 'the door.' " [2]

Both types of faith are present in full strength in Christianity. Consider the use of miracles in the New Testament. We
are told that when Jesus was crucified and gave up the ghost,
the veil of the Temple was rent and many other wonders
happened "in order that you might believe." Jesus, however,
speaks differently of miracles. He tells the woman who touches
his robe and is healed of an issue of blood that it is her faith
that has made her whole, and he tells his disciples that if they
have but as much faith as a grain of mustard seed, they can
move mountains. In other words, for Jesus miracles are not the
cause of faith but at most the product of faith.

Idolatry does not arise through images of God but through
any one image being taken to be God. Certainly the imagelessness of God has been a central emphasis in Judaism, yet there
has been no lack in Judaism of Talmudists, philosophers, and
halachists who have wanted to fix God in one image or another. The problem is not whether the imageless God reveals
himself, as he must if there is to be a relationship to him, but
whether these revelations are taken as universal, objective attributes of God or as God's relationship to man in concrete

[2] Martin Buber, *Two Types of Faith*, trans. by Norman P. Goldhawk
(New York: Harper Torchbooks, 1961), p. 160.

situations, capable of being transformed and renewed in still other concrete situations.

A few years ago I took part in a remarkable dialogue with an English Quaker who is perhaps the leading theologian in the Society of Friends today. The dialogue was before an audience, but the audience was not invited to take part in order that the dialogue might not turn into a debate. So far from seeing Christ as an article of faith that one must hold to, this theologian fully subscribed to Buber's I-Thou trust as the center of the relationship to God or Christ. What is more, in contrast to *both* the universalists and the fundamentalists among the Friends, he and I saw eye to eye on the meaning of the Bible as a history of unique moments of revelation, as demand and response in concrete historical situations. He did not deny the revelation of God at other times and situations than that of Christ nor could I remain indifferent to his witness to Christ: it was a deeply moving statement from a truly religious man that I could not fail to honor. In short, his point of view was much closer to mine than to that of many Quakers, and my point of view was much closer to his than to that of many Jews.

Where then was the difference between us? At one point only, and it is a point which perhaps illuminates the subtle difference between image and imagelessness of God in Judaism and Christianity. If he had only wished to witness that for him the fullest, most complete, and most perfect revelation of God was in Christ, I should not have been troubled by this witness, even if I could not share it. But when he objectified his witness into the theological statement that Christ *is* the fullest conceivable revelation of God, he had in that moment gone over from *trust* to *belief*. "You are my witnesses, saith the Lord," we read in Isaiah, and the Talmud adds, "If you are not my witnesses, then I am not the Lord." What is this but a reiteration of the covenantal relationship in which we witness for God through bringing every aspect of our lives into dialogue with him? But the Jehovah's Witnesses have objectified this "witness" into something that can be handed out in pamphlets, in memorized speeches, in phonograph records. Just such objectification takes place if one claims that the Jews *are* the "chosen people" in abstraction from the covenant—that dynamic of relationship and falling away from relationship which led Hosea to name his son *Lo-Ami,* "Not my People," when Israel had turned away from God.

Martin Buber contrasts the prophet who *speaks* to the people in the historical situation and calls for a decision that may affect the character of the next hour with the apocalyptic *writer* who sees the future as already fixed and is only concerned with foreseeing it. Jesus, in my view, stands in the tradition of the prophets who called on the people to turn back (*teshuvah*) and thought they had the power to do so. Paul, on the other hand, despairs of himself and of other men and sees the initiative as necessarily coming from God—not just in the address to man but even in the grace which enables one to respond to that address. "Put off your old nature which belongs to your former manner of life and is corrupt through deceitful lusts and be renewed in the spirit of your minds, and put on the new nature, created after the likeness of God in true righteousness and holiness." (Ephesians 4:22–24) The contemporary Pauline theologian, Emil Brunner, sees man as sundered from God by his original sin: God bridges the gap with this grace while man receives but cannot initiate.

Paul's cosmic view of all men becoming sinful through the giving of the law at Sinai and of being redeemed from sin only at Golgotha removes from those who have not taken on a new nature in Christ that possibility of turning back to God and receiving forgiveness which is always open to man in the Hebrew Bible. Insofar as Pauline Christianity has held man unable to do any good thing of himself and has seen him as entirely dependent upon the grace that comes through Christ, the apocalyptic lineaments of the despair of man in history and the "Good News" coming from the supernatural breaking into history are there.

Very often, of course, as in the thought of Reinhold Niebuhr, both elements are subtly mixed. Niebuhr strongly objects to what he regards as Paul Tillich's equation of creation with the fall. Creation is good, says Niebuhr, and the fall comes not through man's existence as flesh but through his will which tries to absolutize what is in fact only relative. Niebuhr rejects "original sin" as any biological inheritance, à la Augustine, but he affirms it as our social inheritance and as the sinful overstepping of creaturely limitations that man not necessarily but most probably will fall into again and again.

Insofar as modern Judaism has turned from the literal belief in the coming of the messiah at a specific time, it has turned from the apocalyptic. Insofar, however, as it has turned to a "messianism" which is equivalent to progress toward universal ideals, it has *not* turned toward the prophetic. It is a lamentable fact that a great deal of modern Jewish thinking is far less concerned with the prophetic reality of historical demand and decision than a great deal of modern Christian thought.

Israel, to the Hebrew Bible, means the actual people Israel who became a people through the Sinai Covenant and who remain one insofar as they are faithful to this covenant. This covenant, as we have seen, is to become "a kingdom of priests and a holy people." A holy people does not mean to become a collection of well-meaning individuals but a true community: imitating God's justice, righteousness, and holiness in the life between man and man *and* in the social, political, economic, and international life of the people. There is no distinction here between the religious and the social since the religious for biblical man is not a separate dimension transcending history but the demand that the Transcendent places on man in history. The unity of these two spheres, which have come apart in modern life and thought, is clearly grasped by Jesus when he gives as the first commandment,

"Thou shalt love the Lord thy God with all thy heart, soul, mind, and might," and as the second, "which is like unto the first," "Thou shalt love thy neighbor as thyself." Many uninformed Christians do not realize that these two commandments were quoted by Jesus from Deuteronomy and Leviticus. It was with amazement, however, that I heard so eminent a Christian minister and thinker as Pastor Martin Niemoeller say that what was unique in Jesus' teaching was putting the two commandments together. From the Lord's reply to Cain, "Thy brother's blood cries out to me from the ground," to "Thou shalt love thy neighbor as thyself. I am the Lord," these two dimensions have always been joined in the Hebrew Bible, as in Judaism in general.

If we recognize this, we still have the question of how the old and new covenants differ, since Jesus himself stood so clearly in the tradition of the biblical covenant when he cited these two commandments together. In terms of Jesus himself, it must be said that he addressed men more often as individuals rather than as the people of Israel. So far as orthodox Christianity's understanding of the Covenant and Israel is concerned, however, the difference is a more radical one. For Christianity there is a new Israel, an invisible Church, that unites all who have been reborn in Christ. This new Israel differs from the old in that it is not an actual community able to respond to a demand placed upon it as a people, but a spiritual bond of widely separated individuals whose communal and social lives are lived in practical distinction from their membership in the invisible Church. The one covenant is associated with a task—the realization of the kingship of God through which Israel may serve as the beginning of the kingdom of God. The other is associated with a fulfilled reality—the partaking in the redemption through Christ which is already there for all who share in this communion.

The understanding of the messiah is a corollary of the understanding of Israel and the covenant. For biblical Judaism the messiah is not a divine figure who can bring redemption in himself but a man who can lead the people or a remnant of the people in turning back to God, fulfilling the covenant, and making real the kingship of God. This is evident from the passages on Immanuel in Isaiah in which Immanuel is associated with the tasks of justice and righteousness to which the prophets had continually called the kings. It is also clear in Deutero-Isaiah where the suffering servant takes over this task of leading the remnant in the renewal of the covenant. The suffering of the servant may best be understood, in my opinion, not as vicarious suffering for others but as the terrible suffering which the hidden servant takes on himself by turning back to God while remaining a member of a faithless community.

The Christian conception of the messiah is very different. The root of the word in "the anointed" no longer signifies a tie to the task of realizing the kingship of God. Instead Christ is the divine figure, the Son of God, who in his oneness with God steps on the other side of the divine-human dialogue and effects a redemption which takes the place of rather than fulfills the task of becoming "a holy people." This is not the messiah who leads men to the redemptive turning but the messiah who has already redeemed them through his crucifixion and resurrection if they are ready to accept this grace through their faith in Christ. One of the saddest aspects of the Jewish-Christian dialogue is the failure of even such eminent Christian thinkers as Jacques Maritain to recognize the essential difference between these two concepts of the messiah. As a result, they regularly attribute the Jewish rejection of Christ to a desire for a materialistic messiah who will lead them to worldly victory. This dualism between the spiritual and the material is so strongly ingrained in some strains of Christianity that it is difficult for many Christians to understand the Jewish concept of the messiah, to which such a dualism is entirely foreign.

But how about Jesus himself? Did he think of himself as the messiah in the Jewish sense or the Christian sense? The texts are far from clear, but it is as unthinkable to me that Jesus thought of himself as the messiah in the Christian sense as that he said, "Take up your cross and follow me," with foreknowledge of the central significance of the cross after his own crucifixion, or that he said to Peter, "On this rock I found my church," and meant by it the Roman Catholic Church, a type of religious structure then entirely unknown in the world.

Did Jesus think of himself as the messiah in the Jewish sense? Here too the texts are not clear. Buber thinks that Jesus' "Thou sayest it" in reply to Pilate suggests that he saw himself, in the pattern of the apocryphal texts, as the suffering servant who has had a pre-existence in heaven. To me the most intriguing interchange is the one in which he asks his disciples who people say he is and then asks them who they think he is. "Christ, the Son of the Living God," says Peter, and "Jesus charged them that they tell no man of it." Seen in retrospect, the question is one of what category Jesus fits into. Seen from within as a present event, it cannot be that, for the category does not exist. What do the forty days' wrestling with Satan in the wilderness mean but the temptations of a man who knows himself called and yet must discover again in each new situation just what it means that he is called? When T. S. Eliot's Thomas à Becket is martyred, the category of the martyr, the objective and selfless instrument of God, is there ready-made for him to fill. Jesus, on the contrary, had to go through the terrible tension of a unique call which he could not know objectively but only as he responded with his whole being to the unheard of demand of the new moment. When he prays in the Garden of Gethsemane, "Father, if it be thy will may this cup be taken from me," he is not, like Eliot's Thomas, a man who has lost his own will in the will of God. Rather he is a man in anguish who wills to live, if it be God's will, but who is ready to accept God's will if it is not. And when he prays on the cross, "Eli, Eli, lama sabachthani!" he is not merely reciting a psalm, as those who wish to see him as very God but not as very man suppose; he is experiencing again the terrible anguish of the unique vocation in which he has answered the call but in this moment experiences no confirming answer himself.

It has been customary for many liberal Jews to wish to show their broadmindedness toward Jesus by enrolling him in the ranks of "the prophets" or "teachers" of Israel. In a broad sense of the term, we can agree with this. But he was no prophet in the exact meaning of the term, and though he was certainly a teacher, he played a unique role in his life that bursts the bounds of any such category. A Jewish protest against Jesus often is that he spoke in his own name—"But I say unto you"—and not in the name of God, as did the prophets. At the end of the Sermon on the Mount, we read that the people were astonished, "for he taught them as one who had authority, and not as their scribes." But the prophets also taught with authority and not as the scribes. "I am no prophet and no son of a prophet," says Amos, "but when the lion roars who can but tremble and when the Lord God speaks who can but prophesy?" Jeremiah never tires of belaboring the false prophets while being able to evince no authority of his own other than, "Of a truth the Lord hath sent me." Still, they do speak in the name of God, and even Moses, who is pictured as closer to God than any man, spoke to the people only in the name of God and not in his own name.

But does Jesus speak in his own name as if he were God? The texts do not bear this out. "Not every one who says to me, 'Lord, Lord,' shall enter the kingdom of heaven, but he who does the will of my Father who is in heaven," says Jesus in the Sermon on the Mount. And even in John, the most theological of the Gospels, it says, "Why callest thou me good? Only God is good," and "If I bear witness to myself and not to him who sent me, I witness false." When Jesus cites the two main commandments, he speaks of loving God rather than of loving or believing in himself. Jesus' awareness of a unique calling undoubtedly contributed to the ring of authority in his voice. But equally important, surely, is the reaction against the Scribes who carry on tradition without *kavana*, or inner intention and the fact that, as George Foote Moore has pointed out, this was the age of an individual piety to our Father in Heaven—a piety which Jesus exemplified in a unique and uniquely intense way. To speak, as many Christians do, of Jesus being perfect as man and as showing a way of perfection that other men can follow, has no meaning to me, perhaps because I gave up perfection as something desirable and attainable when I abandoned my mysticas striving for spiritual self-sufficiency in favor of a life in and with the world. If we are going to talk about creation and history, we cannot talk about perfection; for there is no perfection in human existence, any more than there is an innate sinfulness in man. There is only taking up a task with the resources that we have. Therefore, I do not pray with Jesus, "Lead us not into temptation," but rather that we may have the resources to bring the temptation into meaningful human dialogue or at least not to be overwhelmed by it. Every moment is a moment of temptation, as Jesus knew well, for every new moment is unique—a new reality that we must withstand, a new task that we have to face, or a new bit of concrete existence that must be brought into our lives and allowed to affect it.

One of the most important stumbling blocks in the relation of the contemporary Jew to Christianity is the widespread tendency to regard "an eye for an eye and a tooth for a tooth" as a description of a vengeful God and the tendency to contrast this passage with "Love thy neighbor as thyself," as if the latter did not also come from Leviticus but originated in the New Testament. Christianity has rejected the Marcionite gnosticism that wished to cut off the Old Testament as the product of an evil Creator God, but there has lingered in Christianity just enough of the Gnostic apologetic to stamp indelibly in the popular mind the notion that the God of the Old Testament is a God of wrath as opposed to the Christian God of love. The texts, of course, do not bear this out. There is no end of "gnashing of teeth and wailing in the outer darkness" in the New Testament whereas in the Old there is no suggestion of a hell where the wicked are punished. The loving kindness, mercy, and compassion of God are emphasized in countless passages throughout the Hebrew Bible, and God's wrath is seen as but minor in comparison: "For a little while I hid my face in wrath but with long suffering compassion I have loved thee," says Deutero- or Trito-Isaiah. And there are a thousand sayings of the Talmudic Fathers and of the Hasidim that one might adduce in addition.

No amount of citing texts is going to remove this mind-set, however. It can only be removed, if at all, by a new way of thinking. Our mention of the Gnostics gives us a clue to a basic way of thinking about this problem. That is in terms of the meaning of God's oneness in biblical Judaism. "I the Lord make peace and create evil," says Deutero-Isaiah, probably in conscious opposition to whatever Zoroastrian dualism had filtered into the culture. To affirm God's oneness is to affirm that there is no realm or power separate from God, that there is no "devil" in the Christian sense, that Satan is nothing other than God himself tempting man, and tempting him not to damnation but in order that he may realize hitherto unfulfilled possibilities of dialogue with God. It is this basic existential trust that underlies the *emunah* that says, "I shall fear no evil for thou art with me." Job, to be sure, was tempted in such a way that he saw God as mocking the calamity of the guiltless, but he never "appealed from God to God," as the scholar Robert Pfeiffer assumes in his interpretation of "I know that my redeemer liveth." Even in the tension between his trust in God and his insistence on justice, Job never ceases to affirm the dialogue with God into which *all* the evil that he experiences must be brought.

When it is no longer possible for man to hold this tension, then Job's question does indeed lead to the Gnostic dualism in which creation and the God of creation are seen as evil, and redemption is redemption *from* the evil of creation and not *of* it. This is the dualism which is embodied in Dostoievsky's "Legend of the Grand Inquisitor" in *The Brothers Karamazov* in which the merciless justice of Ivan's Inquisitor is complemented by the completely unconditional forgiveness of his Christ, who places no demand of wholeness or authentic existence on the Inquisitor but leaves him sundered into a being whose actions betray Christ while Christ's kiss "glows in his heart." "My God is a nicer God than Amos's," said a freshman student in one of my classes. "Why is your God nicer than Amos's?" I asked. "Because he forgives *everything*," she replied. I thought about this for a moment and then asked her, "If he forgives everything, then what is there to forgive?" The answer was obvious—it was the guilt she had accumulated in that other, everyday sphere of life ruled over by parents and teachers and withdrawn from God's mercy! Even if she had not confessed that she kept her God in the closet when she was a child, it would be evident that we are confronted here with the sort of practical dualism that leads guilt-ridden people like Ivan to imagine, in utmost contrast to Jesus himself, a Christ who forgives everything and demands nothing. Surely it is such a dualism between God and creation that leads Kierkegaard to his unbiblical "suspension of the ethical" and his equally unbiblical picture of Abraham as the "knight of faith" who renounces and receives back the finite (Isaac) in lonely relation with the Transcendent.

The true mercy of God in the Hebrew Bible is that he cares that man become human, that he live a true life, that Israel make real the covenant and the kingship of God by becoming a holy people. It is this caring and concern that lies behind God's anger. It is a demand placed in a situation rather than an attribute of God. The meaning of man's life is found in the dialogue with God; the meaning of Israel's existence as a people is found in the covenant. For God not to ask Israel "Where art thou?" as he asked Adam, would be a "mercy" that was no mercy, for it would abandon Israel to meaningless and inauthentic existence. God's calling man to account is his mercy. It is no cutting off such as the Gnostic dualists fear. Adam and Eve must leave the Garden of Eden, Cain must become a wanderer on the face of the earth, Jacob must flee from Esau's wrath in the wilderness, Moses must stop short of the Promised Land, the suffering servant must die in disease and ignominy, Israel must be defeated and dispersed, but God is with them all in their exile. To seek a God who is all-merciful in the face of an existence that is anything but would be to settle for a practical dualism in which God must make up for the godforsaken creation in which we are flung. To accept the real terrors of existence and bring them into the dialogue with God is to understand, as Job did at last, the mercy that is contained even in God's anger. Not to understand conceptually, of course, but in the uniqueness of one's dialogue with God, as Levi Yitzhak of Berditchev understood when he prayed, "O Lord, I do not want to know why I suffer but that I suffer for thy sake."

If one defines Jewish messianism in terms of becoming a holy people in real community, one must say that an impressive number of small Christian brotherhood groups—such as the Friends, the Brethren, and the Mennonites—come much nearer to this goal than the modern Jewish community center, which often has all the aspects of real living together except actual community, on the one hand, and the centrality of the covenant, on the other. Nonetheless, we cannot regard the Christian brotherhood group, in its Anabaptist and Quaker forms, as the true inheritor of the biblical covenant; for it stands on the ground not of an uncompleted task but of the already accomplished redemption in which it is the presence of the resurrected Christ which unites and transforms.

When we look at modern Christianity, we are bewildered by its variety and seek in vain to find a key that unites it in all its differences. This same variety extends to contemporary Christian thought, but here at least one key comes to our service: the understanding of Christianity as a mixture of the biblical and the Greek, in which the proportions and method of the mixture determine some of the most outstanding differences. When we then look at the spectrum of modern Judaism, we find almost as great a range if not so much variety, and when we look at contemporary Jewish thought, we find some of the very issues in the mixture of the biblical and the Greek that we have found in contemporary Christian thought.

A helpful approach to this mixture of the biblical and the Greek is the contrast between two types of knowing: *emunah* and *gnosis*, the direct knowing of trust and the contemplative, comprehensive, or indirect knowing of philosophical and theosophical faith. We shall certainly not be able to apply this typology as a simple key to the differences between Judaism and Christianity since a great deal of Christianity has been characterized by the simple knowing of a trust relationship whereas *gnosis* has again and again entered into Judaism, from Philo's Platonizing allegory of the Bible through the Merkabah mystics, to the medieval Jewish philosophers and the Kabbala.

For the Judaism of the Hebrew Bible, of Hasidism, and of such contemporary philosophers of Judaism as Martin Buber, Franz Rosenzweig, and Abraham Heschel, knowing is, to begin with, a reciprocal contact, as when "Adam knew Eve" or God knew the prophet Hosea. This knowing takes place within the relationship of trust, the biblical *emunah*. Faith and knowing are not opposites or separate spheres for these types of Judaism, therefore, as they so often are in Christianity. Biblical man does not find his *Torah*, or guidance, in the order

of the cosmos—the Greek *moira*—but in the unmediated dialogue with God who alone causes the sun to rise up and seals
the stars. "He goeth by me and I perceive him not." Therefore, the beginning of wisdom for biblical man is not *gnosis*—
whether that means theology, cosmology, ontology, or even
Plato's poetic vision of the Good—but "fear of the Lord," awe
before the Reality that we can meet but cannot comprehend.
This awe does not mean primitive superstition, as the Russian
Orthodox philosopher Nicolas Berdyaev thinks, but the given-
ness of existence itself, which leads Heschel to declare that
the beginning of religion, knowledge, and art is awareness of
the ineffable. "All religious reality," writes Buber, "begins
with the 'fear of God' "; this is a dark gate through which
the man of *emunah* "steps forth directed and assigned to the
concrete, contextual situations of his existence." [3]

The fear of the Lord has never led in Judaism, as it has in
some types of Christianity, to putting away knowing. It has
led, rather, to the Talmudist's recognition that that wisdom
which is not grounded in existence will not stand, to the essential Talmudic belief that all argument which takes place
"for the sake of Heaven" endures, even though opposite and
mutually incompatible points of view are put forward, to the
recognition that the *doing* of the people in the covenant with
God comes before the hearing, that the hearing of what is
asked comes out of entering into the dialogue with God. This
is a truth which one does not possess but to which one relates.
It is not theology, in the traditional sense of the term; for it
gives no knowledge of God as he is in himself—neither proof
of his existence nor description of his nature and attributes.
Revelation to it is never something objective that God hands
over to men, any more than it is a mere subjective inspiration.
It is address and response in which, as Heschel points out, the

[3] Martin Buber, *Eclipse of God. Studies in the Relation between Religion
and Philosophy* (New York: Harper Torchbooks, 1957), "Religion and
Philosophy," trans. by Maurice Friedman, p. 36.

response is as much a part of the revelation as the address. It is the Word of God, but this Word is not Karl Barth's Word that comes to man from the distance of the Wholly Other. God and man may be radically separate, but as Franz Rosenzweig has said in criticism of Harnack and Barth, the Word of God and the word of man are the same. They *must* be the same for the very meaning and existence of the word. The word does not exist in some hypostasized substantiality, like the Logos of Plato, but is a lived reality of the "between." It comes to man not out of the hyperborean blue but in the concrete, contextual situations of history.

The meaning of history, in consequence, is not an objective one that may be seen from above, but that of dialogue. The meaning of history tells me only what history's challenge is to me, what its claim is on me. This is not subjectivity. It is, rather, the refusal to lose sight of the given of our concrete situation—our existence face to face with a reality that comes to meet us and to which we can respond but which we cannot subsume under a single order or process or the chain of cause and effect. To preserve the existential reality of the present means to preserve history as dialogue. "Lord of the world," said the great Hasidic *zaddik* Rabbi Levi Yitzhak of Berditchev, "I do not beg you to reveal to me the secret of your ways—I could not bear it! But show me one thing; show it to me more clearly and more deeply: show me what this, which is happening at this very moment, means to me, what it demands of me, what you Lord of the world, are telling me by way of it." Levi Yitzhak concludes this prayer with the sentence we have already cited: "Ah, it is not why I suffer, that I wish to know, but only whether I suffer for your sake." [4] "Why I suffer" means here *gnosis*—an objective knowledge of the order of things which would enable Levi Yitzhak to place his suffering in relation to some overall scheme of cause and effect, reward and punishment. "That I suffer for thy

[4] Martin Buber, *Tales of the Hasidim. The Early Masters,* pp. 212 f.

sake" means the meaning found in the dialogue itself—a meaning which cannot be divorced from that dialogue and objectified but which is, nonetheless, a real knowing and not just a statement of blind faith. It is *emunah*, and the knowing that arises from this *emunah* is the open, dialogical knowing of the prophet rather than the closed monological knowing of the apocalyptic writer or the isolated philosopher.

I affirm the biblical covenant as a covenant of trust between God and a people, between God and every people, to be renewed in every age according to the cruel but real demands of that age. The biblical covenant is not the exclusive possession of modern Judaism any more than it is of modern Christianity. Jesus is, to me, one of the unique bearers of the covenant, as is Abraham, Job, Isaiah, and the Baal Shem Tov. He is not to me *the* unique bearer; for no one moment of history may do the work of all other moments: if it comes down to us in its uniqueness, it must be taken up into the uniqueness of this new historical hour. Jesus is not an image of God to me. The paradox of man's being created in God's image lies in the fact that it is precisely God's imagelessness which is imitated and represented in the uniqueness of each new man. But Jesus *is* an image of man to me—along with Job and Saint Francis, Socrates and Lao-tzu, the Buddha and Albert Camus. Even Jesus' denials were a part of his faithfulness to the covenant, his immediacy of relation to the Father, his concern for "the Kingdom." His "Take no thought for the morrow" is an unforgettable renewal of biblical *emunah*, as is that verse without whose commonsense wisdom and whose intimations of the morrow's grace I could hardly live from one day to the next: "Sufficient unto the day is the evil thereof." Jesus' life and his crucifixion are not, for me, the fulfillment of "prophecy," but a true incarnation of the "suffering servant," who has never long been absent—from Abraham to the "Job of Auschwitz."

Jesus' unconditional trust is a demand for wholeness which carries forward the biblical covenant as, for me at least, Paul's either-ors of flesh versus spirit and law versus grace do not. Paul is a figure for whom I have an admiration amounting to awe. He was no mere organizer but a unique religious genius, no mere rhetorician but a man of great passion and anguish— perhaps the first truly modern, truly divided man, who came to Christ in a great turning of mystic faith which rings down through the ages. But I cannot witness for Paul as I can for Jesus, since the "new covenant" of Paul represents, for me and I think even for him, a break with the old.

There is literally no end to the witnesses I might make to this or that strand of Christianity which has, in my dialogue with it, become for me one of my touchstones of reality: Saint Augustine crying out to the "Ancient of Days" that burst his deafness and shattered his blindness, Meister Eckhart confessing that when God laughs at the soul and the soul laughs back at God the Trinity is born, Saint Francis singing his Hymn to the Sun, Brother Lawrence picking up straws for the love of God, the fourteenth-century Brethren of the Common Life renewing Christianity in an unprecedented mystical, communal fervor; Jacob Boehme, George Fox, Blaise Pascal— powerful witnesses and contenders for faith down through the ages, along with that sometimes anonymous "cloud of witnesses" that speak to us out of the Theologia Germanica, the Divine Comedy, Thomas à Kempis, Ruysbroeck and Thomas Vaughn, Francis Thompson and Thomas Kelly.

My personal dialogue with the thought of such Christian thinkers as Søren Kierkegaard, Fyodor Dostoievsky, Nicolas Berdyaev, Gabriel Marcel, Paul Tillich, and Reinhold Niebuhr has been complemented by the impact on me of great Christian poetry, such as T. S. Eliot's "Ash Wednesday," Thomas Traherne's poetic prose "Centuries of Meditations," and Francis Thompson's "In No Strange Land," and of Christian music from "Saint Patrick's Breastplate" and Negro spirituals to Bach's "B Minor Mass" and "Magnificat," Beethoven's "Missa Solemnis," and Brahms's "German Requiem" which I sang with the Harvard Glee Club and the Boston Symphony Orchestra under the direction of Serge Koussevitsky. All of these touchstones return to me with comfort and with grace at various times of my life, some still attached to particular moments of the past, like the poignantly sad final chorus of Bach's "Saint Matthew Passion."

Chapter 10

Jewish-Christian Dialogue
and
the Working Party
for the Quaker Movement

"Maurice, you are a better Christian than any of us," said the young woman who was one of the leading spirits in a group of social actionists and pacifists that I met with in the summers during my college years. It did not occur to her that to be a "good Christian" might not be my own highest ideal, any more than a black might want to be told that he was really white or a woman that she can think "as well as a man." Once I talked for two hours about Martin Buber with a student from a Protestant seminary in Kentucky. "Martin Buber is so good," he said to me as he left, "how does it happen that he is not a Christian?" A number of years ago, one of my oldest friends, now a minister, told me of his hope of establishing a community church which would attract many of the Jews in

New York City who no longer have any religious commitment. "Will you have a cross at the altar?" I asked. "Of course," he replied. "It is a universal religious symbol." "That is where you are wrong," I said. "Even to the nonreligious Jew the cross is a symbol of the antisemitism from which the Jew has had to suffer."

Martin Buber said that when he first went to school in the Austro-Hungarian Empire, all the teachers desired to be tolerant of the small group of Jewish students and no attempt at conversion was ever made. Yet the recital of the Sign of the Cross morning after morning for eight long years, during which ritual the Jewish students stood looking at the ground, stamped itself upon his soul as no intolerance could have done. "To have to participate as a thing in a sacral rite in which no dram of my being could take part," he said, resulted in a life-long antipathy to all missionary effort among people with religious roots of their own. Asked once to speak to an annual luncheon of clergymen about Buber's view of Christianity, I concluded with this story, only to be followed by a benediction in the name of Christ!

What was so difficult for Buber and me in these situations? It was not that our religious position as a Jew was attacked but that it was ignored. This "unanimity" of the majority which overlooks the presence of another vital attitude, remains a central problem for all Jews in trying to come to terms with Christianity. One result of it has been an unconscious disparagement of Judaism that is so much a part of our culture that the average secular Jew shares it—a tendency to look on the religion of the "Old Testament" as a lower, inferior religion of a jealous, wrathful God in opposition to the New Testament's religion of love. Another is that even liberal Jews are often quite unable to have an honest dialogue with Jesus and Paul and the Gospels.

Yet if Judaism is to come of age intellectually in our day, it must be able to enter into this dialogue without fear of losing itself. This fear leads many Jews, including rabbis, to suppose that Martin Buber's influence on contemporary Christian thought must somehow mean that he is not really Jewish. But real dialogue, as Buber himself taught, means going out to meet the other and holding your ground while you meet him. Speaking of Hasidism Buber wrote: "It has often been suggested to me that I should liberate this teaching from its 'confessional limitations,' as people like to put it, and proclaim it as an unfettered teaching of mankind."

Hebrew Union College, and I was the first non-Catholic professor of philosophy and religion at Manhattanville College of the Sacred Heart in one hundred forty years. In all these situations I have enjoyed complete freedom to be myself and to speak from my commitment as a Jew, a freedom that was occasionally astonishing even to me. When Rabbi Soleveichik, the leading thinker of Orthodox Jewry, warns against Jewish-Christian dialogue about faith, I cannot take him seriously. But neither can I get excited about *official* Jewish-Christian dialogues. I am convinced that wherever committed people

---

[1] Martin Buber, *Hasidism and Modern Man,* ed. & trans. with an Introduction by Maurice Friedman (New York: Harper Torchbooks, 1966), p. 42.

> Taking such a "universal" path would have been for me pure arbitrariness. In order to speak to the world what I have heard, I am not bound to step into the street. I may remain standing in the door of my ancestral house: here too the word that is uttered does not go astray.[1]

At times I feel as if I were the original ecumaniac, as far as Jewish-Christian dialogue is concerned. I have for years been connected with Pendle Hill, the Quaker Center, and am now a regular member of its faculty. During the four years of its existence I was the only non-Quaker member of the small and intensive group that called itself the Working Party for the Future of the Quaker Movement. I have twice been a Visiting Professor at Union Theological Seminary, as well as once at

come together they can talk with one another if they share some real concern.

It would be less than honest to suggest that my encounters with Christianity have always been genuine dialogues. If I owe the resurgence of my Judaism on its positive side to the influence of Martin Buber and Abraham Heschel, I must gratefully acknowledge my negative debt to that fellow conscientious objector who, as I have related above, set out to convert me to his own form of high Episcopalianism and bring me with him to take monastic life-vows by Easter. Up till then I had only encountered Christians with whom I shared either social concerns or mystical strivings. Now I was confronted by a Christian who attacked me as stubborn and willful because I would not submit to his Pauline faith in Christ. How he sang Saint Patrick's Hymn and recited the Annunciation at Compline I shall never forget. But every buried vestige of Judaism that was in me rose up in protest against the spiritual violence that he brought to bear on me. Feelings that I did not know I had took hold of me and turned me to the God of Israel.

No similar dramatic experience has happened to me since—only minor reminders of the inequalities of a dialogue in which the representative of the majority religion is often quite unaware of the effect of what he says and does. When I had finished a lecture to two hundred alumni of Union Theological Seminary on Buber's dialogue with Christianity, I was much struck by the difference in the spirit in which two people questioned me. One, a minister, said, "I know this is not the right way to put this question, but why is it that Buber and you cannot accept Christ as the Messiah?" Though his question was couched in the terms of his own religion, his hesitation showed how he was trying to reach beyond his own framework to experience the situation from my side. A woman religious educator then asked me the same question without the hesitation and added, presumably by way of persuasion, "I wish Buber and you could understand how much we Protestants all love you." "I am not really lovable enough," I exclaimed, "to be loved by all Protestants!" What I did not say was that even personal hatred would have been preferable to such an abstract love offered in the name of a total group.

Other encounters have made me aware of my own hangups. In a conversation with an Episcopalian minister with whom I had worked drafting a protest against the war in Vietnam, I learned that he followed the "death of God" theologians in espousing the Son while questioning the very meaning of any "God-talk." I could not understand, I objected, how he could maintain the supreme redemptive power of Christ while denying the Father whom Christ proclaimed. Much to my surprise, it became evident from his reply that he saw our discussion with the context of Jewish-Christian differences rather than of theology in general. I came away somewhat annoyed, only to recognize later that in one respect it really *was* a Jewish-Christian encounter. Since childhood probably I had resented the Christian claim of exclusive salvation through Christ—a claim in effect that the Christian is "inside" whereas I the Jew am forever "outside." Without being aware of it at the time, I was reluctant to grant the death-of-God priest the right to make the same claim of exclusiveness when he no longer acknowledged the God whom the orthodox Christian holds to be incarnate in Christ.

My emotional unclarity became evident to me on another occasion when I went so far as to accuse an old friend and fellow member of the Working Party on the Future of the Quaker Movement of being a WASP because he saw my stress on the differences between biblical Judaism and Christianity as drawing lines between myself and the rest of the group. What made my charge particularly ludicrous was the fact that it was I who had first raised the issue of the place of Christ in the Quakerism of the members of the Working Party and had even implied that my friend was a second-class Quaker because he was more oriented to Zen, Jung, and Teilhard de

Chardin than to Christ. On his side he also tried to affix labels
by assuring me that Albert Camus and I were really Quakers.
"Why can't we have fellowship with you without your having to call us Quakers?" I asked.

There is a new spirit of openness abroad among a great
many young and not so young Catholic, Protestant, and Jewish thinkers. Real listening is already a form of responding,
and real response is not only dialogue but sharing from a different side in a common reality. In a "Third Hour" discussion
at Emmaus House between an eminent Catholic theologian
and myself, I asserted that Judaism could not be expected to
enter fully into dialogue with Catholicism when even after
Vatican II the Church still claims to have superseded the
people of the covenant as the "true Israel." His complete
agreement with what I said was an honest recognition of
difference that was already a step toward overcoming it.

Despite its grandiose title, our Working Party for the future
of the Quaker Movement really consisted of a small group of
eight or nine intellectuals who met three weekends a year for
intensive sharing of where we had come from, where we were,
and where we felt we were going. Sometimes we thought of
our sessions as autobiographical excursions, sometimes as confirming each other in our *daimons*, or callings, sometimes as a
dialogue of metaphors, or the interchange of the myths that
"spoke to our condition."

In an important way these four years advanced my own
understanding of touchstones of reality; for we met across all
differences in an intense mutual sharing and caring that went
beyond the search for common formulae. My very presence
in the group, as a Jew and not a Quaker, already implied that
loyalty to the Society of Friends did not preclude fellowship
with committed seekers outside of it. At times we had to make
a distinction between the Society of Friends and the "Quaker
movement." If the Society of Friends creates an environment

in which its members feel at home, that raised for us the question of whether a feeling of belonging and being a vanguard movement, or thrust into the future, go together. There is a persistent danger of confusing affinity and community. Affinity is based on likeness, community begins with the acceptance of otherness. People feel that they belong because of likeness, or affinity. But is there not a community of otherness that would make Quakerism really a movement and not an institution?

What the Friends call the "gathered meeting"—the silent meeting in which the presence is at once personal and communal—tells us something important about the nature of religious truth. We do not need to use the same words as others or even to affirm that beneath our different words and images we really mean the same thing. In contrast to those like Aldous Huxley, Bergson, Fromm, and Stace who have proclaimed a perennial philosophy, we can accept the fact that we not only have different paths but that these different paths may lead to different places. What matters is that in listening to the other we hear something genuine to which we can respond. The oneness of God, to me at least, is the renewed meeting with the ever unique and ever particular. It is not some type of superabstraction above time and space. Our Working Party could never reach the place where it could agree on Christ-centeredness as a central term for everyone, nor could it reach the place where everyone would agree to dispense with that term. The greatness of the gathered meeting lies in the fact that it does not start with an *a priori* unity but with a genuine trust. We receive from each other without ever being identical with each other; we are able to affirm and respond to what we receive, and grow through it. The genius of Quaker worship, at its finest, lies in the fact that it does not seek any sort of abstract or conceptual unity or criterion of faith. Nor can one speak of an experienced unity attained during the meeting—only community and communion, which enables us to be really different and yet together. To some members of the Working Party, Christ remained an ultimate beyond which they could not go to any sort of higher abstraction that would be more satisfactory to them. Yet in contrast to those who turn their Christology into an exclusive way to God, they were not imprisoned in it and had no trouble talking to non-Christians as well as to Christians for whom Christ was not central.

There is a great illusion in our culture that if people could just arrive at the same terms, they would be in real communication and agreement and could get somewhere. Actually no real communication takes place except by one person speaking from one vantage point and the other listening and responding from a really other vantage point—the ground of his uniqueness. My word is part of my witness. I cannot give it up. But I wish to witness to *you*. Therefore, I cannot impose my word on you. I want you to hear and respond to it *from your side* rather than passively to accept it. The only legitimate demand which I may place on another is that of his being actively what he is in relationship to me. But if this is so, then we cannot have the notion of "one truth" of which our individual truths are so many symbolic expressions. Every one of us has to witness from where he is.

The very meaning of personal and social witnessing is a problem in our day as perhaps never before. What does it mean, in general, to witness? Political activity, social action, civil disobedience, personal example, a way of life, suffering in silence, communicating ideas? Are there times when we must witness violently? Are there times when we must witness anonymously? What do we mean by *effective* witnessing and ought we be concerned that our witnessing be effective? Ought we to be concerned about our witness being confirmed by others? Do we witness for an idea, a political cause, an image of man, the Truth, or the spirit speaking through us?

One of the ways in which the members of the Working

Party shared their witnesses with each other was bringing into the group from one time to the next some of the important life-issues they had had to wrestle with in the interim—operations for cancer, changing one's vocation, moving to a different community, facing death. But an equally important form of witnessing for us was our dialogue of metaphors, our expounding and mutual testing of the myths that best embodied our own touchstones of reality. We were soon forced to recognize that we would never find a common myth that would unite us. We shared our myths with each other and grew in the strength to live without a single or an all-encompassing myth. A decisive turning point in my own life, certainly, was when the comprehensive world-view that I had taken over from Heard and Huxley and within which all reality seemed to be contained was not only shattered but laid bare as something that existed within my head. Reality was larger by infinity than my conceptions of infinity—larger by the emotions I had suppressed, by the evil and the otherness that I had looked away from.

In the course of our discussions of myth I glimpsed one further "myth"—one might call it a "metamyth"—which included both the individual daimons of the members of the group and that spirit which joined us together as a group. This myth I called "the Quaker movement." Taking it out of the context in which it arose, I now call it "The Community of Otherness." In contrast to the myths of process, evolution, and the unconscious which we had, *it* possessed *us*. We could not objectify or articulate it. It removed the very desire for a common myth; for it held us together, borne in a common stream. This inarticulable myth is perhaps greater than any myth that can only be lived out in the lives of individuals. Wherever men of no matter what religion or none at all meet in a spirit of common concern, ready to encounter each other beyond their terminologies, this "myth" can come into being and with it the lived reality of community.

No group is able to confirm all otherness. That is beyond human capacity. But the test of a fellowship is the otherness that it can confirm, which should not begin by going out to gather other people in but by understanding from within the actual people present. If you explain to someone that he is really not a member of the group because he does not fit your conception of the group, you have read him out of existence as far as this moment and this situation are concerned. Trust and openness are the same. It is our lack of trust, our existential mistrust, that makes us feel that we have to have the security of like-minded groups, groups based on generalized affinity rather than on the concreteness of open meeting with the real otherness that is present in every group, down to a pair of friends or a husband and wife. This is no formula. We should have respect for the real limitations of the moment— for our own limits in the situation as well as that of those we have to do with. Above all, we should not promise to be "there" for someone if that promise is conditional upon his reflecting the dominant coloration of the group.

What emerged for me from our four years of the Working Party as the uniqueness of the Quaker movement is also what I should like to point to as a model for the dialogue of modern man in general—a way of being faithful and diverse at the same time. Many people feel that you have to choose between an exclusivist truth and a hopeless relativism. After we had given up trying to come to an articulated myth, movement, or future, we glimpsed the possibility that the distinctiveness of the Quaker movement might be precisely a quality of gathered presence which would give us the trust that would enable us to affirm religious pluralism. The reality of pluralism must be the starting-point of any serious modern faith. We should give up looking for the one true religion and consider our religious commitments as unique relationships to a truth which we cannot possess. We should also give up the notion that some men possess the spirit and others do not. One of the geniuses of the Friends has been the recognition that the spirit moves in the group, and that no one *has* it. The spirit that speaks through us is a response to the spirit that we meet in others, the spirit that meets us in the "between."

The special Quaker form of the "between" is the gathered meeting. If this meeting begins with silence, it is not a "non-verbal" silence that dispenses with and stands in opposition to words. The words that are spoken in Quaker meeting are spoken *out* of the silence, out of a gathered presence which transcends the particular set of words that each member uses. This gathered presence gropes toward and responds to the diversity of individuals without aiming at any final answers or conclusions. We live our lives in a movement between immediacy and objectification. What matters is not the one or the other taken by itself but the spirit that leads us from the one to the other and back again. The gathered silence does not need to articulate moral standards or theological formulae. It transcends any metaphor or myth, even the question of whether you call the Quaker movement Christian or not Christian. Nearly every church has felt collectively true, but the gathered meeting of the Quakers, when it has really existed, has also meant the collective experience of being *led*, of being guided by the stirring and prompting of an "inner light" which is as much among and between as it is within. This is the uniqueness of Quaker mysticism.

The spirit does not stand in contrast to words. It finds its true life in the encounter of words when that encounter means caring and concern, in the contending of words when that contending means witnessing and confirming. Without ever reaching an overarching word, our Working Party glimpsed the meeting of one *logos* and another, felt our "ultimate concerns" touch one another through and beyond all words. This going *through* the word to a meeting *beyond* the word can be a more powerful witness to the imageless God than any dogma, creed, theology, or metaphysic.

Chapter 11

Religious Symbolism
and "Universal" Religion

Although we have by no means surveyed all the major religions, we have looked at those we have surveyed not only as "live options" but also as touchstones of reality: each one can and does speak to us in some way. Having done this, we cannot altogether avoid the question, Where do we come out? Can we extract a universal religion or essence from the religions with which we have entered into dialogue? Can we content ourselves with being eclectics who take a bit from here and a bit from there? Or must we make a decision between climbing one ladder or the other?

There is quite a range of people who have suggested that we can get hold of a universal religion, that it is something, indeed, that we as modern men must do. We are confronted as no previous age has ever been with the variety of cultures and religions. We are in a position to distill the essence from this variety, they say, and we owe it to ourselves and mankind to do so—to ourselves for the sake of truth and to mankind for the sake of ending those endless internecine wars that men perpetuate on one another because they do not believe the same thing. In particular, there are many in our age who claim to have rediscovered the secret of the mystics who offer us, in one form or another, keys with which to uncover their hidden treasures of meaning. Seeing the essential unity in the varied forms of religion, they quicken our hope for a universal religion that will unite all generations and all cultures in a common brotherhood. Aldous Huxley, Gerald Heard, Ananda Coomaraswamy, Carl Jung, Henri Bergson, Erich Fromm, Bahai, the Ramakrishna Society—these are but a few of the many thinkers and groups who seem to be moving in that direction. "The truth is one," says the Vedantist. "Men call it by different names."

The danger of these attempts lies in the failure of these thinkers to understand the impossibility that their own formulations can ever be universal religious essence divested of particular cultural form. As a result, either they fall into a relativistic pansymbolism which affirms all religious manifestations indiscriminately, or they naively overlook the really important differences between religions and force them into a mold quite foreign to their spirit. As soon as we say that this or that is the "essence" of all religions and all the rest is only "manifestation," we are, of course, making a selection. Every particular formulation of a universal religion runs the danger of being an expression of a particular culture, even when one is least aware of it. Take, for example, the Ethical Culture Society. The members of this Society are much to be applauded for the seriousness of their ethical concern and the seriousness with which they have gone about realizing it. But when they claim that the essence of all religions is ethical and that the ethical is essentially the same in all religions, they say something that is patently untrue to anyone who knows a number of religions well. They do not say it knowing it to be untrue, however. It is because they are, in fact, so very American, Western, and more or less modern that they see it that way.

It is a perfect example of seeing the whole world through the cultural lenses of one's particular culture.

The only way by which we can keep our foothold on the narrow path between the forbidding cliff of a too rigid literalism and the abyss of a too flexible symbolism is by an examination of the problems of religious symbolism. The symbolic is not a negation of the literal but another and deeper level. The "intrinsic symbol" points to some object which can also be known literally and directly without the aid of symbols. The "insight symbol," on the other hand, points to a referend which cannot be known literally and in itself because it is beyond the rational or the empirical or because it is utterly transcendent and unconditioned. Thus the cross in its Christian usage is an intrinsic symbol which points to the suffering of Jesus and the way of life of those who seek to follow him. But the sufferings of Jesus are themselves used as an insight symbol for a hidden process of redemption which can never be known directly and nonsymbolically, yet is nonetheless an article of faith with the majority of Christian sects. The concept of God as a loving father, the concept of the Holy Spirit as the wind which bloweth where it listeth, the concept of Christ as the Word, the Jewish concept of the Shekinah or Glory of God, which is exiled from the Infinite, the Hindu concept of the avatar or incarnation of the Absolute—these are all insight symbols, and it is symbols such as these that form the primary material of all religions.

If we recognize the central significance of insight symbols in all religions, we must also recognize the importance and the difficulty of proper interpretation of these symbols. It is on the basis of a careless, too easy, and one-sided interpretation of these symbols that many forms of occultism and universalist religion thrive, even as many religious sects keep their ranks by a too literal, exclusivist, or traditionally distorted interpretation. Every true symbol speaks to us in its own name, and yet it informs us that it is merely a re-presentation of something beyond it. For this reason we cannot entirely accept it as true or reject it as false. The same applies to myth. People find it much too simple to say that a "myth" is something that is untrue. That is not so. On the contrary, many myths contain a truth that we cannot get in any other way. It is a dramatic capturing of truth in an event rather than in a concept. But that does not mean that a myth is "literally true" any more than it is "literally false." A myth is a way of thinking, pointing, speaking which altogether eludes the criteria of "literalness"; nor can it be entirely captured within the category of the "symbolic," since it speaks out of events in time and involves the listener in the happening itself as many symbols do not.

The paradox of symbol interpretation lies in the fact that all symbols need to be interpreted and expanded, yet in this process much of the concrete reality that we held by the tight mesh of myth and symbol falls out of the frame of rational categories. The only fruitful course, then, is a dialectic between symbol and interpretation or, to speak more accurately, between one type of symbol and another—that of poetry and that of philosophy, that of religion and that of metaphysics, that of myth and that of concept—for, in matters relating to the transcendent, even the most literal and rational language can only be symbolic.

Positive theology undertakes to describe the attributes of God, believing that these attributes, even if anthropomorhpic in character, have at least analogical significance in pointing to something that is actually true of God. It aims to divest theology of the cruder anthropomorphisms and yet to retain those anthropomorphic images, such as the Wisdom, Justice, and Mercy of God, which are insight symbols behind which we cannot see. Negative theology, on the other hand, emphasizes the utter unknowability and transcendence of God and contents itself with statements not of God's perfection but of all the many things which God is not. This is the *via nega-*

tiva of Plotinus and the *neti, neti,* or way of discrimination, of the Hindu Vedantist. For this school, God is not good but is more than good; he is not being but the ground and abyss of all being; he has neither attributes nor qualities and is unutterably beyond human comprehension. Even to speak of him as God or person is symbolical and misleading, and for this reason many mystics distinguish between the personal God and the Godhead, the Ground, the Eternal, or the Infinite.

It is in the differing conceptions of God that we see most clearly the fallacy of those who seek a universal essence in all religions and ignore the very real conflicts between religions as to the nature of God. Even in the final stage of the great religions there is no agreement as to whether God is to be ultimately understood as Thou, I, He, or It. To the mystic, time and space sink into unreality before the awful being of Eternity; but to the prophet and the Jewish or Christian theologian the events of history are of the greatest significance and a God who does not in some sense enter into time is felt to be an unreal, philosophical absolute. Again there is a radical difference between those who conceive of God as entirely transcendent and wholly Other, as Barth and the neo-orthodox theologians have tended to do; the dualists, who divide the universe between good and evil, light and darkness, God and the devil; the pantheists, who see God as entirely immanent in the world; and the panentheists and mystics, who see God as both immanent in the world and at the same time utterly transcendent. If this last position is paradoxical, it is also the one that many of the profoundest religious thinkers of all ages have come to.

We confront another paradox when we attempt to decide whether God is personal or impersonal. If it is impossible for us to conceive of God as really like man, on the one hand, it is equally impossible for us to conceive him as entirely impersonal in the way that we regard the rest of the world that is not man. If we do the former, we are uneasily conscious of the fact that our God is an idol which we have created in our own image. If we do the latter, we lose God altogether in some monism of matter, energy, or abstract consciousness. This paradox is often solved or at least transformed by referring to God as the superpersonal or as the Absolute which appears personal when turned in the direction of man. One of the profoundest expressions of the latter concept is Martin Buber's description of God as the "absolute personality," who "if he was not a person in himself . . . so to speak, becomes one in creating man, in order to love man and be loved by him." Religious symbols do not give us an objective knowledge, says Tillich, but only a real awareness. Through religious symbols we experience the unconditioned as the boundary and source of everything conditioned, but the knowledge we attain of God through these symbols is not a theoretical, but an existential, truth, that is, a truth to which one must surrender in order to experience it.

If all our knowledge of the divine is symbolical, what, then, are the possibilities of getting direct contact with God or at least of discovering what part of the symbol is true and what part fiction? This is a question that cannot be answered with assurance. Every religious person tends to make his own interpretation of insight symbols on the basis of his religious tradition and his religious experience, and, by this same token, those who have neither tradition nor experience usually draw a blank when confronted with such symbols. The mystic claims to get beyond all symbols in direct contact with God, and the Hindu Vedantist claims that all religious traditions and all religious paths—those of devotion, discrimination, meditation, and action—lead to the same Absolute. But even the mystic and the Vedantist express themselves symbolically and mythically when they try to characterize what it is that they experience in their direct contact with the Divine. Aldous Huxley has called this mystical contact "unitive knowledge"

—the union of subject and object in which one loses consciousness of one's self in the greater consciousness of the Divine. But if this is so, it also follows that when one returns to objective self-consciousness, one can find no literal or undistorted way of describing what one has experienced. Neither Huxley nor his philosophical counterpart, W. T. Stace, seems adequately aware of the difference between mystical experience and mystical philosophy or of the fact that experience can quite properly be interpreted in terms of quite different philosophies, each with equal metaphysical claim. No interpretation is going to add up logically, for we are beyond the border of where logic holds. The relationship of the One and the Many will always baffle the mind of man. It cannot help but do so. Neither monism nor nondualism necessarily follows from mystical experience, nor is the abstract concept of nonduality the only or best means of representing the experience in which the intensity of reciprocal relationship temporarily submerges the awareness of one's self as a separate person, so that, as T. S. Eliot says, "you are the music while the music lasts."

Because we cannot get beyond the symbolical in our description of the divine, all religions are constantly faced by the problem of idolatry and demonism—elevating to the status of the unconditioned and absolute that which is only conditioned and relative.

What, then, is our hope for attaining a universal, if still symbolic, essence of religion? Men like Whitehead and Urban would bid us look in the direction of metaphysics, and here surely we shall find universal concepts, if any place. Yet metaphysics is, at its height, inevitably symbolic. It provides us with insight symbols that we cannot see beyond, but metaphysicians are by no means agreed, and their differences stem as much from differences in their basic insights and assumptions as from the differences in their logic. Moreover, metaphysics always runs the danger of emptying the religious symbol of its living content and turning it into an "It"—a philosophical absolute with which no one could be in meaningful existential relation.

Even less promising are the efforts of such men as Huxley, Coomaraswamy, Stace, and Jung. Huxley follows the modern Vedantists of the Ramakrishna Society in asserting that the identity of Brahman and Atman, the Absolute and the innermost soul, is the essence of all religions. Like them, he distorts all other religions in favor of one and makes a futile attempt to formulate a mystical essence which cannot be formulated. Coomaraswamy bases his perennial philosophy on the myth of the dragon and the dragon-slayer—the emergence of the many from the One and the re-entrance of the many into the One. He, too, sets up a false universal which is contrary to the spirit of many religions.

W. T. Stace's *Time and Eternity* contains a more systematic, but ultimately no more satisfactory "perennial philosophy." Here God and the mystic are identical within the mystic experience of the infinite and eternal which intersects time but is not in time. Not only are all mystical experiences identical, but all mystics are identical within this experience. "There is, from within, no relation at all between one mystic experience and another, and therefore no likeness or unlikeness, *and therefore no concept*" (italics mine). But this statement is itself a concept, and no less so for being a concept of the absence of concept. Nor is Stace justified in identifying this concept with the nonsymbolic and nonconceptual reality to which it refers, for it operates in the realm of subject and object in which even the memory of the mystical experience cannot guarantee the validity of the leap from experience to expression in this and only this way. Stace's claim that "the eternal moment . . . is the one God . . . one self-identical point . . . which is everywhere, coextensive with the universe" is not derived from the mystical experience itself, for this experience gives the mystic no information that he may carry away with

him about the nature of God and the universe. It is derived
rather from metaphysical speculation, stimulated, no doubt, by
Stace's own mystical experience and his sympathetic reading
of certain kinds of mystical philosophy.

Still less is the order of the world and scale of being with
which Stace explains the intersection of the timeless with time
a valid conclusion of mystical experience per se. How does
Stace know that the divine order and the natural order co-
alesce in the mystical moment and "God is totally God"? Is
the mystical experience the proof of the truth of these metaphysical statements, or are the statements intended to be only
symbols of the mystical experience? In either case we are faced
with an immense gap between an experience which is defined
as beyond discursive thought and a world-picture which presupposes stages in God's self-realization and the separate, yet
overlapping, existence of natural and divine orders.

Stace's uncritical identification of mystical experience and
mystical symbol finds a corollary in his still more questionable
attempt to solve the problem of how one may judge the
adequacy of religious symbols. The "more adequate" symbols,
we are told, are those which are "higher" on the stage of
consciousness, with the highest of all being the mystic who is
one with God. "The relation between the symbol and the
symbolizandum is not that of resemblance, but that of greater
or less *nearness* to the full self-realization of God." This "criterion," far from being easy to interpret, as Stace suggests,
can hardly be applied at all, for it begs all the essential questions. It provides no support other than mere assertion for
Stace's claim that "to find the scale of values . . . we have to
look . . . to the eternal moment as viewed from within, . . .
to the experience of the mystic." Nor does it provide any
criterion as to which type of mystic experience is "higher,"
which type nearer "to the full self-realization of God." It
assumes, but in no way supports, the nondualist mystical
philosophy which Stace, unlike most mystics in the history of

religions, holds to be the most valid interpretation of mystical experience. Finally, and most remarkable of all, it clearly depends for its truth upon an articulation of stages and degrees of mystic experience that only a mystic who had reached the "highest" level could properly make! Since Stace would hardly claim to have reached the highest level himself, what entitles him to judge which mystics have attained a "higher" stage of consciousness than others and which have come "nearer" to "God's self-realization"? Certainly not the testimonies of the mystics themselves, for they are by no means in agreement as to which experiences, symbols, and philosophies are the highest, nor can we divorce their statements from their immersion in particular cultures and religious traditions which lead them to interpret their mystical experiences in terms of one symbol or philosophy rather than another. The apparent tolerance of the modern Vedantist for all forms and manifestations of religion masks a value hierarchy in which the nondualist stands higher than the qualified nondualist, the yoga of discrimination than the yoga of action or worship, the impersonal Absolute than the God who can enter into personal relations with man.

Jung substitutes for the intended meaning of the religious symbol an unconscious process in which the individual reconciles himself with the collective unconscious and thus attains both personal integration and spiritual power. Jung has made a real contribution to the understanding of comparative religions, insofar as he has substituted the insight symbol for the Freudian sign as the proper means of interpretation. He is guilty, however, of religious vitalism and relativism. Ultimately, "personal integration" is meaningless unless it is in terms of something. Jung's "collective unconscious" fails to provide an adequate integrating center because, for all its great energy, it does and must fall short of any conception of God as really transcendent and unconditioned. Unlimited psychic energy cannot be identified with the divine without running the risk of falling into a demonic identification of spirituality and psychic power which leaves unanswered the question of motivation of the will. This criticism can be leveled against many of the forms of occultism, spiritualism, and scientific mysticism that are in vogue today.

Jung's psychology of religion is only one among many manifestations of the strong modern tendency to reduce religion to symbolism, in which the "symbol" no longer corresponds to a transcendent reality or derives from a meeting with the divine but is merely a manifestation of the psyche or an imaginative projection of man's own ideals and aspirations. When Jung advises his Catholic patient to go to the confessional, the pragmatic effect for which Jung hopes depends upon the patient's believing in the objective reality of divine forgiveness and not himself being a Jungian! "In earlier times, symbolism was regarded as a form of *religious thinking*," writes Abraham J. Heschel in *Man's Quest for God*. "In modern times religion is regarded as *a form of symbolic thinking*." This reversal of roles "regards religion as *a fiction*, useful to society or to man's personal well-being. Religion is, then, no longer a relationship of man to God but a relationship of man to the symbol of his highest ideals." No pragmatic "will to believe" can make such "symbols" believable. No psychological or social need to act "as if" these symbols had some reality independent of man can enable us to worship them.

"Symbols can be taken seriously," writes Heschel, "only if we are convinced of man's ability to create legitimate symbols, namely, of his ability to capture the invisible in the visible, the absolute in the relative." Heschel's insistence that our indirect symbolic knowledge must be constantly referred back to the direct knowledge of religious reality is of the utmost importance as a corrective to the tendencies toward an idolatry that fixes the divine in the objective, visible symbol, toward a relativism that accepts all symbols as equally valid, and toward a subjectivism that reduces religion to "mere" symbolism. But is Heschel justified in treating the real symbol as a static, visible object that represents and gives indirect knowledge of an invisible divine object rather than as something that communicates the relation between man and the divine? Metaphysical analogies, as Dorothy Emmet has shown, are analogies between relationships rather than between one object which is familiar and known as it is in itself and one which is either abstract or unknown. To say "The Lord is my Shepherd" does not mean that the shepherd is a known, visible object corresponding to an unknown, invisible God. It means that my relationship to God is, in one of its aspects, analogous to the relationship of a good shepherd to his sheep (a shepherd such as we can imagine the young David to have been and not some modern employee of a slaughterhouse!). Heschel himself treats symbols in this active, relational way when he speaks of man as a symbol of God and interprets man's being created in the image of God as man's potentiality of becoming like God through imitating his mercy and love. "What is necessary is not *to have a symbol* but *to be a symbol*," writes Heschel. "In this spirit all objects and all actions are not symbols in themselves but ways and means of enhancing the living symbolism of man."

The "nonsymbolic" knowledge to which Heschel refers is, in the first instance, "the awareness of the ineffable," and it is this awareness, in his opinion, which represents the one universal element in all religions—the essence of religious experience which is both the source and the criterion of religious symbols. The sense of the ineffable alone leads us to meaning —meaning which can never be fully expressed but only indicated. We encounter the ineffable as a powerful presence outside us, a spiritual suggestiveness of reality which gives knowledge without certainty. The ineffable is the "something more" in all things which gives them transcendent significance. It is an allusiveness of all beings, which teaches us that "to be, is to stand for." We do not proceed from God's essence to his presence, but from his presence to his essence. The transcendent significance in things and self is not a mystery at the edge of being but that which we are immediately and concretely given with the things themselves, an awareness that is within all our experience, closer to us than the experience itself.

The "awareness of the ineffable" is not the knowledge of God as an object but of ourselves as known by God, embraced by his inner life. We know only our relation with God, and we discover this relation when we perceive ourselves as perceived by him and respond to his demand. We come to understand the wonder as a question that God asks of us, and through this question and our response we come to the awareness of God "in which the ineffable in us communes with the ineffable beyond us."

Heschel frequently falls into a tendency to identify his categories and symbols of the ineffable with the ineffable itself. "The categories of religious thinking . . . are unique," he writes, and "on a level that is . . . immediate, ineffable, metasymbolic." But "categories of religious thinking" are already, as such, a step beyond the "awareness of something that can be neither conceptualized nor symbolized." "Religious thinking is in perpetual danger of giving primacy to concepts and dogmas and to forfeit the immediacy of insights," Heschel writes. Yet "insights" are not themselves immediate, even though they are derived more directly from the awareness of the ineffable than concepts. The fact that he is referring to a metasymbolic reality leads Heschel, like Huxley and Stace, to regard the images that he uses to point toward that reality as themselves beyond the symbolic.

The symbol stands in twofold relation to the direct relationship that gives rise to it. As long as it is recognized as symbol, it may point back to the nonsymbolic religious reality. But when "the finger pointing at the moon is taken for the moon itself," as it says in a Zen Buddhist text, then it may stand in the way of man's meeting with God. The approach we have taken of touchstones of reality is less likely to fall into this danger than religious symbolism in general since the symbol all too often has static and visual connotations which easily lend themselves to false objectification.

This attitude toward religious symbolism implies a radical reversal of the idealist and mystical view which sees the symbol as the concrete manifestation of some universal, if not directly knowable, reality. The meaning of the symbol is found not in its universality but in the fact that it points to a concrete event which witnesses just as it is, in all its concreteness, transitoriness, and uniqueness, to the relation with the Absolute. The symbol does, of course, become abstract when it is detached from a concrete event. But this is a metamorphosis which deprives the symbol of its real meaning just by giving it the all-meaning of the "universal" and the "spiritual." This all-meaning is always only a substitute for the meaning apprehended in the concrete. Any symbol is, of course, itself a step toward the more general. If we speak of Adam and Eve and the myth of the Garden of Eden, this is certainly universal, but only in the sense that it happens with every man anew, not in the sense that it arises from something beyond space and time and concrete human existence. If we speak of the legend of the parting of the Red Sea, we are talking of a particular moment in history. As soon as we say that the Passover is a symbol of freedom, however, we have lost the immediacy of the historical moment—its uniqueness and concreteness—and have gone over into the realm of vague abstractions. Actually it is the other way around. Freedom is a symbol of the Passover. It comes from that moment of history, and others like it, and it becomes alive again in all concreteness in the Negro spiritual, "Go down, Moses," arising, as it does, out of the slavery of the black man in America.

At a "Dialogue of Underground Churches and Communes" at Pendle Hill, a well-known Protestant leader of "The Submarine Church" stated that "at Auschwitz Christ was a Jew." "Was he not always a Jew?" one of those present asked in bewilderment. "I am speaking of him as a symbol," the underground theologian replied and added, "Christ died six million times at Auschwitz." My friends later told me that I have never spoken with more passion than when, in my part in this "Dialogue of Men of Faith," I insisted that it was not a symbolic Christ who died in Auschwitz but six million actual persons, each of whom died his individual death! Quite apart from the fact that he appropriated the extermination of the Jews for his Christian purposes, it is precisely this "universal" approach to symbols that enabled the Nazis to see the Jews not as unique human beings but as so many manifestations of the hated universal, "Jew." For Adolf Eichmann six million murders of persons like himself was transmuted into the abstract symbol of "the final solution"!

We do not have to put aside particularity and the reality of time to find our touchstones of reality. On the contrary, they have to do with the full seriousness of the moment. The fact that this moment will not come again does not mean it is an unreal or illusory moment. It is the only moment that is given us now to make real. Because the symbol means the covenant between the Absolute and the concrete, its meaning is not independent of lived human life in all its concreteness. Not only does this lived concreteness originally produce the symbol, but only this can renew its meaning for those who have inherited it and save it from becoming merely spiritual and not truly existential. When the prophet Hosea takes as his wife a whore and then she betrays him, it is not what he says to Israel but the actual event of her turning away, as Israel turns away and goes whoring after strange gods, which is the symbol. If the religious symbol is grounded in such a concrete and particular event, how then does it carry over from that moment of history to this? It can only do that if it is renewed again in all concreteness in another moment of lived history to which it speaks. William Blake bases his poem-preface to "Milton" on the historical fact of Jesus walking in Jerusalem: "And did those feet in ancient time," but he transposes the setting immediately to contemporary England: "Walk upon England's mountains green?" And he ends by demanding that that ancient event be real in the present, "Among these dark Satanic Mills":

> I will not cease from Mental Fight,
> Nor shall my Sword sleep in my hand
> Till we have built Jerusalem
> In England's green & pleasant Land.

Blake ends his preface to "Milton," after his poem, by quoting a statement about the Hebrew prophets from the Old Testament: "Would to God that all the Lord's people were Prophets." (Numbers 11:29).

"All symbols are ever in danger of becoming spiritual and not binding images," writes Buber. "Only through the man who devotes himself is the original power saved for further present existence." Buber does not mean the man who devotes himself to the symbol the way a theologian might. He means the man who devotes himself to the hour, who involves his whole being in his response to its claim. The life of such a man, his nonsymbolic meeting with the people and things that confront him, may ultimately, indeed, be the truest and most meaningful symbol of our relation to the divine. For the modern man, too, the highest manifestation of the religious symbol is a human life lived in relation to the Absolute, and this relationship is possible even when there is neither image nor symbol of God but only the address which we perceive and the demand to which we respond in our meeting with the everyday. Those who have tried to safeguard religion by reverting to tradition and those who have tried to safeguard it by seeking some universal essence of religion, not to mention the "God is dead" theologians who wish to preserve all the icing of religion without the cake, have alike fallen into the dualism of our age in which people live in one world and have their ideals and symbols in another.

In an age in which our alternatives seem increasingly to be reality divested of symbols or symbols divested of reality, the prerequisite to an image of God may be the rediscovery in our lives of an image of man: an image of authentic human existence such as that which Albert Camus has provided us in Dr. Rieux, the atheistic helper of men who stands his ground and faithfully encounters the plague that comes again and again "for the bane and the enlightening of men." Rather than develop an objective theory of hermeneutics, such as my teacher Joachim Wach did in his book on "Understanding" *(Das Verstehen)*, I prefer to understand less precisely and more relationally by way of touchstones of reality. Starting with touchstones, we can understand the unique relationship of the person or group to the event. We can also understand the problem of the renewal of touchstones in future events and the problem of communication and handing down of touchstones. Last and perhaps most important of all, we can understand the problem of the "dialogue of touchstones." My answer to the dilemma of religious particularism versus religious universalism is the mutually confirming pluralism of touchstones of reality. Religious witnesses are renewed when a situation or event speaks so powerfully that a John Woolman can suddenly hear in the American wilderness the teaching of George Fox, not as a doctrine to be preached but in his whole life—in his relations to the Indians and the black slaves, and his fellow Quakers.

The importance of touchstones of reality as an approach is that it does not claim to be the absolute truth, but it also does not abandon us to some completely subjective relativism. It witnesses to as much reality as we can witness to at that moment. In opposition to both the *via negativa* and the *via positiva*, therefore, I would make bold to call touchstones of reality the *via humana*. Only through it can we keep close to the concrete reality, without pursuing theology at the expense of the fully human or humanism at the expense of closing man off from the nameless reality that he meets in his meeting with everyday life.

Man does not have to have "a religion" to exist as man, but he does have to have basic trust, he does have to have touchstones of reality. A great many people do live without formal religion. Anyone who says that these people do not have ethical concerns or spiritual qualities is mistaken. I am more concerned with basic attitudes than belief, with religious reality than with religion. Every religion perhaps originates in and points to religious reality, but it also often obstructs it. Even the community in which we meet and confirm one another at times also obstructs the immediacy from which our touchstones spring and to which they have the power to point back.

PART III

Religion, Psychology, and Moral Action

Chapter 12

The Crisis of Religious Values

The notion of touchstones of reality clearly has to do with relevance, but "relevance" is sometimes like a will o' the wisp. If we seek "where it is at," we may find ourselves pursuing it from one place to another while all the time "it" may be under our own hearth. Actually the very phrasing of the question is misleading. For the true question is not Where is *it?* but the question which God addressed to Adam—Where are *you?* Only this latter question is relevant to what claims and addresses us in our situation. Otherwise we simply follow the latest fashion—whether in the realm of intellect and culture, of social action, of "walking the straight and narrow" or "hanging loose." For touchstones there cannot be two separate spheres of religion and morality, but only one indivisible sphere of the concrete hour in which our awareness of what speaks to us and our response to that address are two aspects of a single reality.

One way in which touchstones of reality come to us is through those moral dilemmas and value conflicts that force us to dig deeper, as I was forced to do in order to make my decision as to whether to become a conscientious objector.

This means that we cannot take our values for granted but have to seek the source of those values in the basic attitudes toward reality in which they are rooted. For more than twenty years, I believed that this insight necessarily implied that modern man can *not* be ethical without being religious. Now I would no longer say that; for I must recognize that there are men like Albert Camus who face value conflicts at the deepest level without drawing on religion or anything that they would recognize as religious reality. On the other hand, I still believe as strongly as before that moral values do not rest in themselves, that they necessarily presuppose an image of man—an image of a meaningful direction of personal and social existence—or a basic stance in life—or, in the language of this book, a touchstone of reality. Where they rest, instead, merely on custom, convention, tradition, or inheritance, they cannot stand up before the terrible, the anguished moral problems of our time. For the problem of the ethical is at once, and indistinguishably, the question of the *sources* and the *resources* for answering the question of what *ought I* or *we* to do in *this situation?* The crisis of values in our time lies in the manifest inability of most modern men to find either a ground for moral action or the continual renewal of personal integrity and genuine spontaneity necessary for answering the calls that come to them in their everyday lives. The religion of America is middle-class culture; for that is where the touchstones of reality are for most Americans and that is the basic content of most churches and synagogues. Sometimes this means wealth, sometimes security, sometimes status, sometimes having the smattering of culture that gives status, and now in addition "realizing human potential."

Twenty years after my own confirmation, I returned to a liberal temple, this time as the leader of a post-confirmation discussion group. One Sunday when the rabbi was called away, he asked me to take over his confirmation class. Informed that each student was reading in preparation for his confirmation speech (in this temple the rabbi did not write them), I asked each in turn what subject he was studying. One girl said she was studying theology and explained that according to the book she was reading this was really a matter of psychology—what psychological needs cause an individual to believe one religious concept or another. Another girl said that she was studying man and explained that, according to the Bible, man was created in the image of God.

"But if theology is really psychology," I queried, "does that not mean that God was created in the image of man?" Since no one was disturbed by this, I put on the blackboard two propositions, "God is created in the image of man" and "Man was created in the image of God," and went round the room to find in which each individual really believed. I discovered that without a single exception this class believed that God is created in the image of man and that religion is really a matter of psychological needs. Like myself at their age, they considered this in no way incompatible with their being confirmed as Jews. Nor did the loss of God seem to distress them since, as one student said to comfort me, "We still have the Ten Commandments."

One of the consequences of preserving the Ten Commandments without a God who commands is that they are converted into universal and timeless values but they are in no sense commandments addressed to a people at a particular juncture of history, to an individual at a crucial moment of his personal life. We have not taken seriously enough the question of what answer our emotional allegiance to "peace, justice, and brotherhood" can give us when we are confronted by concrete moral dilemmas. We have affirmed the oneness of God in temple and church and denied it in our lives, removing values from the present to the "dawn of a new day" or to a messianic era at the end of history. We have used values as sources of emotional satisfaction or as consolations for the God-forsaken everyday world, rather than as the growing point of our existence. We have substituted for the judgment of the biblical prophet in the specific historical situation the "progressive revelation" of values which are too self-evident to need to be revealed, too universal to apply to any concrete present. We have lost that demand on the present moment, that judgment on present history which has held the present and future in tension throughout millenia of Jewish and Christian messianism. We have two sets of values—one that we profess as our "ideals" but relegate to the future as un-realizable at present, another that we live by in the present but do not admit even to ourselves. These latter are the real life-attitudes with which we respond to the situations which con-front us. If we are aware of them at all, we assure ourselves that these are practical necessities imposed on us from without. Yet it is only in the perplexity and heartache of trying to dis-cover what it means in practice to deal lovingly with our neighbor as one equal to ourself that our values are tried and that we rediscover the Thou who speaks in "Thou shalt."

Society wishes to preserve the Ten Commandments for their socially integrating value. But it translates the personal and specific "Thou shalt" of religion into the impersonal "one must" of morality, and it translates this morality, in turn, into objective law. By then it is neither religious nor moral since it does not help us answer the question, "What *ought I* to do?" but only tells one what *one must* do if one does not wish to pay the penalty.

Many of us have inherited moral values from our parents without having inherited that way of life in which those values were originally grounded. Our children, as a result, do not even inherit our moral values, and it becomes increasingly clear that what we took to be the sure ground of liberal, ra-tional, commonsense morality is really an abyss. In the face of depressions, wars, the atomic bomb, the Middle East, Viet-nam, and Biafra, the young person of today knows that much of what has been handed down to him is inadequate for confronting the concrete situations in which he finds himself. *Or* to the horror of his parents, he begins to understand what has been "handed down" not as rhetoric or idealism but as a serious word that speaks to his condition as he could not before have imagined.

The corollary of the loss of absoluteness in values is that relativism which accepts all moralities as descriptions of the culture of this or that group or subgroup while removing their normative status as values with any binding force from without or any existential reality from within. Moral relativism seems to begin with the simple act of looking around, comparing, and then deciding that the Eskimos do one thing, the Tahitians another, the Samoans a third. Actually it goes beyond that to the nonposition which I call "the Abominable No-Man"! when I encounter it among my students—the position of one who says, "It's all relative" in such a way that he imagines he remains above it. Those who apply the social sciences or anthropology so naively as to reduce everything to the particular culture and leave themselves out, forget that they too are relative—not only as Americans or Europeans but also as social scientists or anthropologists. Relativism is actually the inverse of absolutism. It is a way of saying, "Unless I can find the same value everywhere, it is nowhere." Thus relativism, which seems to deny universality, is, in fact, the sickness of universalism turned inside out. It does not accept things as they happen in their *uniqueness;* for it knows only *difference* —comparison and contrast in terms of categories.

Moral relativism must be unmasked as not being a moral position at all since it tries to reduce the normative "ought" to a purely descriptive "is" and substitutes a statement of what people *do* value for real valuing from within. For all that, our choice is not, as some contemporary theologians think, between moral absolutes and moral relativism. For any particular individual, this may still be a live option. But for the wide spectrum of individuals from different walks and ways of life who are concerned with contemporary morality, it is not. There is not any one set of moral absolutes on which general agreement could be found. The appeal to unanimity and universality is a thing of the past since we live in dialogue with other individuals and peoples with different cultures and values from our own. This fact has forced men with a serious moral concern to a deeper searching for a basis for morality which they can really believe and live.

One of the most serious consequences of the "death of God," or the "eclipse of God," as Martin Buber puts it, is the dominance of an approach which *recognizes* no consequences of the absence of an image of meaningful human existence but puts forward an "as if" ethic in its place. Mordecai Kaplan, the founder of the Reconstructionist Movement within modern Judaism, offers the clearest possible example of this pragmatic inversion in which moral values—both the sources and resources for which he takes for granted—are treated as the source of religion. Kaplan defines religion pragmatically as "a dynamic response to man's need to give meaning to his life," the "Torah of the Lord" functionally as "whatever is perfect and restores the soul." "To make for the good life, the God of Israel is assumed to have revealed to His people the Torah. . . . To hold out hope for the future, God is conceived as certain to send the Messiah for Israel's redemption." Though we cannot demonstrate the correctness of the assumption that the universe is congenial or favorable to human fulfillment, "we hold to it, because it is indispensable to mental health and the sense of moral responsibility." Without faith in God, i.e., "in a Cosmic Process that makes for . . . personal integrity in the individual, and for unity and mutual helpfulness in society . . . there can be no valid ethics, because without it, one can find no rationale for that measure of self-sacrifice and self-transcendence which is indispensable for ethical living." [1]

[1] Mordecai Kaplan, *A New Zionism* (New York: The Reconstructionist Press, 1955), *Questions Jews Ask* (The Reconstructionist Press, 1956), pp. 89, 128, 137.

In other words, we do not know that God exists even in Kaplan's sense of an impersonal natural Process beneficial to man, yet we must act *as if* he existed in order that we may have a rationale for ethical living. But the man who rejects self-sacrifice and self-transcendence will hardly be moved by Kaplan's appeal to retain them for the sake of "ethical living," for he will reject "ethical living" too. While it may be true that if one believed, it would have beneficial human results, one cannot bring oneself to believe *just in order to attain* those results. Either our meeting with reality produces meaning or it does not. There is no meaning "as if."

An even more insidious relativization of values than the pragmatic inversion that defines them functionally rather than intrinsically is the psychologism that pervades every aspect of our culture. Psychologism is not psychology or psychoanalysis. It is the subjectivist reduction that leads us to turn events that take place between ourselves and the world into psychic happenings within ourselves. Love is not an event that happens between two people: it is merely "that old feeling." To psychologism, religion is either the projection of our wishes and illusions onto the cold and empty sky (Freud) or it is a purely psychic phenomena—the integration of the self in the depths of the collective unconscious (Jung) or it is, in its good form, a humanism in which God is merely a symbol of the potentialities of man and religion a means to the end of realizing those potentialities (Fromm). Moral values by the same token are defined in pragmatic psychological terms, the good being that which contributes to the mature and integrated personality, vice being that which destroys it (Fromm, *Man for Himself*). When applied by the logical positivists and the linguistic analysts, who do not use the tools of depth psychology, this psychologism results in the "death of God by a thousand qualifications." God dies through semantics, or rather he does not even need to die. It is only the word 'God' that has to die, and it is dead already since it has no real referent

aside from subjective feeling. Any sort of immediacy in relationship to God is reduced to an inner feeling in the same way
that any value statement is reduced to: "This is the way I feel.
I wish you would feel this way too." Thus if I say anything
about religious reality, I am making an unjustified inference
from a feeling which is real in itself but has no referent or
content beyond itself. The linguistic analyst and his theological
fellow travelers chop off the "inference" and leave us with our
subjective feeling—now neither numinous nor momentous.

The corollary of psychologism is the emphasis upon "experience" and "self-realization." Once a perfectly good word,
"experience" has gotten turned inside out. You go abroad
and find yourself in conflict again and again between looking
at a beautiful scene and taking a picture of it. We are more
interested in *possessing* the experience than in going out to
meet the really unique moment that faces us. People now talk
about sex experience, drug experience, and religious experience
in exactly the same terms. They are all means of *having* an experience. Experience is now something inside you, not something that seizes and transforms you. It is an individual "trip"
rather than a relationship into which you enter or an event
that catches you up. This enables you to remain, in the most
gripping of experiences, partly an observer—a "drip-dry tour-
ist." If it is a "bad trip," you can always find someone to tell
you how to get a better one. In other words, the emphasis on
experience can reach the point where experience itself is
empty of what it formerly was: going out from yourself to
what is not yourself. Earlier the experiencer was like the hero
of a picaresque novel, a David Copperfield who set out into the
world. Today the "experiencer" is like the reader of such a
novel or the viewer of a TV movie. He stays home, and the
experiences are injected into him like vaccine.

An article comparing the teachings of a Hasidic rabbi and
Alan Watts' *The Joyous Cosmology* concluded by conceding
that the rabbi was more serious about his mysticism. But he

had spent years getting there, whereas we can attain the same thing just by taking a pill. So naturally it is all a cosmic joke for us. While the rabbi remains stuck at the level he reached, we can move along to higher levels by means of still another pill. Religion becomes like a good shot of whiskey or a good drug or any other means to "self-realization," to be judged or set aside in terms of whether it produces the desired effect. The drug cult, the whiskey cult, the TV cult, the movie cult, the sport cult, the sex cult, the sensory awareness cult, and the "basic encounter" cult are all so many means of planning "spontaneous" happenings, and the "religious" cult is often the same.

There is one good aspect to this, namely the fact that people today do not just want to take someone else's word for it. Each seeks his own touchstone of reality. This does not mean that he can reduce reality to his experience, but he has to have some share in reality. He has to be able to witness for something. People demand today, and rightly, that values be humanized, that they be really represented and lived by actual human beings in concrete situations. We live in an age of social conflict, of social change, and of the demand for social justice. We cannot say to the black man, "Wait for another four hundred years. Something is bound to work out," or to the peoples of the world that do not have our standard of living, "In another millenia your turn will come around." Today when a value is espoused, there is likely to be someone nearby ready to apply the acid test of "Do you really mean it? And if so, what are you willing to do about it now?"

Along wtih the current polarizations and confrontations, some of them real and good and some of them based on slogans and caricatures, there is today a widespread questioning of every kind of authority and with it the breakup of the certainty and structure of the old values. Along with this questioning of authority is the growing distrust produced by the "generation gap"—the mistrust that arises from and is exacer-

bated by the weakness and vulnerability of the young in relation to the "establishment." Young people look for simple
cues to categories and see through the elders with their "re-
pressive" values. The unhappy truth behind this rebellion,
problematic though it often is, is that young people often
accept the values of their elders not through genuine response
but through the suppression of their own uniqueness. A parent
or teacher or minister may try with the best motives in the
world to instill values in the young person only to discover
that the latter accepts what he says as just another part of an
internalized oppressive force which is keeping him down. He
does not yet have the strength to throw it off, but when he
gets his strength, he will throw off the good along with the
bad. He has related to it only externally as something that
oppresses him. This is one of the sad things about witnessing,
especially to one's own children. How can we make a witness
that does not impose and is not simply brushed off into ir-
relevancy? We have to accept the fact that many people—the
youth, the black revolution, the women's movement—are going to say, and rightly so, "We want to do it for ourselves.
We want to find it for ourselves. We don't want you to tell
us what is right."

Chapter 13

Psychology and Religion: The Limits of the Psyche as a Touchstone of Reality

In the many years that followed the collapse of our amateur "psychodrama," the psychological—in the double sense of the experience of the psyche and the theories of psychology— often became for me a touchstone for the reality of religion. I was influenced most strongly at first by Carl Jung and Erich Fromm, but later also by the "nondirective" or "client-centered" therapy of Carl R. Rogers and the "interpersonal theory of psychiatry" of Harry Stack Sullivan. These were also the years when I was mastering the total corpus of Martin Buber's philosophy and seeking out its implications for many fields of thought, including psychotherapy. Thus in the "Psychotherapy" chapter of my book *Martin Buber: The Life of Dialogue*, I brought Buber into comparison and contrast not only with Freud, Jung, Fromm, Rogers, and Sullivan but also with such European psychiatrists as Hans Trüb, Ludwig Binswanger, and Viktor von Weizsäcker.

These studies fused into a point of view toward psychotherapy which is expressed by the title of Hans Trüb's posthumous book, *Healing through Meeting*. Trüb, like myself, moved from immersion in Jung to an approach thoroughly transformed by Martin Buber's philosophy of dialogue, or "the between." Only Trüb had had years of personal contact with Jung that I myself did not have, and the revolution in his therapy which led him to "healing through meeting" arose less from Buber's writings than from the impact of his personality—an impact which I only experienced seven years after first reading Buber's writings. Like Trüb, I understood that what was at issue was an anthropology, an understanding of man, and the whole question of epistemology, of how we know. This radical change in my philosophical understanding has issued into a critical approach to the very men who had helped me on my way—Jung, Fromm, and Rogers.

During this period I came into ever closer contact with various therapists and schools of psychotherapy, particularly Leslie H. Farber and the Washington School of Psychiatry onto the Faculty of which he brought me. Farber and I worked together in planning Buber's visit to America in 1957 to give the Fourth William Alanson White Memorial Lectures and the series of seminars that issued into Buber's theory of the unconscious. I also came into close association with Rollo May, through whom I taught for two years in the William Alanson White Institute of Psychology, Psychoanalysis and Psychiatry in New York. For more than a decade I have been on the Executive Council of the Association for Existential Psychology and Psychiatry which Rollo May founded, and for two years I was a member of a group composed of Rollo May and three other therapists who discussed their cases from an "existential" point of view. If one adds to this enough years of individual and group therapy to give me some solid insight from within, it is evident that the psyche has remained for me a touchstone of reality, even though in radically different ways from the part it played in the beginnings of my way a quarter of a century ago. Particularly important in the last fifteen years has been my active and growing concern for the relation of the image of man and psychotherapy which has expressed itself in central sections and themes of my books.

Religion has much to learn from psychology because religion has so often fallen into a false prating in the higher spheres quite opposite to its real motives underneath. Religion cannot blink what psychology tells us about the depth and complexities, the problematic and irrational aspects of man, nor about the task, which I believe is an essentially religious one, of bringing the whole of oneself—and not some conscious, willed part alone—into one's life relationships. But psychology also has something to learn from religion. A great deal has been written about the psychology *of* religion, but, with the exception of Joe Havens,[1] very little has been written about psychology *and* religion. As long as we think in terms of psychology *of* religion, then psychology is given license to dispose of whatever in religion falls, or seems to fall, within its jurisdiction. Whatever does not is conveniently referred to some other discipline. But as soon as we think in terms of psychology *and* religion, then a meeting is envisaged on equal terms between two essentially different realities: a body of knowledge within the structure of a science and a body of tradition, ritual, history, and experience accessible in parts to many sciences and as a whole to none. To envisage this meeting is to raise a question which is almost by definition never raised within the field of psychology *of* religion, namely, the limits of the psyche as a touchstone of reality. "Psyche" here is used in the most general sense possible—mind and soul, conscious and unconscious, thought, feeling, intuition, and sensation.

[1] Joseph E. Havens, ed., *Religion and Psychology* (New York: Van Nostrand Insight Books, 1968).

Today the psychological in the sense of objective analysis and the psychic in the sense of subjective experience are confusedly intermingled. Yet this confused intermingling has taken shape in the popular mind not only as a single phenomenon but as *the* modern touchstone of reality in the way theology was for the Middle Ages, physics for the Newtonian age and the age of Enlightenment, and evolution for the mid-nineteenth to mid-twentieth centuries. Here I am using the phrase "touchstone of reality" in a derivative, objectified, and cultural sense rather than in an existential sense: as a product of some direct encounter or contact with an otherness that transcends our own subjectivity even when we respond to it from that ground. These two senses of "touchstones of reality" are often quite distinct but seldom entirely so since we live in culture and our contacts with any reality whatever are refracted through culture—including language, concepts, world-views, ways of seeing, thinking, and experiencing, attitudes and expectations.

But if there is no contact with reality which is wholly separate from culture, there *is* culture which is far, far removed from any direct contact with reality. In this latter case our "touchstones" become both obstacle to and substitute for any immediacy of apprehension or reapprehension of the reality known in mutual contact. The limits of the psyche as touchstone of reality is a problem for this very reason. For those who take the psychological or the psyche on faith as ultimate reality, the question of touchstones of reality in the more immediate and concrete sense in which they derive from concrete encounters or events can hardly arise.

"It cannot be supported for a moment," writes Freud that there can be some other way of regarding man aside from the scientific. "For the spirit and the mind of man is a subject of investigation in exactly the same way as any nonhuman entities." The result of Freud's application of the science of psychoanalysis to the region of the mind was the unmasking of religion, conscience, and morality as mere products of the economy of the libido in the interaction of ego, superego, and id. Religion, to Freud, is an illusion, and one that has no future.

> The final judgment of science on the religious *Weltan-schauung*, then, runs as follows. While the different religions wrangle with one another as to which of them is in possession of the truth, in our view the truth of religion may be altogether disregarded. . . . Its doctrines carry with them the stamp of the times in which they originated, the ignorant childhood days of the human race. Its consolations deserve no trust. Experience teaches us that the world is not a nursery.[2]

Even odder than that reality should correspond to our wishes, writes Freud in *The Future of an Illusion*, would be the notion that "our poor, ignorant, enslaved ancestors had succeeded in solving all these difficult riddles of the universe." In the end Freud not only allows for no *meeting* between religion and psychology but does away with any reality transcending man or beyond the reaches of exact science: "No, science is no illusion. But it would be an illusion to suppose that we could get anywhere else what it cannot give us."

Erich Fromm is more significant for the *meeting* of religion and psychology than Freud, because instead of insisting on the rape of religion by psychology he has left room for a decent marriage between the two so long as each comes from a respectable family and comports itself according to approved values. But just for the same reason, Fromm's marriage of the "right" sort of religion and the "right" sort of psychology is more problematic if also more valid than Freud's. The nature of an individual's love for God corresponds to the nature of his love for man, states Fromm. But this is hardly true for Fromm himself, whose usual recognition of the otherness of the other

[2] Sigmund Freud, *New Introductory Lectures on Psycho-Analysis,* trans. by J. H. Sprott (New York: W. W. Norton, 1933), "A Philosophy of Life," Chap. 7, pp. 217-219, 229 f.

partner in the healthy, mature relation between man and man entirely disappears in his various discussions of religion. In human relations Fromm affirms the self *and* the other and denies that one must choose between self-love and love of others. In religion Fromm posits the self *or* the other, denying *a priori* the possibility that man may "fulfill himself" in relation to what transcends him.

What matters to the psychologist, writes Fromm in *Psychoanalysis and Religion,* is what human attitude a religion expresses and what kind of effect it has on man, whether it is good or bad for the development of man's powers. "Authoritarian religion," according to this formula, is "bad," and therefore presumably untrue, because in it man projects his own powers on a transcendent God and crushes himself under a burden of guilt and sin. Like the sado-masochistic relation between man and man, authoritarian religion is a means of escaping from the feeling of aloneness and limitation through losing one's independence and integrity as an individual. Completely at God's mercy, he feels himself a "sinner," without faith in his fellow men or in himself. Incapable of love, he tries in vain to recover some of his lost humanity by being in touch with God. "The more he praises God, the emptier he becomes. The emptier he becomes, the more sinful he feels. The more sinful he feels, the more he praises his God—and the less able is he to regain himself."

Fromm characterizes "humanistic religion" as "centered around man and his strength," developing the power of reason, experiencing the solidarity of all living beings, experiencing "oneness with the All," achieving the greatest strength and realizing the self. "Inasmuch as humanistic religions are theistic, God is a symbol of *man's own powers* which he tries to realize in his life." But Job did not look on the God with whom he contended as "a symbol of man's own powers," nor did Saint Francis or the Baal Shem Tov remove their God from a reality met in meeting the beings over-against them to a potentiality within them. To interpret them in this way is fundamentally to distort them.

Carl G. Jung, in contrast to Freud and even Fromm, is open to every variety and manifestation of religion. So far from considering religion an illusion, as Freud does, Jung finds in the religions of mankind the golden ore which, when it is extracted and refined, becomes the alchemist's stone not only of healing but of personal integration and spiritual fulfillment.

Jung sees the necessity of sacrificing oneself to one's "vocation," of consciously assenting to the power of the inner voice. This means that one must choose between one's conscious will and one's unconcious will, at the price of becoming neurotic if one chooses the former. The latter, the voice of the unconscious, Jung freely indentifies with "the will of God." He sees this obedience as a necessity, rather than growing out of the freedom to respond of biblical man. Psychic experience, informed by the archetypal and transpersonal "collective unconscious," here takes the place of the traditional God as address and guidance. Jung ascribes certain qualities of otherness to the archetypal unconscious, to be sure, in particular that sense of numinous awe of which Rudolph Otto has spoken. But he has robbed his commanding voice of its essential otherness by identifying it with one's own destiny, one's law, one's daimon, one's creativity, one's true self, one's life-will. This "voice" never comes from the other that one meets (other people are seen by Jung in the first instance as projections of one's own anima or animus) but from within. While Jung may retain a certain amount of inverted divine transcendence or "wholly otherness" in his view of the transpersonal objective psyche, he rules out of *primary* consideration as revelation and command the life between man and man. Jung's ineffable and unconscious "objective psyche" is "other" than one's conscious ego and even one's personal unconscious, but it is not other than the "Self" in the larger and more complete sense in which Jung uses that term. The mutuality of relationship that enabled Abraham and Job to contend with God seems to be entirely lacking in Jung's understanding of the relation between the personal ego and personal unconscious, on the one hand, and the "objective psyche" on the other.

If anything, the collective unconscious, or objective psyche, is a more basic and all-inclusive reality to Jung than God. God too is a "psychic reality like the unconscious," an archetype that already has its place in that part of the psyche which is pre-existent to consciousness. Our problem is thus transformed from the limits of the psyche as touchstone of reality to the limits of a psychologism which tends to swallow up all other reality. "Not only does the psyche exist, it is existence itself," writes Jung in *Psychology and Religion: East and West*. He defines religious experience, by the same token, "as that kind of experience which is accorded the highest value, no matter what its contents may be," and by value he means psychic value. The only action that Jung recognizes as real is from the unconscious and never from any independently other person or reality. Hence he states, "God acts out of the unconscious of man." "It is only through the psyche that we can establish that God acts upon us," and, "Only that which acts upon me do I recognize as real and actual." God is indistinguishable from the unconscious or more exactly from the archetype of the Self within the unconscious.

The placing of the divine in the unconscious, however archetypally and universally conceived, still psychologizes God *and* reality, robbing our meetings with "the things of this world" of any revelatory power other than the mimetic relection of our forgotten and buried inner truths. If Jung did not need to assert the psyche as *the* exclusive touchstone of reality, he could show great honor to a realm which undoubtedly has profound meaning, whether that of the shadow, the anima, the animus, or any of the other life-symbols that slumber in our depths, without hypostasizing that realm into an inverted

Platonic universal and elevating this larger-than-life-size sphere to the now empty throne of the Absolute.[3] He might even recognize that the shadow and anima arise to begin with in the sphere of the interhuman.

Once when I was teaching the biblical Prophets in a class at Sarah Lawrence, I was startled by a freshman who insisted that Isaiah was a paranoiac. "How can you call him a paranoiac?" I asked. "A paranoiac is one who lives in a sealed-off world of his own whereas Isaiah was more aware of the realities of history than any man of his time." "Well then," the freshman replied, "he was an educated paranoiac!" While few of us would express ourselves with such frankness and naiveté, most of us are really on her side, even if we are not aware of it. If any of us had Isaiah's vision in the Temple, we would be more likely to consult a psychiatrist than to exclaim, "Holy! Holy! Holy!" Though we are far beyond Freud's dogmatic and simply negative approach to religion, popular Freudianism still dominates our thoughts and provides our most tenacious cultural "touchstone of reality." The search for linked causes, the distrust of motives, one's own and others, the distrust of the conscious, the conceptual, and the "merely verbal," the loss of trust in the immediacy of our feelings, intuitions, and insights, the loss of trust in our own good faith and that of others, enclose us round in a well-nigh hermetically sealed psychic ecology. Even in the age of the "group explosion," the search for joy, sense relaxation, non-verbal feelings, and gut-level hostility is leading many of us to new and more deadly forms of psychological self-preoccupation, and planned

[3] For a full-scale treatment of the psychology of religion of Fromm and Jung, see Maurice Friedman, "Religion and Psychology: The Limits of the Psyche as Touchstone of Reality," with comments by Elined P. Kotschnig, Joseph Havens, J. Calvin Keene, and Chris Downing, and responses by me in *Quaker Religious Thought*, Vol. XII, No. 1, Winter 1970. For a treatment of the psychology of religion of Freud, Jung, and Fromm within the context of their total thought, see Maurice Friedman, *To Deny Our Nothingness: Contemporary Images of Man* (New York: Delta Books, 1968), Chaps. 9, 10, and 13.

"spontaneity" is making a mockery of the grace of true immediacy.

If the psyche is not given to us as an object that we can analyze, dissect, or even interpret according to the universal hermeneutic of myths, folklore, and fairy tales, neither is it given to us as sheer immediacy. Not only is it never accessible to us from without or in abstraction from a living person in relationship with other persons and with nature, but we never experience it directly minus an attitude toward it, a personal stance which already constitutes an interpretation of it.

The psychologizing of reality can be directly traced to the psychologizing of our understanding of experience, which now is something that happens *within* us rather than *between* us and the world. It means by the same token the abdication of our responsibility before the situations, events, and meetings of our existence, for we see "experience" as happening to us, or as "a happening," and we become the passive enjoyers, users, and observers of our turned-on lives. To face the fact that we cannot grasp the psyche either as an object or in sheer immediacy is to come face to face with a whole host of basic problems, no one of which can be located simply within "psychology" minus the wholeness of reality. If the "I" is not merely the passive servant of three masters, as Freud saw it, or the "persona," or social role, as Jung saw it, then what is its relation to the psyche? To speak, as Jung does, of an integration of the self which takes place in the unconscious with or without the consent of the "I" and without the active relationship to and valuing of what is not the self, to speak of an individuation which discovers personal uniqueness through a combination of one's archetypal destiny and the limitations of one's environment, to speak of individuation without personal uniqueness or that direction of meaningful personal existence which I have called the "image of man" is, to my mind, a contradiction in terms.

An equally grave problem is the relationship of the psyche

to consciousness. Consciousness is not the sum total of reality, Jung to the contrary; nor is Freud's goal of making the unconscious conscious an adequate aim for either therapy or personal or social fulfillment. The world in which we live is more than consciousness, and our existence itself is more than consciousness. An alteration of consciousness, even in the form of an intercourse between the archetypal depths and the personal unconscious and conscious, can never be the sum and substance of concrete existence.

Another problem that arises from the tendency to take the psyche as touchstone of reality is that of time. The fleeting moment, the full present, the flow of present to past, and the anticipation of the future carry within them an undeniable fact of existence to which the psyche itself can never bear adequate witness. The psyche, indeed, is the very seat of illusion in much of the literature of mankind. Nothing suggests the unreal and illusory quality of life more poignantly then to compare it to a dream, an image, a tale that is told.

The psyche, to be sure, has its revelations to make to us in anger, hate, rage, in love and mystic ecstasy. Yet we cannot follow Huxley in identifying the interpretation—the mystical philosophy or metaphysics—with the experience itself. Nor can we follow the "basic encounter" cults in absolutizing individual feeling as the one incontrovertible authority on where you are. Even Abraham Heschel's awareness of the ineffable, which includes far more than the psyche alone, cannot be identified with the *insights* which derive from this awareness. The attempt to identify the psyche and truth—never more boldly made than by Jung in his universals of meaning originating in the psychic depths—must always shipwreck on the fact that truth means a relationship to *existence*. It can never be restricted to one aspect of existence—the inner—to which all the outer must *de facto* if not *de jure* be subordinated. Like the nineteenth-century theory of social harmony arising from *laissez faire* in which each follows his individual interests, this necessitates a magical assumption of one universal which guides each of us separately in such a way that all is somehow for the best together. Either truth is reduced to the psychic and becomes mere tautology or the psychic is elevated to Truth and becomes a false hypostasizing.

None of this is to deny the overwhelming experience which we all have at some time or other of a revelation that comes to us through the psyche, whether it be dreams, intuitions, or the liberation and expression of emotions so deeply suppressed that we did not even suspect their existence. But this is revelation precisely because the psyche is thus brought into the fullness of human existence and interhuman coexistence, not because the truth already exists as such "down there" in the psychic depths or "in there" in the hidden recesses of our being.

[Chapter 14]

Toward a New Social Ethic

All religious ways of life and all touchstones of reality, even when they are not thought of as religious, have ethical implications. For ethics in the serious sense is not just a body of external rules. It is the way that we go out to meet what comes to meet us, what impinges on us, what accosts us, what demands us. Much of what we have considered in our dialogue with the religions need only be mentioned for its implications for ethics immediately to spring to mind: the *ahimsa*, or non-injury of the Bhagavad-Gita; Gandhi's *satyagraha*, or non-violent direct action; the Buddha's refusal to give or accept injury; Lao-tzu's *wu-wei* or the action of the whole being that flows with the Tao and does not interfere; the love of enemies preached by Jesus and the Hasidim; the importance of *kavana*, or inner intention; "the action that is in inaction"; "the way to do is to be."

If there is one thing that is perhaps in common to all of these, it is a philosophy of action that makes doing integral with being and rejects any ethic that is less than a claim on the whole person. This also means that we ought not deny or neglect action for the sake of inwardness. We cannot achieve wholeness by going inward and leaving the outward secondary and inessential, anymore than we can achieve it by going outward and neglecting the inward. If we have such a split between inner and outer, then our so-called "inner, essential self" is going to atrophy, and it will not be a real person at all.

"Who shall stand on God's holy mountain?" asks Psalm 24. "He who has clean hands and a pure heart"—the two together. The wholeness of man cannot be attained in isolation from other men and from community. What we do is what we are, and what we are is what we do. There is no concrete reality underlying that way of thinking that sets the individual in conflict with society; for there is no individual who lives outside of society. We are bound into society whether we like it or not, and our contending, if contend we must, is as one part of society confronting another.

There are two, closely related kinds of life that are not worth living, according to Plato's Socrates: an unexamined life and an unjust life. Plato found a link between where you are, what you are, and what you do, based, like the Hindu caste system, on the progression of the soul within the cosmic and the social order. It was obvious for Plato, as it is not for most social scientists and philosophers today, that there is a connection between being, knowing, and valuing—that what we know takes place within what we are and what we do. The teaching of the Bhagavad Gita is closely similar, especially in its central sentence, "He who knows the action that is in inaction, the inaction that is in action is wise indeed." The "inaction that is in action" is that "metalled appetancy," that has no purpose or meaning, that chain of cause and effect that is merely driven and has no spiritual freedom.

The Buddha's refusal to deal with metaphysical matters— with "questions that tend not to edification"—focuses us in on what we are doing in the here and now. Zen too stresses that real action and real being have to do with "this moment," the now, with where we are now and what we are doing now. The center of Taoism, similarly, is "The way to do is to be." This statement is entirely misinterpreted if one thinks it means to turn inward and away from the beings with whom one lives. In my mysticism there was something inherently disconnected between the means and the end. I thought to reach others by turning away from them. I was, in fact, perpetuating a dualism between the inner and the outer. The more the outer became empty, the richer became my dreams and the more intense my meditation. Lao-tzu, in contrast, teaches a swinging interaction, for the Tao is not located in any particular place. "You do not need a window for better seeing," says Lao-tzu. "Rather abide at the center of your being." But the Tao is never found except through opening one's center to one's fellow beings and the world: "A sound man's heart is not shut within itself."

In contrast to the currently popular dualism between "words" and "feelings," Lao-tzu says, "Real words are not vain and vain words are not real." A *real* word embodies the movement of theTao between being and being. A *vain* word prevents this movement of the Tao. It shuts the Tao out and hides itself away; for it will not risk itself, it will not give itself. The way of Lao-tzu is *inner* and *outer* both, and it is *between*. In the end no structure is going to take the place of spontaneity. "He who is anciently aware of existence is master of each moment." I do not have to split my existence into a phenomenal "unreal" present as opposed to a "real" but not present essence somewhere transcending it. I can take each moment as it comes. "What more do I need to know of origin than this?"

The injunction of the Hebrew Bible to love God with all your heart, soul, and might implies loving your neighbor as one equal to yourself; for you cannot bring your whole existence into relationship with God minus your relationship to your fellow men. We do not love other men because of God. We meet God in loving other men. Only in this moment, in this concrete situation can I love you. Even then I may not have the resources to love you; for it is not a matter of what is in me or in you but of what occurs between us. The whole approach customary from Aristotle down—that action is simply *potentia* made actual—is in error. We do not know what our potentials are minus the situation that calls us out and our response to it.

We cannot accomplish real effective action unless we bring the whole of ourself into that action. The whole of ourself is not some mystical or psychological state of being. It is a becoming whole through finding our direction in this moment. Our uniqueness is not *in* us. It is something which comes to be as we respond to what is not ourselves. This sort of love, this sort of relationship takes place *between* persons and cannot be counted on as a social technique at our disposal. Our whole notion of action—that we use this means to that end—is a plain violation of the concrete reality, which is that we do not know what the consequences are going to be of almost any action that we do. We must have social planning and social action, but we cannot string together events in such fashion that they become links in a chain of cause and effect or moves in a chess game. We think that we know what will happen because we imagine it happens *through* us. Yet we do not even know our own resources, much less the situation that will confront us. If we are so well "prepared" that we carry the situation off the way we expected, we may be sure that we have not really been present, that we have not heard the real address of the situation. We have to founder and flounder before we can discover what is asked of us. The sociologist Kurt Wolff in his study of the Loma Indians reports that he first had to surrender all his categories and set questions before he could make the "catch": discover the uniqueness of that particular culture.

When Danilo Dolci spoke at Pendle Hill, a man got up and said, "when you tell us of your work to build community in

Palermo, you are talking about little skirmishes, minor tactics. You are not telling us about the larger strategy for revolution." To this Dolci replied, "No, I am concerned about strategy; for what we do in Palermo affects New York, and what is done in New York affects Palermo." It is not a question of a choice between action and cultivating our own garden. It is a matter of saying where we can effectively begin to build community and peace in the situation where we are. Clean hands *and* a pure heart, *kavana*, "the way to do is to be"—all of this takes place in the integument of the family, the group, community, and society. When we succeed in uncovering the concrete reality of the situation, then we shall discover what is asked of us. This approach is neither "evolutionary" nor "revolutionary." It is a call that lies the other side of both optimism and despair—the call to do what we can in each situation in which we find ourselves.

This approach has great meaning for the contemporary crisis of values and its manifestations. Especially relevant for this crisis is something which, while we take it for granted as a part of our culture, has been largely lost to it—modern biblical morality, biblical trust issuing into personal and social action. Ethics is *both* the meeting with the other that comes to you in the situation and it is that turning inward, and perhaps looking upward, that is necessary to find the resources to meet the situation. If we get down to where man really exists, where he lives from, we discover basic attitudes that have to do with the way in which we go out from our own ground to meet what is not ourselves. Ethics is grounded in such basic attitudes.

Modern biblical morality attacks every attempt to separate our life into inner and outer, individual and social, or spiritual and material. It speaks of and from the actual situation—the demand placed on us now—and this cannot be relativized, any more than it can be absolutized in the metaphysical sense of the term. It sees man's existence as living in open relationship to a creation other than himself. It would never see his relationship to God, to man, and to the world as merely a function of his own becoming.

One reason that we have lost the biblical vision of wholeness is because of a dualism deeply ingrained in our culture—a dualism between law and spirit, between the material and the spiritual world, between the practical and the ideal. We have settled down in this dualism. We have accepted it. But today many, many people from all sides—from all religions and from the nonreligious—are trying to break out of this dualism to some relevant form of personal, social, and communal living. There is a new spirit abroad in the land which expresses itself in the growth of fellowships and cells of renewal, within established churches and organizations and also outside them, in "underground churches" or informal communities of seekers, and in communes of every type—urban and rural, religious and nonreligious, young people and people of all ages. For this spirit modern biblical morality has precisely the relevance of making present one of the sustained great refusals in the history of mankind to separate personal integrity and the fight for social justice, inward light and social witness, expanded awareness of the wonder and beauty of nature and active political concern.

The biblical covenant rested upon the actual existence of the people as a people. Its task was to build real community. But you cannot build real community out of the sprawling agglomerates which so many of our modern cities have become. We live in a time in which we find ourselves painfully trying to rebuild real communities within the larger social bodies. One of the dangers, of course, is the temptation to betray the "community of otherness" by designating one's own commune or cell "the blessed community" and consigning everything else to total meaninglessness, if not to the profane. Everything is the "real world," including the "godforsaken" part of it. But our responsibility has much to do with our humble awareness

of the factual limitations of our resources in any actual situation. That "radicalism" which would cut us off forever from
anything outside of a chosen community is a denial rather than
a fulfillment of creation. That is why I cannot accept Harvey
Cox's notion of an "I-You" relationship in between the "I-
Thou" and "I-It" relationships, to be used for impersonal,
one-dimensional relations that one does not allow to flower
beyond this limited structure. One of the serious aspects of a
moral way of life is the repeated, ever-renewed decision as
to where to draw the line of responsibility in any particular
situation. But this must not be allowed to become any sort of
"once for all" by protecting ourselves in advance and ruling
some people out of "I-Thou" relationships *a priori*.

Modern biblical morality is grounded in what we have already seen as basic to biblical faith—in basic trust. This is not
trust that something is so but the willingness to meet what
comes. It is grounded in man's real freedom, but his freedom
as co-creator with God, as the partner who walks with God
in history, a freedom, therefore, which realizes itself in again
and again turning to God—bringing one's existence into relationship with God. The moral and social responsibility which
it implies is grounded in real hearing and real responding—the
root meaning of responsibility. It is grounded in the awareness
that it is the whole existential person who is addressed and
claimed and that one's social relationships make up an essential
part of this whole personal existence.

Man's creaturehood does not mean the denial that man has
a ground to stand on—the ground of his created freedom. But
it does mean a recognition that man lives in perpetual contact
with an otherness that he has not created himself, with creatures that exist for their own sake and not just for human
purposes. In the human sphere, this recognition of otherness
means setting a limit to the tendency to regard one's own point
of view as absolute and the other's as relative. It means the
recognition of the other as a brother who is created in the

image of the imageless God and whom one cannot deny without denying God. The failure of communication between men cannot be cured through the simultaneous translations of the United Nations Assembly, since the basic obstacle to communication remains—that each people sees itself as absolute and the other peoples as questionable and relative. Without the recognition that in meeting the other we meet a unique person or group that we cannot reduce to a means to our end or to a function of our self-realization, no basis for true social responsibility can possibly exist. Here the true meaning of "love your neighbor" unfolds itself: "Deal lovingly with your neighbor as one equal to yourself," as your fellow creature, your brother, your "Thou."

You cannot "deal lovingly with your neighbor as one equal to yourself" as a general principle, but only in a mutual relationship in a concrete situation. What did it mean not to bear false witness during the McCarthy era of recent American history? Many people bore false witness by keeping silent, others did so by innuendoes, selective reporting, or simple unwillingness to risk themselves. Every commandment takes on meaning only when you are the one addressed in all the complexity and anguish of a real life-choice, such as John Proctor had to make in Arthur Miller's play *The Crucible*—a play set in Puritan New England but explicitly growing out of Miller's own experience in the McCarthy era.

There is thus a morality which is both modern and biblical. This is not the morality of Dostoievsky's Grand Inquisitor—the morality of compulsory order and compulsory good—but neither is it the morality of the Christ of that legend—the morality of a freely given love which places no demand, which does not ask that man authenticate his existence by becoming genuinely human, the morality which does not demand that man bring his inner feeling and his outer social behavior into one unity but leaves him split in two. It is not the morality of absolute pacifism and liberal perfectionism—it is not the morality of any "ism" at all, but of the concrete historical situation. Yet neither is it the morality of those who make the moral demand relevant to "immoral society" only as a judgment but not as a call to "drive the plowshare of the normative into the hard soil of political fact."

Although I do not necessarily cease to deal lovingly with another even when I am no longer in dialogue with him, it is just in the concrete that I meet reality, and it is this which prevents dialogue from degenerating into "responsibility" to an abstract moral code or universal idea. Man is created in the image of God. But I do not respect my fellow man as a deduction from this premise. On the contrary, I realize him as created in the image of God only when I meet him in his concrete uniqueness as a person. What is meant by love your neighbor, if it is to become real and not just remain a warm glow in the heart, can only be discovered in the situation. This is the only way in which I discover that men are equal in the only way that they really are equal—that each is of unique value, of value in himself, and that in the meeting with this unique other my own existence is authenticated.

In that relationship which claims my whole being, which I must enter as a person, and in which I find the meaning of my existence, in that relationship which calls me forth and to which I respond, in that relationship of freedom, direction, mutuality, and presentness, there is no room left over to speak of a separate relationship with God. No matter how "inward" I may be, I still live in the world facing my fellow men. My relationship to God is not apart from my relationship to man but is its very foundation if the latter is understood deeply enough.

Modern biblical morality implies that we find the absolute ever again in the relative—not as timeless essence or universal, but just in and inseparable from the unique, the unrepeatable, the new. If we do not live our lives in such a way that we rediscover our ground again and again, we shall have nowhere from which to respond and nothing to give. We program ourselves so that we have no time for spontaneity, and we end up turning paradise into hell—a life full of good causes and of total frustration since no activity gets the attention it deserves. To be fully present we must be able to do one thing at a time. Not to be really present is not to be truly alive. This, if anything, is inauthentic existence.

Basic to modern biblical morality is hearing and responding —not imposition or obedience in the sense that we have to split ourselves into an obedient and rebellious part, but becoming ourselves in responding to what addresses us in the situation. This hearing and responding is linked with the basic biblical understanding of creation, as in the last four chapters of the Book of Job. As Job is confronted with the otherness of nature and of the rain that falls on the land where no man is, so we are called to respond in so far as our resources allow to every other—human or nonhuman—that comes to meet us. This is not because the other is God or contains the essence of God, or "that of God in him," but because he and we are set in one creation, are creatures who find our access to true existence only through the encounter with and response to genuine otherness. If we are co-creators with God, we are also co-redeemers, but our redemption depends neither upon our will nor upon grace but upon each of us doing his share to build the "community of otherness." Reality is not given in me alone or in some part of reality with which I identify myself. Among primitive tribes, the members of other tribes were often not even considered human beings. Even the civilized Greeks saw the rest of the non-Greek world as "barbarians" and therefore by nature unequal to them and properly forced into permanent slavery when conquered. On the coast of Africa there are still great castles in which for four hundred years the Portugese, the Dutch, and the English vied with one another as to who could get the most profit out of shipping fifty million slaves to America for sale there. The ravaging of the frontier and of the whaling industry, similarly, shows that a good deal of what has characterized modern man, long before the Nazi exterminations, has been a lack of respect for the otherness of creation, including the nonhuman. If in the first creation story in the Book of Genesis man is given dominion over creation, in the second all the other creatures are created first and creation is pronounced good before man is created.

The respect for the otherness of the other does not mean that I love everyone or even that I have the resources to meet everyone in genuine dialogue. But it does mean that just everything that confronts me demands my attention and response—whether of love or hate, agreement or opposition to the death—just because it is the reality, and the only reality, that is given me in that moment. The corollary of this presupposition is that there is no thing and no event that is absolutely meaningless or absolutely evil, even though meaninglessness and evil are inescapable components of all human existence. This is the *emunah*, the trust, underlying modern biblical morality. There is a growing tendency today, on both sides of the generation gap, on both extremes of the political spectrum, and on both sides of every militant social and racial confrontation, to regard some people as totally irrelevant because they are not "where it is at." The acceptance of the otherness of creation stands in uncompromising opposition to this tendency. I have freedom, but I am not the whole of reality, and I find my existence in going out to meet what is not myself.

In an age of the "eclipse of God" can we still meet, can we still hear, can we still respond? Or are we like Kafka's scholar-dog in "Investigations of a Dog" who said that in the old days the Word was with the dogs but that now dogs have become so fond of their doggishness that they can no longer hear the Word? Is that the way it is with us? Is biblical morality no longer relevant for us because we can no longer believe in a loving Father who counts the hairs of every head and sees the fall of every sparrow?

The answer to this question is implicit in the words that we have quoted from Deuteronomy: "It is not in heaven. . . . But the word is very near you; it is in your mouth and in your heart so that you can do it." If we take this seriously, that means that the word is not simply the possession of those who claim to have unlocked the esoteric mysteries, whether it be the Gnostic elect, Plato's Philosopher King, or those who specialize in the interpretation of the ancient Vedas, the Bible, the Talmud, the Kabbala, the I Ching, or the Buddhist sutras. Certainly the word may come to us through anything we make our own, including the scriptures of any religion. But the word is not tucked away in any special drawer for the privileged. Hearing and responding is a part of our existence itself. This is the basic biblical trust to which we have pointed, a trust all but obscured in a world in which psychologism so dominates that again and again we miss both the real otherness and the real address of the events that make up our lives. We stunt and cripple our own touchstones of reality by looking only for the byproduct: how the event helps us realize our potentialities or adds to our "growth." We can, nonetheless, hear and respond because the given of our existence cannot be abrogated, namely, that we live meeting situations that place demands upon us. What is really asked of us may be entirely other, even diametrically opposite, to what some person consciously demands. But to the real address of that person we *can* respond as long as we have the courage again and again to bring our touchstones back into that lived reality from which they arose. I agree with Kafka that, "No one knows the tasks of the present, and therefore we all have a bad conscience." But I would not agree with those who think there is no possibility or need to act and no value in acting unless and until we have comprehensive certainty and objective assurance of the rightness of our hearing and responding.

All ethics rests on a basic attitude toward reality—on a touchstone of reality that waits in the depths until it is summoned by a concrete situation. No matter what his religious beliefs or lack of them, modern man lives in an age of the "death of God" in the sense in which I use the term: an age in which men no longer have a direction of meaningful personal and social existence such as gave some sureness and meaning to bibilical, Greek, Christian, and Renaissance man, even in the midst of tragedy. Yet two possibilities remain open for modern man. The first is being ethical within given, inherited structures—the family, the culture, the state—ordinary living which because it *is* within these structures and because it rests on some genuine interhuman contact is ethical in practice, whatever the names by which its source is called or miscalled. The second is the vastly more difficult and painful discovery of the ethical in limit situations, in the "dialogue with the absurd," in the "eclipse of God."

The ethical in this second sense takes a deeper grounding, whether one wants to call it religious or not. It means not putting up with the merely surface, and it means the testing of resources. It may mean living with guilt, anxiety, and the absurd. What is common to both types of ethical possibilities is that for them moral values are not authenticated in the abstract through finding rationally consistent positions. It is not in logical consistency but in our withstanding and being true in the situations that confront us that they are authenticated. We do not have to live every moment in a limit situation, and for this we must be grateful; for we do not have the resources to do so. But at times in our lives when we are confronted by the abyss, we do have the resources to respond from the depths and become ourselves in responding.

[Chapter 15]

The Covenant of Peace

We live in an age of compounded crises, an age of hot and cold war and the constant threat of total annihilation by the weapons that we ourselves have perfected. It is an age more and more bereft of authentic human existence, and even the image of such existence increasingly deserts us. Those who cannot accept the compromises of our age run to the extremes: the yogi and the commissar, the mystic and the social actionist. The one prayer which seems least likely to be answered, the prayer we have almost ceased to pray, is *Dona nobis pacem*, "Give us peace." War, cold war, threatened war, future war, has become the very atmosphere in which we live, a total element so pervasive and so enveloping as to numb our very sensibility to the abyss which promises to engulf us.

My first image of man as peacemaker was Mohandas Gandhi, who found the meeting point of religion and politics in *satyagraha*, a laying hold of the truth, or "soul force," which proved effective in liberating India as, under the leadership of Martin Luther King, it also proved effective up to a point in liberating the Black communities of the South. I still hold the Mahatma in reverence and regard his form of resistance through nonviolent direct action as the most significant political experiment of modern times. But my present understanding of the origin and nature of social conflict has led me to turn increasingly to Martin Buber and to the dialogue which meets others and holds its ground when it meets them. Like Buber, I have found in the biblical covenant a base for real meeting between peoples and real reconciliation between conflicting claims.

The "covenant of peace," a phrase which I have taken from Deutero-Isaiah, is an extension of the biblical covenant and like it has implications for social responsibility and the contemporary crisis of values. In the eighteenth century Immanuel Kant searched for "eternal peace" in terms of the rationality, the dignity, and the universal humanity of man. In our day it is faith in these very things that has broken down. The search for a simple universality has gotten us nowhere, and we are as far as ever from overcoming nationalism. New nations keep coming up all the time in the Middle East and Africa, and these nations are not going to be satisfied always to have a lesser share in the "universal" order.

The greatest task of contemporary man is not to build "enlightened" utopias but to build peace in the context in which he finds himself. The true peacemakers are those who take upon themselves, in the most concrete manner conceivable, the task of discovering what can be done in each situation of tension and struggle by way of facing the real conflicts and working toward genuine reconciliation.

The God of the covenant of peace is not a God of theology, whose attributes can be defined. "My God is a mighty man of war," says a Negro spiritual paraphrasing a biblical passage. The God of the Hebrew Bible does indeed often appear as a man of war. The Hebrew Bible does not, Kierkegaard to the contrary, call for "a suspension of the ethical" in favor of an absolute duty to God. Yet no one can read the stark happenings of the Bible and the intimate mingling of the word of

God with the violent conflicts of men without fear and trembling. For all that, the God of the Hebrew Bible is not a God
of war. He is the God of the historical situation, of the cruel
historical demand, of the wars against the Canaanite nations
and against the Amalekites. But he is not the tribal God who
is there simply to protect the tribe. He is the God of David,
the mighty warrior, but also of David the just king and the
compassionate man who will not destroy Saul, who seeks his
life, even when twice he has him in his hand. He is the God
of the Psalmist who prays for protection and even for revenge.
"O daughter of Babylon, you devastator! Happy shall he be
who takes your little ones and dashes them against the rock!"
But he is also the God who says, "Vengeance is mine"—the
God who "Will abundantly pardon, for my thoughts are not
your thoughts, neither are your ways my ways, says the
Lord." (Isaiah 55:7–8)

This is the God of the covenant. He is the God of the historical demand, but he is also the God of compassion whose
covenant of peace shall not be removed from man, the Holy
one who dwells in the high and holy place "and also with him
who is of a contrite and humble spirit." He is the God of
Israel, but he is also the God whose house is a house of prayer
for all peoples. "In that day," says Isaiah (19:24), "Israel will
be the third with Egypt and Assyria, a blessing in the midst of
the earth, whom the Lord of hosts has blessed, saying 'Blessed
be Egypt my people, and Assyria the work of my hands, and
Israel my heritage.' "

On Israel, or on the holy remnant of Israel who remain
faithful to the covenant, is laid the task of initiating the kingdom of God, but the kingdom itself will only come into being
when all nations have come to Zion to receive the law. "How
do the nations so furiously contend?" says the Psalmist. "The
nations rage, the kingdoms totter, God is our refuge and
strength, a very present help in trouble. . . . He makes wars
cease to the end of the earth; he breaks the bow, and shatters

the spear, he burns the chariots with fire! 'Be still and know that I am God.' " (Psalm 46) If the wars of David stand at the beginning of the covenant, it is the descendant of David—the true king—who will lead the people back to the task of making real the kingship of God, who will judge the poor with righteousness, and decide with equity for the meek of the earth. It is the descendant of David who shall usher in Isaiah's "peaceable kingdom." "The wolf shall dwell with the lamb, and the leopard shall lie down with the kid. . . . They shall not hurt or destroy in all my holy mountain; for the earth shall be full of the knowledge of the Lord as the waters cover the sea." (Isaiah 11:4–9)

The realization of the kingship of God means the realization of peace. Conversely, Isaiah's great vision of peace coincides with his vision of the fulfillment of the covenant, when all nations shall flow to the mountain of the house of the Lord that he may teach them his ways and they may walk in his paths:

> For out of Zion shall go forth the law,
>   and the word of the Lord from Jerusalem,
> He shall judge between the nations,
>   and shall decide for many peoples;
> And they shall beat their swords into plowshares,
>   and their spears into pruning hooks;
> Nation shall not lift up sword against nation,
>   neither shall they learn war any more. (Isaiah 2:2–4)

Isaiah's "universalism" is not an alternative to the task of the people but a continuation of it. His vision of peace is an integral part of the historical covenant between God and Israel, an integral address from God to the people in a new historical situation.

Out of the biblical covenant grows the covenant of peace. The covenant of peace is not only Isaiah's vision of peace "at the end of days." It is the comfort that God gives man now, "the very present help in time of trouble." It is *emunah*, that

unconditional trust that enables man to enter into the historical situation without guarantees or security and yet know
that there too he will meet his "cruel and kind Lord." "The
mind stayed on Thee Thou keepest in perfect peace," says
Isaiah, and adds, "because he trusts in Thee." This is "a peace
that passeth understanding," but it is not a peace beyond
history and daily life. The biblical covenant of peace is not a
consolation at the end of history or an eternity above it: it is
an integral part of history, of the tension between present
and future, the dialectic between comfort and demand.

As Hasidism took up again, in a new historical situation, the
task of the biblical covenant, so it also continued the task of
the covenant of peace: the task of building peace in the actual
interhuman, communal, and political contexts in which men
found themselves. Once the rabbi of Apt shouted, "Adul-
teress!" at a respected woman who came to ask his advice.
To this the woman replied, "The Lord of the world has patience with the wicked . . . he does not disclose their secret to
any creature, lest they be ashamed to turn to him. Nor does
he hide his face from them. But the rabbi of Apt sits there in
his chair and cannot resist revealing at once what the Creator
has covered." Commenting on this incident, which was a turning point for the rabbi of Apt, Martin Buber writes:

> He learned step by step that human justice as such fails
> when it attempts to exceed the province of a just social
> order and encroaches on that of just human relationships.
> . . . Man should be just within the bounds of his social order,
> but when he ventures beyond it out on the high seas of
> human relationships, he is sure to be shipwrecked and then
> all he can do is to save himself by clinging to love.[1]

Hasidic realism recognizes that true love and true reconciliation cannot be based upon altruism and selflessness and
self-denial, but only upon genuine dialogue, real mutual contact and trust between men. "The motto of life is 'Give and

[1] Martin Buber, *Tales of the Hasidim. The Later Masters*, p. 19.

take,'" said Rabbi Yitzhak Eisik. "Everyone must be both a giver and a receiver. He who is not both is as a barren tree." A person who sets out to be responsible toward others but will not receive from them is actually more and more limited in what he can give. He is not renewed by the flowing interaction, the wellsprings of life that come to a man, not when he takes it upon himself to do good but when he allows reality to work with him and through him. But this also means that one must demand for himself as well as others. It is a false humility which denies the very ground on which one stands—that of one's created existence as a self whose freedom one can neither absolutize nor surrender. Rabbi Pinhas cautioned that anger not only makes one's own soul impure but transfers impurity to the souls of those with whom one is angry. But he also said, "Since I have tamed my anger, I keep it in my pocket. When I need it, I take it out." Many people confuse anger with hostility and wish to suppress it entirely. Also, they see anger as destructive of relationship when often it is anything but. Sometimes anger is the real demand that we have to make because we care—not about ourselves but about the relationship. There is a very important difference between anger that can be tamed, however—that is, anger that can be an expression of one's person in its response to a situation—and anger that rips through one because one has been suppressing it and has given it thereby a life of its own.

Rabbi Mikhal commanded his sons to pray for their enemies that all may be well with them, for "more than all prayers, this is, indeed, the service of God." Rather than give testimony against a guilty man, Rabbi Rafael died. Rabbi Wolf declared all his possessions common property every evening before going to bed so that in case thieves came they would not be guilty of theft. Rabbi Schmelke prayed so powerfully that his enemy should suffer no ill because of him, "even though there are persons who are hostile to me and try to make me an object of ridicule," that the rich man who had tried to make him drunk in order to discredit him when he conducted the service on the eve of the Day of Atonement, dropped his malice and became a devoted follower.

None of these attitudes is incompatible with the fight for justice; Rabbi Wolf went to court, not to defend his wife, as she thought, but to help the servant girl against whom his wife was bringing a suit for having broken a dish. "You know very well what to say," he said to his wife. "But the poor orphan, your servant, in whose behalf I am coming, does not know it, and who except me is there to defend her cause?" But justice must be attained by just means not by unrighteousness, as the holy Yehudi said. Commenting on the Yehudi's statement, Martin Buber wrote: "What knowledge could be of greater importance to the men of our age, and to the various communities of our time" than that "the use of unrighteousness as a means to a righteous end makes the end itself unrighteous?" Buber was not saying that from the standpoint of some absolutist morality concerned with purity of the soul. He was saying that out of the experience of what in fact happens to one's end when one uses means unlike it, the realization of how the goal is altered in the accomplishment. In *Paths in Utopia*, for example, Buber discusses at length what happened to the socialist revolution in Russia where the original Marxist idea of the gestation of the new order in the womb of the old—hence of a *social* change—was replaced by the notion that first one must have *political* change through state centralization and then the state will magically "wither away." The result was the destruction of the cooperatives to which ten million people belonged, the destruction of the labor unions, and of the local Soviets, with a final product not too different in its form from Western capitalism.

Human togetherness is seen by one *zaddik* in the figure of a divine vehicle whose unity man must preserve: "When you see that someone hates you and does you harm, rally your spirit and love him more than before. That is the only way you can make him turn. . . . If your neighbor grows remote from you in spirit, you must approach him more closely than before —to fill out the rift." A humorous but profound example of how reconciliation was effected in this way is that of Rabbi Zusya and his wife. Zusya did not moralize at his wife but appealed to her at such a deep level that in her response to him, she was able to change herself:

> Zusya's wife was a shrew. She kept nagging him to give her a divorce and his heart was weighed down by her words. One night he called her name and said to her: "Look!" And he showed her that his pillow was wet with tears. Then he went on: "In the Gemara it is written that if a man puts his first wife away, the altar itself will shed tears for him. My pillow is wet with these tears. And now— what do you want? Do you still want a letter of divorce?" From this moment, she grew quiet. And when she was really quiet, she grew happy. And when she was happy, she grew good.[2]

Like Jeremiah, the Hasidim warn against the false peace that people proclaim to avoid looking at the real issue and conflicts in a situation. When Rabbi Yitzhak of Vorki informed his friend Rabbi Mendel of Kotzk that their quarreling disciples had made peace with each other, he was astonished by the latter's angry response. "Controversies in the name of Heaven spring from the root of truth," Rabbi Mendel explained. "A peace without truth is a false peace." What "truth" means here is made clear by the Talmudic statement Rabbi Mendel partly quotes: controversies for the sake of Heaven endure. This is completely contrary to Aristotelian logic with its assumption that a statement and its opposite cannot both be true. If controversies take place for the sake of heaven, then *both* sides will endure. It does not mean that eventually one will be proved right and the other wrong. The knowledge that the other also witnesses for his touchstone of reality from

[2] Martin Buber, *Tales of the Hasidim. The Early Masters*, pp. 244 f.

where he stands can enable us to confirm the other in his truth even while opposing him. We do not have to liberate the world from those who have different witnesses from us. The converse of this also holds, namely that each must hold his ground and witness for his truth even while at the same time affirming the ground and the truth of the other.

In an encounter seminar I once conducted, the members were asked to read Buber's *Tales of the Hasidim* and select one to bring to the group, telling what it meant to them and why they selected it. One woman read to us the tale entitled "Drudgery":

> Rabbi Levi Yitzhak discovered that the girls who knead the dough for the unleavened bread drudged from early morning until late at night. Then he cried aloud to the congregation gathered in the House of Prayer: "Those who hate Israel accuse us of baking the unleavened bread with the blood of Christians. But no, we bake them with the blood of Jews!"[3]

When she had finished reading, she told us that her father, a simple man from a poor background, used to tell her and her sisters about his childhood in the Ukraine and about how all the children in his village were warned not to go near the Jews' quarter for fear of being captured and killed to make blood for the Jewish matzoh at Passover. Her father still believed this millenial superstition that has sprung up again and again from the fear and hatred of the alien. The story of Rabbi Levi Yitzhak struck the woman who read it to us not because she too believed this naive yet tenacious myth, but because it removed the fear of the alien that lies at its base. It enabled her to experience the situation from the other side—from the side of Rabbi Levi Yitzhak, of the Jewish girls whom he befriended, and of the Jewish employers whom he called to account! The imaginative task of comprehending a relationship from the other side is essential to the goal of overcoming

[3] *Ibid.*, p. 225.

war. For every war justifies itself by turning the enemy into a Manichean figure of pure evil. A number of American prisoners of war, having been released from captivity by the Vietcong, said that they would think twice about fighting the Vietcong again because they were so well treated. They had a personal experience which would make it difficult for them *not* to imagine the other side of the relationship.

In Hasidism, the reality of peace and reconciliation is that of the biblical covenant. Man's task as God's partner in creation is not to work for his own salvation or for harmony with any already existing spiritual order but to create justice and peace in each new situation. By the same token, creation is not seen as already redeemed but constantly in need of redemption.

To fulfill our task as co-creators and redeemers is to discover that moral action which constitutes our own unique response to the ever present reality of war. It is only when I ask, "What ought *I* do in this situation?"—not what ought *one*, but what ought I do?—that I begin to understand the problem of moral action from within. It is my involvement in the situation, my decision, my commitment, my acceptance and seeing through the consequences of this commitment, that are the real stuff of moral decision and not the logical games of professional moral analysts. Morality is not a spiritual ideal hovering mistily above our heads: it is the tension, the link, the real relation between the "is" and "ought"—between what I can do in this situation and what I ought to do. To answer the question of the morality of war in general and objective terms means to identify oneself with some non-existing universal perspective or corporate entity and to lose the only real perspective for moral judgment and decision: the ground on which I stand and from which I respond to the claim of the situation upon me. It is conceivable to me that here and there a man might place a prophetic demand upon a group faced with a fateful historical decision, but not that any man in our age could presume, like Plato's philosopher king, to hand down from above absolute moral dicta on war. I sometimes think that draft boards require the eighteen- and nineteen-year-olds to be junior Platonists by declaring how they would act in response to *all* wars rather than how their opposition to war has formed in response to the particular war that has confronted them and demanded of them decision.

A peace witness based on the covenant of peace cannot be an "absolute" pacifism; for in history there is no room for absolutes. Absolutes have to do with a "morality" abstracted from the total situation in which any moral conflict arises: the situation of a person facing other persons and called on to act in relation to those persons. The absolutist, in so far as he is one in practice as well as theory, acts unilaterally and monologically. He knows what is right *a priori*, before he reaches the situation, and this means that his action is not a true response to the situation but something imposed on it. The absolutist thinks he is being uncompromising and true to his ideal when, in fact, he is simply not responding to what is asked of him. For what is asked of him is not the perfection of his own soul or the moral purity of his actions but the most adequate response possible in a situation which, just because it is human, is always in need of redemption and never entirely redeemable.

This is the old quarrel between Plato and Isaiah. Plato's philosopher king is so identified with "The Good" that he may safely impose his single consciousness upon all men of the state, holding them in submission through royal myths and royal lies, knowing better than they do what is best for them since only he knows the Good. In contrast to this, Isaiah's vision of peace is no utopia abstracted from the historical situation but is itself a demand placed upon man in history, a dialogue between God and man. It does not necessitate leaving the concrete world—the world of Plato's cave—in order to reach some timeless absolute, but believes that reality can be met in the "lived concrete." Plato, and the absolutist after him, sets a timeless ideal that history is supposed to approach. The result of such an ideal is all too often a dualism between "is" and "ought," real and ideal. The very existence of the ideal becomes the excuse to dissociate oneself entirely from the actual state, as Plato recommends that his philosopher should do since, as he rightly recognizes, the philosopher never will be king nor the king philosopher. Or, as with the absolute pacifist and the absolute social-actionist, it becomes a temptation to impose the truth on the situation in such a way as to recognize neither the possibilities of the situation nor the need for communication with those actually involved in the situation.

Taking seriously the covenant of peace, in contrast, implies risk—one *responds* without certainty as to the results. It also implies trust—the trust that if one responds as best one may, *this* will be the work that one can perform toward establishing the covenant of peace. And it implies humility—the humility which says I cannot take on myself the remodeling of the world according to some great blueprint or even the armchair administration of the United Nations. This is not asked of me, and this is not my task. What I can do is to make real that portion of existence that is given to me—including the political, but not the political alone.

The peacemaker "is God's fellow worker," writes Buber. We make peace not by conciliatory words and humane projects, however, but through making peace "wherever we are destined and summoned to do so: in the active life of our own community and in that aspect of it which can actively help determine its relationship to another community."

If the present crisis leads us to succumb to the merely political, we shall have reinforced the mistrust between nations that makes them deal with each other not in social or human terms but in terms of political abstractions and catch-words. "Our work is for education," one of the leaders of an organized protest against atomic bombs said to me. If this is so, then this work cannot afford to be purely political, purely external. It must start from some organic base. It must build on social reality and find its roots in the community already there. It must be concerned about real communication with the people whom it approaches. For the distinction between propaganda and education does not lie in whether one is a communist or a pacifist but in whether one approaches another wishing to impose one's truth on him or whether one cares enough for him to enter into dialogue with him, see the situation from his point of view, and communicate what truth one has to communicate to him within that dialogue. Sometimes that dialogue can only mean standing one's ground in opposition to him, witnessing for what one believes in the face of his hostile rejection of it. Yet it can never mean being unconcerned for how he sees it or careless of the validity of his standing where he does. We must confirm him even as we oppose him, not in his error but in his right to oppose us, in his existence as a human being whom we value even in opposing.

"One absolute surely stands," a leader of the Committee for Nonviolent Action once said to me, "and that is that nonviolence is the way to solve conflict." No, even this absolute cannot stand. Even this absolute reveals itself as an idol as soon as we look at it carefully. "Nonviolence" claims too much, and it claims too little. To claim that nonviolence is possible in every situation is to ignore the most obvious facts of personal and social existence. How often even a literal turning of the other cheek masks a violence we cannot extirpate, no matter how we suppress it! How often a tiny word, or gesture, or facial expression betrays the latent violence in a relation between persons where each is trying with all his might to act positively toward the other! And in social and international relations it is no different. The congealed violence that lies just beneath the surface in so much family life, civic administration, government administration, the "cold war" that has been the dominant note in international relations ever since the Second World War, give glaring evidence of how much the alternatives "violent" and "nonviolent" falsify the concrete situation. One can no more know that one will be completely nonviolent in a given situation than one can know that one will love—really love in genuine caring and response—every person one meets or that one will meet every temptation with Kierkegaard's "purity of heart that wills one thing—the good in truth." We do not know our resources in advance of the situation which calls them out of us, the situation to which we respond. What is more, our insistence that we shall deal with every situation in a nonviolent way may actually limit our resources by curtailing our open awareness of what is asked of us and our readiness to respond from the depths with the spontaneity of the whole being.

On the other hand, nonviolence also says too little. One may be nonviolent and still be monological, offering one's answers to others without first listening to their questions. One may be nonviolent and still be the propagandist imposing one's truth on people with whom one does not care to communicate as persons, placing political abstractions above social realities. Amos said, "There will come a famine not of bread or water but of thirst for the words of the living God." If we consider what is being done in our day to the most ordinary media of communication—the incredible distortion, whether in the interests of politics or advertising, and with it the production of universal mistrust—we can see how rapidly we are reaching a place where we shall not even be able to hear if we want to. We shall have a famine for some word of reality that could reach or touch us. One may use nonviolence as a technique divorced from the laying hold of truth of Gandhi's *satyagraha*. One may use nonviolence without dialogue and without love. Nonviolence, in fact, may be, and sometimes is, covert violence, congealed violence, suppressed violence, apocalyptic rage, perfectionist intolerance. It *need* not be these things. It *was* not these things in a Gandhi, an A. J. Muste, or a Martin Luther King. But that is because in them nonviolence was grounded in personal existence and in genuine relation to other persons, rather than objectified into an omnicompetent technique.

I came to my position as a conscientious objector through the belief that only good means will lead to good ends. I still believe this—but in a radically modified sense. A "good end" I would define neither as merely social and political welfare nor as inner spiritual perfection, but as the good that is created again and again in lived relations between persons, within and between groups. Justice cannot be based on the personal or the interhuman alone; yet justice remains only a name for the interests of the state or a mere formality until it is concretized and realized in the interhuman sphere. Peace, too, is only an abstraction unless it means a genuine peace based on real community and relations between communities. A "good means" I would define as the whole of the present situation as it leads into the future, and this situation includes all that I am. I cannot work with the situation or with myself as an instrument to be manipulated to some good end. I cannot speak of using good means abstracted from my or our actual resources at any moment, and these resources may make the means that are used something far less than purely good. The absolute pacifist who insists on purely good means is sometimes very little different from the communist who says that the end justifies the means: both are moral absolutists who ruthlessly abstract from the concrete present situation, who treat the present as if it merely exists for the future, who think of action in terms of an external definition of it.

In the end the purity of the means I use, while not unimportant, is less important that the faithfulness of my and our response. Beyond that I can only trust. Biblical *emunah*, the trust that walks with God through the valley of the shadow of death, precludes the calculations of results whereby we glean a false security about a future that no one in fact can anticipate. The word of the biblical God that addresses man in history is not, "I shall protect you from all danger," but "I shall be there *as* I shall be there." Faithful response to the demand of the historical situation begins with awareness and responsibility, but it ends with trust. The total situation is never our responsibility, but only what is asked of *us*.

My present view of ends and means is thoroughly dialogical. Neither the outer action nor the inner person is essential alone, but the call and the response. Even the "inner light" shares in this dialogue. It is a stirring, a prompting, a leading, that comes in a particular situation and calls for one's active concern. One senses it "within," to be sure, but it exists in the *between*—between a man and the situation that calls to him, between a man and the message or event that "speaks to his condition," between a man and the divine spirit that enters into him and works through him, between a man and the "still small voice" that addresses him from the depths of his conscience.

For the covenant of peace, both the means and the end are the building of true community—the community of otherness. It is not requisite upon a community to forego all action for the sake of the lone dissenter. But much depends upon whether it takes the action as a real community or just as a majority which is for the moment able to override the minority. The reality of community is polyphonic; it is many-voiced. In real community the voice of the minority is heard because real community creates an atmosphere of trust which enables this minority to make its witness. I have been in very few groups in my life, including the finest, where real community has not been violated day after day by a few "weighty" persons imposing their will upon the less sure in the name of what *should* be done. The true opposite of this imposition is that trust through which my wife Eugenia elicits the "other voice" in teaching poetry—the voice, for example, of the student who does not like Emily Dickinson because of her poems about death but would never say so except in an atmosphere that weights every voice equally no matter how hesitant or how much in the minority it may be.

Shalom, peace, is not merely a negative conception—the absence of war, disarmament, draft resistance, getting the troops out of Vietnam—but a positive one. The covenant of peace, *brith shalom*, does not find its sphere of action simply in international relations and foreign policy. It begins with the building of peace wherever we are, in the actual conflicts within community, between community and community, between nation and nation. I know of no better illustration of this positive approach of *shalom* than a public letter which Martin Buber wrote to Gandhi in 1939. Gandhi, in December 1938, criticized the Jews for settling in Palestine, an Arab country, rather than keeping Palestine only as an ideal within their hearts. In his reply Buber pointed out that the Jews cannot be responsible without experiencing from the side of the Arabs what it means for the Jews to have settled in Palestine, but neither can they give up their own claim based on their historical task—the task of making real the biblical covenant by creating a community of justice, righteousness, and lovingkindness. "I belong to a group of people," wrote Buber, "who from the time when Britain conquered Palestine, have not ceased to strive for the concluding of a genuine peace between Jew and Arab"—the *Brith Shalom* (Covenant of Peace).

> By a genuine peace we inferred and still infer that both peoples should together develop the land without the one imposing its will on the other. . . . We considered it a fundamental point that in this case two vital claims are opposed to each other, two claims of a different nature and a different origin, which cannot be pitted one against the other, and between which no objective decision can be

made as to which is just or unjust. We consider it our duty
to understand and to honour the claim which is opposed to
ours and to endeavor to reconcile both claims. . . . Where
there is faith and love a solution may be found even to what
appears to be a tragic contradiction.[4]

Gandhi suggested in the same statement that the Jews in
Germany use *satyagraha* as the most effective reply to Nazi
atrocities. Buber pointed out, in reply, that pure spirituality
divorced from the concrete, martyrdom without a ground to
stand on, protest when there is no way for the protest to be
organized and to be heard, is futile and ineffective as a means
of political or social action. From 1939 until his death in
1965 Buber continued to insist that the Jews live *with* the
Arabs in Palestine and later Israel and not just *next* to them
and to warn that the way must be like the goal—*Zion bmish-*
pat, Zion with justice—that the humanity of our existence begins just where we become responsible to the concrete situation by saying: "We shall do no more injustice than we must
to live," and by drawing the "demarcation line" in each hour
anew in fear and trembling. The covenant of peace—between
man and man, between community and community, and between nation and nation—means dialogue.

Dialogue means the meeting with the other person, the
other group, the other people—a meeting that confirms the
other yet does not deny oneself and the ground on which one
stands. The choice is not *between* oneself and the other, nor
is there some objective ground to which one can rise above
the opposing sides, the conflicting claims. Rather genuine dialogue is at once a confirmation of community *and* of otherness, and the acceptance of the fact that one cannot rise above
that situation. It is the living embodiment of the biblical creation in which man is really free yet remains bound in relation

[4] Martin Buber, *Israel and the World. Essays in a Time of Crisis*, 2nd ed.
(New York: Schocken Books, paperback edition, 1963), "The Land and Its
Possessors," pp. 231 f.

with God. "In a genuine dialogue," writes Buber, "each of the partners, even when he stands in opposition to the other, heeds, affirms, and confirms his opponent as an existing other. Only so can conflict certainly not be eliminated from the world, but be humanly arbitrated and led towards its overcoming."

During three years of work as Chairman of the American Friends of Ichud (the Israeli association for Israel-Arab rapprochement led by Judah Magnes and Martin Buber), I was again and again surprised to encounter among men of good will, including men working for reconciliation of the conflict, either an attitude which simply did not take into account the real problems to be reconciled, one that saw these problems from one point of view only, or one that proceeded from some pseudo-objective, quasi-universal point of view above the conflict. Every conflict has at least two sides. Even if one of the two sides is "dead wrong" in its opinion or stand, it represents something real that cannot be done away with, namely its existence itself. In that sense it literally has a different point of view which must be recognized quite apart from the question of the rightness or wrongness of the position it takes. All too often, the word "reconciliation" becomes associated with a sentimental good will that looks away from the very conflict that is to be reconciled, or assumes that, with this or that action or approach, a tragic situation can be transformed into a harmonious one. Genuine reconciliation must begin with a fully realistic and fully honest recognition of real differences and points of conflict, and it must move from this recognition to the task of discovering the standpoint from which some real meeting may take place, a meeting which will include *both* of the conflicting points of view and will seek new and creative ways of reconciling them.

Self-preservation, the self-understood basic principle of the modern nation-state, no longer has much meaning in a world where self-preservation means total domination or total annihilation. The way is hid in darkness, and even appeals for the return of moral sensibility do not grasp our real situation. We are morally insensible because we are morally and in every other sense overwhelmed. The cold war, the wars in Korea, in Indochina, in the Middle East, the pervasive mistrust, the atom and hydrogen bombs, the intercontinental ballistic missiles and the antiballistic missile systems, the rockets and satellites and competition for the moon and the planets, the pseudo-disarmament conferences, the pseudo-peace talks, and the jockeying for world position—all these make mockery of traditional categories of moral or defensive war. What statesmen could justify the entrance into war in our day as an action in any remote sense calculated to preserve the integrity of his nation or even the lives of its people? Who can take the responsibility for starting or engaging in a "contained" and "local" war—a limited defensive retaliation—and say that it will not lead to total war and total annihilation?

America was shocked awake by Soviet spacemanship but only to an awareness of the need for more technology and not to any basic questioning of the assumption that the steady and continued militarization of the total national life is the best means to national safety or world peace. Conscription and the cold war are the environment in which the young men of this generation have grown up, and their ministers, priests, and rabbis serve a turn as military chaplains, occupying the dubious and paradoxical position of serving God through serving the nation. Preparedness for war is called by our government preparedness for peace while in fact, as well as in official pronouncements, the distinction between peace and war has lost much of its meaning. How can any of us stand outside this cold-and-hot-war-world of competitive militarism since it permeates every aspect of our lives and bounds it at its far horizons? "The spokesmen of each side say they know that war is obsolete as a means of any policy save mutual annihilation," C. Wright Mills wrote in 1958, "yet they search for

peace by military means and in doing so, they succeed in ac-
cumulating ever new perils. Moreover, they have obscured
this fact by their dogmatic adherence to violence as the only
way of doing away with violence." Today even more than
when he wrote them, these words seem to me the simple,
incontrovertible facts of our situation.

War—war as we know it, was as we can only dimly and
horrifiedly imagine it— is immoral from almost any moral point
of view one takes. But I do not think we have accomplished
very much by saying this. Our real responsibility is not making moral judgments from some superior perspective, but responding to the claim of the present situation. If we ask what
is the claim of the present historical situation on *us*, on
America and on all of its citizens, we must answer: a great
deal more than the politicians who think in purely political
terms, are willing to face. They cannot see the debacle in
Vietnam, the starvation in Biafra, as judgments against the
country which is not laid waste by napalm or threatened with
any curtailment of its standard of living, the highest in the
world—a country which has no "plumb line" to judge it, a
country which, after occupying the stage as *the* world power,
must increasingly and far more seriously than ever before take
into consideration the real existence of the "other"—the other
civilization, culture, values, political power. This hostile
"other" may threaten our very existence and way of life; yet
a positive relationship to it, a dialogue with it, is the only way
in which we can continue to exist as a nation, both in the
physical and moral sense.

The covenant of peace is neither technique nor formula, and
still less is it a universal principle which needs only be applied
by deduction to the particular situation. It takes its start from
the concrete situation, including all of its tensions—tensions
which we can never hope or even desire to remove entirely
since they belong to the very heart of the community of

otherness. The covenant of peace is no ideal or ought that one holds above the situation but a patient and never-finished working toward some points of mutual contact, mutual understanding and mutual trust. It builds community by way of the mutual confirmation of otherness, and when this community shipwrecks, as it again and again must do, it takes up the task anew.

To some of the white workers in the Civil Rights Movement the appearance of the black revolution came as a tragic rupture of the black-white cooperation and fellowship which the Movement had engendered. Yet we cannot doubt that the revolution itself—not only in the more dialogical and affirmative form it took under Martin Luther King but also in the harsher postures and more strident outcries of Malcolm X and of the Black Panthers—has been a step forward in the covenant of peace. For all the polarization that it has introduced, it has also initiated the beginning of a situation in which the black man will be able to stand his ground and enter into dialogue from his unique position. Only thus can he make *his* contribution to the *genuine* reconciliation of conflict as opposed to the pseudo-harmonies covering over congealed violence that existed before. Tragic conflicts remain, of course, and these may as easily lead to bloody violence as to peace.

The Middle East conflict has again and again threatened the world with a general conflagration or, at the very least, with endless years of mutually bellicose activities between the island of Israel and the hostile sea of Arab countries that surround her. Even here, indeed especially here, the covenant of peace has relevance ultimately far greater than the political and diplomatic moves in the international chess game. No hope is possible in this area short of some beginning of genuine human dialogue, of real mutual contact, of a recognition by each of the existence of the other and of the fact that the other's "point of view" is in the last analysis grounded in his very existence. The realism that recognizes that each side has vital interests that it cannot simply surrender has as its corollary the realism that calls for an ever-new reassessment of the situation and with it of the possibilities of concrete steps toward a détente, a de-escalation of hostilities, and eventually even toward cooperation on such matters as the resettlement of refugees, the use of canals and river waters, the joint cultivation of the area. The Arabs cannot push Israel into the sea or carry out a second Nazi extermination, nor can Israel survive by winning one disastrous war after another. Already the voices on either side are a trace less belligerent, the feelers for peace a touch more vigorous. In this, as in every situation, the covenant of peace means a movement *in the direction* of the community of otherness, such movement as each new hour allows.

The war in Vietnam, Laos, and Cambodia is perhaps the most difficult situation of all to see within the context of the covenant of peace. The widely held view in the United States that this is a war of communism against democracy, cannot be sustained once we look at the way in which the United States has imposed and maintained a minority government over the active protests and martyrdom of many of the South Vietnamese.[5] Political conflicts there are, to be sure, but the peace-loving Buddhists of South Vietnam whom the government puts into jail by the tens of thousands cannot be considered communists, nor can all of the Vietcong, for all their active military opposition to the United States. Whatever the complex factors that prolong this war, we are forced to ask whether it is not perhaps the residue of the *otherness* of white and yellow races which has made it possible for the government, if not the people, of the United States to accept the

[5] See Alfred Hassler, *Saigon, U.S.A.*, with an introduction by Senator George McGovern (New York: Richard Baron, 1970).

napalm burning and the tragic decimation of the people and land of South Vietnam as well as North, with more attention paid to the statistics of American and "communist" dead than to the far greater toll of the civilians whom we are supposedly defending?

Is there room for a community of otherness in such a situation? Yes, even here. The coming to America of the Buddhists in exile Thich Nhat Hanh and Cao Ngoc Phuong brought home to the hearts of many of us that the South Vietnamese are a gentle, sensitive people and that it is we, without wishing or meaning to, who have played the role of barbarians. When they have recited poetry or sung, we have understood their cry to be saved from the unmitigated disaster which our "saving" them has brought about. Polarized and politicized as the North Vietnamese situation is, there have been contacts there too—of the Golden Rule, the Phoenix, A. J. Muste, delegations of students and of clergy. Even some of the more "violent" peace actions—such as the destruction of draft board files—have been, on the part of many, witnesses *for* the covenant of peace and *against* the system that perpetuates a war that nobody wants for reasons that nobody knows.

Protests alone cannot build the covenant of peace; for peace, like the community of otherness grows out of reconciliation of conflict within mutual cooperation, mutual understanding, and ultimately mutual trust. But in bedrock situations even a negative protest may be a positive step toward dialogue if it is done in the spirit of dialogue by men like the Berrigan brothers who embody that spirit. Can the rulers of the hour avert the pantechnical war by ceasing to talk *past* one another and beginning to talk *to* one another about *real* mutual interests? asks Martin Buber. If they cannot who shall come to the rescue but the disobedient, "those who personally set their faces against the power that has gone astray as such?" "Must not a planetary front of such civil disobedients stand ready, not for battle like other fronts, but for saving dialogue?" [6] Men like Dan and Phil Berrigan and many, many others, whether they engage in civil disobedience or not, witness for the covenant of peace by their obedient listening to the voice that addresses them from the situation of the human crisis.

The covenant of peace implies a "fellowship of reconciliation"; yet it is precisely here that we have fallen short. We have tended to turn "reconciliation" into a platform to expound, a program to put over, and have not recognized the cruel opposition and the real otherness that underlies conflict. We have been loathe to admit that there are tragic conflicts in which no way toward reconciliation is at present possible. We have been insufficiently tough-minded in our attitude toward love, turning it into an abstract love for mankind or a feeling within ourselves rather than a meeting between us and others. We cannot really love unless we first know the other, and we cannot know him until we have entered into relationship with him. To assume that we *will* be able to love before we have met the person and responded to his need is sheer presumption. Love is a two-sided grace arising in the relationship itself. It cannot be counted on in advance as a political or spiritual resource waiting to be tapped. Freud wrote to Einstein in a famous exchange of letters that there can never be peace because man has a "death instinct" which makes him prey on other men even when it is not to his advantage. I do not agree with Freud; for I consider the word "instinct" unscientific and the attempt to extract some universal "human nature" out of the social and cultural contexts in which we know man doomed to failure. But I do agree that man is often

[6] Martin Buber, *A Believing Humanism: Gleanings*, trans. with an Introduction and Explanatory Comments by Maurice Friedman (New York: Simon & Schuster Paperbacks, 1969), "More on 'Civil Disobedience,'" p. 193.

indeed, as Freud said, "a wolf to man," and that we are not going to attain love or peace by building a thin surface of placid goodwill over a boiling volcano.

The peace movement has tended to make political action the criterion of effectiveness and has failed to recognize forces working in the depths that cannot be expressed in laws, demonstrations, and public statements. Real dialogue and real social change have often been lost sight of and the peace witness clouded and compromised while the pacifist minority overstrains itself playing the political game as if there were some real possibility of the majority adopting pacifism. The political responsibility of a citizen of a democracy ought not to mislead the peace worker into spelling out the political blueprint that he would impose if *he* were running the country. He should think rather of the contribution that he can make to building the covenant of peace by witnessing *as what* he is and *from where* he is, including, of course, all the groups, large or small, to which he belongs.

A genuine movement has a dynamism toward the world, but this dynamism cannot rest at conversion, which shuts off the other before talking with him. It must extend to brotherhood, and brotherhood means standing on the boundary between one's own group and others and meeting the others at that boundary. Theology can clarify and face issues for the benefit of the believers themselves, but it cannot establish direct communication with the secular world or offer itself as a superior arbiter in its conflicts. Yet the religious man has resources of trust that *can* break through, can meet the other, can build real community. But he must distinguish between genuine dialogue and mere togetherness, between the willingness to affirm the other even when opposing him and the shifting alliances formed on the basis of expediency. More than anything, a genuine meeting is necessary with those who do not banner themselves under any church or organization yet are ready to build real peace.

Only a real listening—a listening witness—can plumb the abyss of that universal existential mistrust that stands in the way of genuine dialogue and peace. The peace movement has not adequately recognized the power of violence in our day and its roots not just in human nature in general or in the stupidity of men but in the special malaise of modern man—his lack of a meaningful personal and social direction, his lack of an image of man, his loss of community, his basic loss of trust in himself and others and in the world in which he lives, his fear of real confrontation with otherness, his tendency to cling to the shores of institutionalized injustice and discrimination rather than set out upon the open seas of creating new and more meaningful structures within which the dispossessed and the systematically ignored can find their voice too. Only if the peace movement confronts this crisis, more basic and threatening than the division between theist and atheist, can it offer genuine hope to the religious and the secular, caught alike in confusion and despair. Only thus can it offer a hand of brotherhood to those everywhere who witness, where they stand, for the covenant of peace.

In the world in which we live the tragedy of the contradictions has been increasingly borne in on us, the possibilities of reconciliation seem to have grown fewer and fewer. Yet reconciliation there must be, and we cannot cease, in each new situation, to discover and proclaim what concrete steps may be taken toward some amelioration of conflicts, some first step toward communication, some laying of the ground for future cooperation. The covenant of peace must be carved out of the resistant granite of our own current history. True reconciliation will come, if at all, only on the soil of tragic opposition. We cannot cease to work for it. We cannot fail to do our share as God's partners in the covenant of peace. Though we live under the shadow of the hydrogen bomb, we stand under the cover of the eternal wings.

> The mountains may depart and the hills be removed
> But my steadfast love shall not depart from you,
> And my covenant of peace shall not be removed,
> Says the Lord, who has compassion on you.

PART IV

Dialogue,
Trust,
and
Meaning

Chapter 16

The Partnership of Existence

Man is given freedom. Man exists as freedom, and with that freedom is possibility undreamt of in the realm of the animals. This includes destructive possibilities quite as much as constructive ones. Aggression does not need to mean destructiveness. It is possible to direct one's aggression into positive channels. But when wedded to existential mistrust, aggression inevitably becomes destructive. Existential mistrust quickly becomes reciprocal. If you reflect suspicion on someone else, it is reflected back on you until you find the very evidence you are looking for: the other also mistrusts you and acts in ways to confirm your worst fears about him. The typical behavior of large groups and societies in relation to one another is exactly what we would call paranoid if we encountered it in individuals. Each group has a shut-in, closed world, sealed off from seeing in the way that the other sees. Each interprets the motives of the other in terms of its own world of defenses, fears, and suspicions.

Objective clear analysis—psychological, social, economic, political, and/or international—will never by itself overcome man's destructive tendencies; for it does not get at what is essentially at issue: existential mistrust. Perspective alone will not do it. What we need is a direction, and direction has to do with our existence as persons in relationship to one another.

Aristotle told us a long time ago that man is a *zoon politikon*. But to say that man is a political or social animal does not tell us *per se* of any partnership of existence. It might only be a social contract, a *modus vivendi*, a *mariage de convenance*. In order that we not bash in one another's heads all the time, we act *as if* we believed in not doing to the other what we would not want done to ourselves—as long as we cannot get away with treating him as we would like to! Aristotle's teacher Plato faced this question as honestly as he could in his great dialogue *The Republic*. But the only thing he could come up with as an alternative to Thrasymachus' "Justice is the interest of the stronger" and Glaucon and Adeimantus' justice as a social contract based on mutual fear was the good of the individual soul. As the Hindu conceived the destiny of the individual as bound up with cosmic and social *dharma*, so Plato saw the harmony of the soul as connected with the harmony of a society divided into classes of guardians, merchants, and workers very similar to the Hindu caste system. But this too has nothing to do with the partnership of existence. There is no room in Plato's *Republic* for a direct, unmediated relationship between man and man; there is no room for genuine community, for real fellowship. There is only the totalitarian state run by the aid of the "royal lie" which has been imposed upon the people by the one man who knows "the Good, the True, the Beautiful"—the Philosopher King—in order to get them to behave the way they ought according to his theories.

If we speak of the "partnership of existence," we are suggesting, in contrast, not that people can live by some altruistic ideal but that our very existence is only properly understood as a partnership. We become selves *with* one another and live our lives with one another in the most real sense of the term. Put in the language of "touchstones of reality," we cannot find reality simply by remaining with ourselves or making ourselves the goal. Paradoxically, we only know overselves when we know ourselves in responding to others.

To say I become a self with others does not mean I ever reach symbiotic unity with them or that I can always be in relationship with them. On the contrary, the ground on which we stand is not only the ground of our uniqueness but of our singleness. We are like that marvelous myth that Plato puts into the mouth of Aristophanes in his great dialogue *The Symposium*. In this myth people are pictured as originally having four arms and four legs and rolling around the world and challenging the gods themselves to combat. Then Zeus cuts them in half. Immediately each half throws its arms around the other, and they cling together until Zeus intervenes once again and makes them separate. From that moment they go around the world, each looking for his other half. They are not self-sufficient as halves, but neither can they ever become whole again even if they should find their other halves. This is a wonderful paradigm of human existence as such. While we are unique persons, we are not so in the sense of nineteenth-century American individualism.

There is a paradox here and a hardly comprehensible one. I cannot regard my "I" merely as a product of social forces and influences, for then it is no longer an "I." There has to be that in me which can respond if I am going to talk about any sort of personal uniqueness. Therefore, I cannot say with George Herbert Mead, "The self is an eddy in the social current." I cannot turn the self into a mere confluence of social and psychological streams. On the other hand, if I speak of our having an "essence," that is misleading because it suggests something substantive that is within us as a vein of gold runs through a mountain waiting to be mined. What can we really say more than that we have in us the potentiality of response which can be awakened? But we must do the responding. No one can handle our side of the dialogue even from the beginning. There is an irreducible uniqueness that has to do with the fact that each person, even identical twins, has a very personal way of responding that can be discerned at six months and even earlier.

This does not mean that we are born already a self, or an "I." If we did not grow up with human parents, we would never become a person—not just in the sense that we would not take on the conventional social adaptations but that we would not be called into existence as an "I." Eric Erickson remarks in *Childhood and Society* that if the parent smiles at a child and the child does not smile back at the parent, there comes a time when the parent no longer has the resources to smile at the child. It is a two-way street. This does not imply that we do not exist as a self when we are not with some other person, any more than that in being with another we are automatically in mutual relationship. There is a distinction between our awareness of our self as some sort of continuity and our becoming ourselves in the meeting with others—with everything that meets us and calls us out.

We must respond to this call from where we are, and where we are is never merely social or merely individual but uniquely personal. We need to be confirmed by others. Our very sense of ourselves only comes in this meeting with others. We do not begin as isolated consciousness. Yet through this confirmation we can grow to the strength of Socrates, who said, "I respect you, Athenians. But I will obey the god and not you." Socrates would have been willing to drink the cup of hemlock even if not a single Athenian had voted for him. Not that Socrates saw himself as responsible only to the god. He expressed his responsibility to his fellow Athenians precisely in opposing them.

Responsibility means to respond. I cannot respond until I am in the situation, until I am face to face with you. I must really respond to you before I can love you. If I can then deal lovingly with you, that means that something real has taken place in our actual relationship. I have not simply manifested or expressed an intellectual or emotional attitude which I possessed before entering the relationship. Genuine response is response of the whole person. Yet we ought not think of the question of how to be a whole person but only of how, in any given situation, to respond more wholly rather than less so. A more whole response in one situation may help us to a still more whole response in a succeeding one. But we never become "whole persons" as a state of being, attained once for all. In every situation we are asked to respond in a unique way. Therefore, our wholeness in that situation is unique too. Although I am an Eagle Scout, I cannot accept the Scout motto, "Be prepared," if it means being prepared with the answer before one reaches the situation in which one has to answer. The only real preparation we can have is our preparation to respond in so far as our resources allow in the situation.

The deceptive aura that clings to the phrase "integration of the person" is the notion that you can become a perfect sphere in abstraction from and in advance of your relations to what is not yourself. In fact, you always integrate yourself in terms of a particular moment, in terms of a particular situation. If the situation calls you, you do not have the choice of not responding at all; for even a failure to respond is a decision, and even a halfway response is some sort of response. But you may bring yourself into wholeness in responding or you may fail to do so. Each moment of personal wholeness is unique even though you become more and more "yourself" through such response—hence more and more recognizable by others in a personal uniqueness that extends beyond the moment.

The "integration of the person" does not take place before the response, as a goal in itself. It only takes place in the act of responding. There are many people who hold that one must first be a "real person" and only then will one be able to enter into real dialogue, make real decisions. But the fact is that we do not become whole for our own sakes or in terms of ourselves. That is because we *touch* on reality at the moment when we touch on what is not ourselves, on what calls us, and we bring ourselves into wholeness from the depths of our being in response to this call. This is what the Hasidim mean by "serving God with the evil urge." Serving God with the "evil" urge does not mean actually doing or taking part in evil. Nor does it mean, in the manner of Jung, the integration of the evil and good in yourself. It means, rather, integrating yourself in responding—in making a real decision. Decision here is not a conscious matter but the movement of the whole person. Real guilt, by the same token, arises because you have failed to respond, have responded with less wholeness and awareness than you might have.

When we are called out in a fundamental way, we discover that we have resources of which we would not have dreamed. Our ordinary, casual responses are put aside, and we bring ourselves together in a rare act of whole decision. Or, if we do not, we know the genuine remorse that comes from not having been able to collect ourselves in the face of what we recognize as a call to our inmost depths. Abraham Lincoln responded with greatness to a unique historical situation and became the unique person that he was. You only really exist when you exist in a situation, and you become yourself in responding to that situation.

Our resources in each situation are limited, of course, but we do not know what that factual limitation will be before and apart from the situation. Our freedom is a "finite freedom," as Paul Tillich says, and that finite freedom varies from moment to moment. Insofar as we have freedom within the situation, we have the possibility of responding more wholly. But to respond more wholly we must be more fully aware. Full awareness here is the awareness of dialogue itself, the awareness of what addresses you. In talking with another person, for example, you may pick up only the intellectual level of what he says while, consciously or not, he is addressing you on many levels at the same time. It may make you anxious to recognize and respond to that address; so you block off your awareness of it. Later on though, the anxiety will probably come into the circle of your awareness—through dreams, fantasies, memories, twinges of pain or embarrassment. When that happens, it might become possible in a new situation to enter into relationship with a greater awareness and a wholer response than before. Much of our guilt is not deliberate commission or omission but simply that fuzzy awareness—"If only I'd really known!" We are responsible even for our lack of awareness, for that failure to hear which eventually turns into an inability to hear.

What is true of our awareness is also true of our response. We can be guilty even when we do and say all the right things if we do not respond with our whole being. One of the most terrible responsibilities in the world is that of really being present, of being a presence for the other. We cannot achieve dialogue by an act of will, for dialogue is a genuinely two-sided affair. We cannot know in advance that there can *not* be dialogue in a particular situation, but neither can we know that there *will* be dialogue. We cannot will that the other respond, nor can we even will our own presence and presentness. We are, nontheless, responsible for what we are, for our presentness or lack of it. To know that it is you that the other is demanding and nothing that you can hand out, whether it be prescriptions or wise sayings, to know that what is really demanded is that you be present for and to him is terrifying. The demand is total and uncompromising, and we are often not able to be fully present even when we really want to. Our lack of awareness is the limitation of the *given* situation. But in the long run our degree of awareness is not necessity but possibility, something for which we can be responsible.

When we become aware and do respond, we respond not to the way the other is regarding and treating *us* but to *him*— to that in him which calls out to us even when *he* does not speak to us. Even though he is not conscious of our answering his call, in some way he will feel our response. He may be asking us for help without knowing that he is doing so. If we refer his existence only back to ourselves and how he regards us, we will fail to hear the question that he puts, we will fail to answer the real need that he has. Because we repress our awareness of our own negative characteristics, we dislike those people in whom they are manifest. Yet even then, it is possible to ask ourselves whether, over and above what upsets us in them and we find so threatening, there is something they are trying to tell us, something to which we are called to respond. This applies even to those who are unjust to us. If someone upbraids and accuses us falsely and with great passion, that very excess and unfairness suggests that there is some hurt in this person that is expressing itself in this distorted way. In the depths he may be asking for understanding and reassurance from us. Listening and responding at a greater depth is the direction away from a specious individualism to the reality of the partnership of existence.

Those people who relate to the world only as a function of their own becoming will not change no matter how concerned they are about changing. But those people whose trust is grounded in the partnership of existence are changed every time they go out to meet another. They become anew and are reborn in each new situation. We can help allow this, and in this sense we can will it. But there is another will that easily falls into despair because it sees everything as depending on it alone. If we change, it is because someone or something comes to meet us as we go to meet it—not because we decide to change. Our will may be necessary to break the inertia, to

overcome the obstacles, but then we have to allow ourselves
to be taken up into the flowing interaction.

We are all persons to a certain extent by courtesy of one
another. We call each other back into being persons when
sleepiness, sickness, or malaise have divested us of our person-
hood. What makes us persons is the stamp of uniqueness, of
personal wholeness, and this is not anything that can ever be
looked at or grasped as an object. This stamp of uniqueness is
not something we can know directly in ourselves. We know
it of each other as we enter into relationship, but we know it
of ourselves only in that dim awareness that has to do with
becoming more and more uniquely ourselves in responding
to what is not ourselves.

The whole self is not what I am aware of when I am simply
self-conscious. For then I am turning myself into an object
and lose my intuitive grasp of the person that I am. That intuitive awareness that comes in responding is not incompatible
with objectivity, analysis, or psychoanalysis. But it *is* incompatible with making these latter the final court of appeal as to
what is real. It is ultimately an interhuman awareness that is in
question here. Our awareness has to guard itself against becoming completely reflective self-consciousness or completely
objective analysis. Our intuitive awareness of ourselves grows
in listening and responding if we use ourselves as a radar
screen: hearing not just how the other responds but also how
we ourselves respond to him. We can do this without turning
our self into an object.

Our wholeness is most there when we have forgotten ourselves in responding fully to what is not ourselves. It is not just
ekstasis, mystic ecstasy, that occasionally lifts us out of the
burden of self-consciousness. Any genuine wholehearted response—"When the music is heard so deeply that you are
the music while the music lasts"—can bring us to this immediacy. Our self-consciousness returns when we go back, as
we must, from immediacy to mediacy. Yet even it need not

get in the way as much as we usually suppose. The fact that we are reflective can be handled lightly instead of heavily, especially if we do not make the mistake of identifying our "I" with that reflective consciousness and regarding the rest as just the objects that the "I" looks at. The more we do that, the more we become Dostoievsky's Underground Man, "twiddling our thumbs" and totally unable to act. One of the forms of lack of personal wholeness, correspondingly, is that endless self-preoccupation which splits us into two parts, one of which is the observer and the other the actor who is being observed. This bifurcation of consciousness prevents us from having any sort of spontaneous response, from ever really going outside of ourselves.

An equally important and frequent form of lack of personal wholeness is that which comes because we do not have the courage to stand our ground in a situation and to make our unique personal witness in response to it. Afraid of what other people think, we fear the consequences of real decision. The antidote to this is not to set our self-becoming as our end. Our becoming whole is merely the corollary of the reality that we find again and again in meeting others. To meet others and to hold our ground when we meet them is one of the most difficult tasks in the world. We tend, as a result, to alternate between two opposite forms of not meeting: "meeting" others through leaving our ground—taking on other people's thoughts and feelings while losing our own—and "protecting" our own ground through closing ourselves off and holding others at arm's length. But we have to discover in the wisdom of our own daily living the right movement between the two and not make openness, going out to others, meeting the "Thou," or loving others a principle. If we do, we shall lose what would make it a real going out, namely, the renewal of our resources that comes in this swinging movement. It will become a theory —something imposed on ourselves—and we shall more and more lose the genuine resources, the spontaneity, necessary for real outgoing. That part of our lives which we cannot live joyfully is that part to which we do not bring our real resources. We have, instead, imposed upon ourselves an idea of what we *ought* to do. That includes the image that we have of ourselves and that we keep up at the expense of spontaneous interaction with others.

We do not help another if we bring anything but our self. Our seeming compliance with his demands is really a deception which makes us as guilty as he may be. We allow the other to believe that we are going along with him, and we suppress from our awareness as well as his that part of us which does not go along with him—until, sooner or later, the time comes when we throw off the suppression and him with it. When the person who has repressed himself breaks out, he usually lays *all* the blame on the person whom he has allowed to dominate him, not admitting to himself what in some part of his being he knows very well: that submission is also a form of domination and manipulation.

How are we so sure that what the other is *really* asking of us is that we comply with his demands, that we distort ourselves for his benefit? We rationalize, "He wants my help. Why should I not give it to him? Why should I not put myself aside for his sake?" What he really needs from us is ourselves, even if that means that we oppose him. He may seem to be asking us to be nothing but "the good mother" or "the good father" to him, but in fact his deepest need and his real question to us is, "Are you going to meet me as the person that you are so that through you I may come up against real otherness and find a touchstone of reality?" The more he appears to be asking us to distort reality, to enter into compliance with him, the more insistently is he asking us that question. Family studies of the National Institute of Mental Health have shown that children in homes where no conflict is allowed to become manifest tend, when they go out into the world, to become schizophrenic. They have not been able to become persons through coming up against real opposition. They have always been smothered in the miasma of pseudo-harmony.

Central to holding our ground is the problem of firmness and anxiety. Do we have the courage to hold our ground—not as a Stoic stance but simply as trust? It is only by holding our ground that we can experience the other's side of the relationship. We are inclined to think that we have to choose between being ourselves and shutting him out, on the one hand, and being "unselfish" and going over to his side, on the other. Actually we cannot know *his* side of the relationship without standing our ground because we can only know him *as a person* in a relationship in which his uniqueness becomes manifest in coming up against our uniqueness. Otherwise, what we see is a distortion of him—the way he is when he has no real person to come up against. Some people would be halfway decent if we gave them a chance by demanding that they start with us. Our notion that they are totally evil may be because we have let them be and have not asked of them what we have not only a right but a duty to demand: that they turn toward us as the person or persons encountering them at this moment, the persons the meeting with whom is, *in this moment*, their access to reality and meaning.

One reason people do not have the courage to show themselves to others as they are is that they wish to avoid conflict. They propitiate and conciliate the other, not wishing the wrathful parent to make his appearance in the form of the friend, the beloved, or the teacher. The truth is the exact opposite. Instead of being afraid that we shall come into conflict with the other if we stand our ground, we should recognize that the only way we can *avoid* coming into conflict with him is standing our ground. We must hold our ground, imagining the other's side of the relationship but also letting him see our side. Otherwise, we are moment by moment making a false, deceitful contract in which we are letting the other think that we are going along with him freely and gladly while, in fact, underneath the resentment builds up. Then it is inevitable that conflict will come; for we are not affirming and responding as a whole person, and one day that part of us which is denying him will be revealed—in small ways and in big.

Each successive meeting gives us a little more strength and trust for the next one, especially when we discover that we can allow conflict to be expressed and the relationship is not destroyed. This does not mean that it is possible to express conflict and hostility in every relationship. It depends very much upon the amount and kind of hostility that is expressed and the strength of the relationship. There are some relationships that have so little resources that as soon as the volcano of hostility erupts, the relationship bursts asunder with no possibility of reconciliation. But to assume that we cannot express conflict without automatically destroying every relationship that we value means *either* that we are suffered only under the intolerable condition of never allowing the porcupine quills to show or, still worse, that what is in us is so murderous that were it to come out, it would necessarily destroy the other. The more we have repressed, the greater the fear is that what is underneath will be murderous if released. There are people who become more and more fixed in their own benevolent image and can never show any other face because of their terror of what lies beneath. The more they suppress, the greater the malignancy that accumulates under cover of their benevolence.

We discover the real limits of our resources in the relationship itself. We cannot be present simultaneously for everyone, and we often have to choose in a particular situation between our responsibility to one person and to another. If we stand in relationship to more than one person—and who does not?— we frequently find ourselves caught in genuine dilemmas of responsibility that are not easy to resolve. We learn we can only give so much. We do not shut other people out, but neither do we have the illusion that we can be there for every-body. Part of our holding our ground, moreover, is the realiza-tion that we can never *wholly* take responsibility for anyone, even though we were the one person on earth to whom he could turn. We can only really help others if we recognize what is essential in the situation: the limits of the grace of each hour. There are no formulae that can help us in these some-times tragic situations. There is only the growing sureness about what we can give and what we cannot, the sense of our own limits and of our resources, and our willingness to risk ourselves and make mistakes.

The word "person" bridges over and unites three separate realities of personal existence. On the one hand when one speaks of person and personality, one speaks of the mysterious imprint of uniqueness on an incessantly changing, varying process which could have no essential unity as an "I" were it not for this imprint. Secondly, however, the person finds his full reality in the present, and personality exists in an actu-alized form only in the present. When we speak, as we must, of personality extending over time, it is the alternation be-tween actual and potential personality that we really mean. The existence of the person in time is not a smooth process but an alternation between moments of real presentness and other moments—of sleep, of semiconsciousness, of distraction, inner division, illness—when a person falls from actualized presentness into mere subsistence, or potentiality.

A person finds himself as person, thirdly, through going out to meet the other, through responding to the address of the other. He does not lose his center, his personal core, in an amorphous meeting with the other. If he sees through the eyes of the other and experiences the other's side, he does not cease to see through his own eyes and experience the relationship from his own side. We do not experience the other through empathy or analogy. We do not know his anger because of our anger; for he may be angry in an entirely different way from us. But we can glimpse something of his side of the relationship. That too is what it means to be a real person. A real person does not remain shut within himself or use his relations with others as a means to his own self-realization. He realizes himself as an "I," a person, through going out again and again to meet the "Thou." To do this, however, he must have the courage to address and the courage to respond—the existential trust that will enable him to live in the valley of the shadow.

Chapter 17

Existential Trust:
The Courage to Address
and the Courage to Respond

The beginning of dialogue is the acceptance of the reality of separation, of that ever-renewed distancing that is the prerequisite for all relationship. Dialogue begins with reality, with trust. I can go forth again to meet present reality, but I cannot control the form in which I shall meet it. We continue to care about and to be responsible for the person who has been our partner even when we are not in actual dialogue with him. But we cannot *insist* that he remain a partner for us. When Pagliacci murders his wife because she has a lover, he says to Nedda, "I loved you more than God himself." He had fixed his Thou in Nedda, and he could not allow her the freedom to exist any longer when she was unfaithful to him. The very meaning of jealousy is the inability to allow the other to be. The more jealousy there is, the more one person feels that he is possessed or dominated by another and the worse the relationship becomes. But this is also the exact meaning of idolatry: to limit the partnership of existence to a given form, condition, or image so that it cannot come again in a new, unique form. I do not have a continuity of relationship to present reality. I have only my readiness to meet it at each new moment in whatever way it comes. This does not mean that every meeting with present reality must be brand new or that we do not look forward eagerly to seeing our friends and those we love. But when we insist that it has to be in a certain form, when we try to control it, then our friendship, love, or marriage will wither even if it continues because we shall not allow it to be spontaneously what it can become in the new moment. We shall be constantly trying to repeat and cling to what it was before. The everyday is not the ordinary, the repetitive, the usual. It is the unique, the ever new, the never-to-be-repeated. It is only in the dialogue with the everyday that I meet God. I do not meet him as an abstraction. The philosopher may talk about the aseity of God, his independence of any relation. But the religious man must enter into relationship with his whole being, and he can only know a God that he meets, that he meets ever anew.

The trust in existence that enables us to live from moment to moment and to go out to meet what the new moment brings is the trust that makes it possible that in new meeting we again become whole, alive, present. If I trust in a person, a relationship, this means that despite what may and will happen, I shall enter into relationship again and bring all the past moments of meeting into present meeting. The particular person who is my partner may die, become sick, disturbed; he may betray me, rupture the relationship, or simply turn away and fail to respond. Sooner or later something of this does happen for most of us. When it does, it is trust which enables us to remain open and respond to the new address of the new situation. If we lose our trust in existence, conversely, we are no longer able to enter anew into real dialogue.

It is our existential trust that ultimately gives actuality and continuity to our discontinuous and often merely potential relationships to our human partners. And it is this trust, too, that gives continuity and reality to our own existence as persons; for in itself personality, as we have seen, is neither continuous nor always actual. If it is the confirmation of others and our own self-confirmation that gets us over the gaps and breaks in the first instance, it is our existential trust that enables this individual course to become a personal direction rather than a meaningless flux.

Trust accepts the fact that a genuine relationship is two-sided and therefore beyond the control of our will. The question again and again arises in our lives, "Why should I go out to meet this person unless I am sure that he will move to meet me?" Many people hold back for fear of being hurt. But this is true in our relationship with God as well. In 1898 William James said in his essay "The Will to Believe": "For the religious person, the universe is not an It but a Thou, and every relationship that is possible between persons is possible with the universe." The situation is comparable, said James, to a man who has joined a club. If he will not go halfway to meet the other members of the club, they will not come halfway to meet him. What can be known in this situation can be known only by taking the risk of entering the relationship. This is a real risk, without guarantees of any sort, for you may find a response and you may not. Therefore, trust must never be understood as trust that in this particular occasion I know that there will be a response. Genuine trust is the exact opposite of this. It is a readiness to go forth on this occasion with such resources as you have, and, if you do not receive any response, to be ready another time to go out to the meeting. Many people imagine that they are justified in a settled mistrust or even despair because once or twice they ventured forth and encountered a stone wall or a cold shoulder.

After this they anticipate rejection and even bring it about, or they protect themselves from it by never risking themselves. The genuine freedom of both sides of the dialogue means that there can be no guarantees written in the heart of the universe, no ontological ground that assures us that this or that is the nature of the universe.

In this entirely non-theological sense we can speak of "existential grace" as a corollary of existential trust. When grace comes, it comes to us from the other who meets us in the situation and from our own resources, which are not simply waiting for us to use them but come and go, only partially subject to our will. Even our ability to respond at times is also a grace. We cannot control our response by an act of will power. The people who believe that their potentialities are entirely subject to their will are people who are misusing and cutting back their potentialities because they have made spontaneity impossible. Spontaneity and genuine responsibility are two sides of the same coin. It is a sad thing that so much of our morality has been characterized by the very opposite of spontaneity and true joy. The essential combination of trust and grace lies in the fact that we are given a created ground on which to stand, yet we can never make that ground self-sufficient. Each time we are granted a new breath, a new day, we are granted a new ground from which to go out and meet life. Therefore, we can neither honestly say, "I can do this all by myself," nor, "I must deny myself entirely and recognize that I can do nothing of myself." Saint Francis prays, "Oh divine master, grant that I shall not so much seek to be comforted as to comfort." But one must also know how to accept being comforted. Toward the end of his life Saint Francis realized that he had been too hard on himself, on his body, "Brother Ass." There is such a thing as compassion for one's self which is not to be confused with self-pity. There are times when only you can know what was really involved in a situation. At such times, when everyone else is eager to be hard on you, you should perhaps have compassion for yourself. Such compassion is really a form of humility, just as being hard on oneself is often a form of pride.

Existential trust cannot be inculcated by autosuggestion. Yet we do not have so much ground for mistrust as we usually think. We cut the ground from beneath our feet by a self-fulfilling prophecy. We were confirmed so little as children, perhaps, that we are used to living with just the crumbs from the table. Therefore, we already know in advance that nothing really joyful can happen to us, and we make sure that nothing joyful does happen. We impoverish our lives a great deal more than they need to be because we live on a scarcity economy in which we exclude *a priori* much of the grace that is waiting to come to us if we are really open, and we imagine our resources to be far less than they are. We are not able, we are not even willing to understand that new resources come to us all the time as we move into the situation that awaits us. It is said that the Red Sea would not open for the Israelites to cross until the first Israelite had put his foot in the sea. We wait on the bank, demanding that the river open before we venture forth. It is necessary to go out to meet the grace that is coming to meet us.

We need the courage to address and the courage to respond. I use these terms in conscious contrast to Tillich's "courage to be"; for we are not directly concerned with our being, and we cannot aim at it, or even at being a "centered self," in Tillich's phrase. The real courage that is asked of us—a greater and more terrifying courage—is the courage to respond, the courage to go out to meet the reality given in this moment, whatever its form. My trust is not that this reality will be such as I might wish it to be, but only that here and here only is meaning accessible to me, even if not without horror, suffering, and evil.

The courage to address and the courage to respond must

include the recognition that there are no formulae as to when and how to address and when and how to respond. This is what it means to walk life's way step by step. We are not first of all placed before Camus' ultimate philosophical question of, "Should I or should I not commit suicide in the face of the absurd?" Nor are we placed first of all before Tillich's question, "Can I affirm the negative in order that I may also have the positive?"—important as both these questions are. Rather, moment by moment, day by day, we are placed before the question, "Do I have the courage to address—to go out to meet —and the courage to respond to what comes?" This includes the courage *not* to speak out and *not* to respond when we cannot do so in this situation as a whole person in a meaningful way. Our response ought not be triggered off—that is merely a reaction. We ought not to respond to what we know somewhere in our being is not a true address. "Because of impatience we were driven out of the Garden of Eden," says Kafka, "and because of impatience we are prevented from returning to it."

If it is important not to allow ourselves to be "triggered off," it is equally essential not to withhold ourselves. One of the forms we have of withholding ourselves is that protective silence which makes us feel we never have to speak out, that we are merely observers in the group, that nothing is demanded of us. Another of the forms of withholding ourselves, however, is that anxious verbosity that overwhelms the situation so that we are not present and we do not allow anyone else to be present either. Still another form of withholding ourselves is substituting technique for trust.

Many encounter groups operate on the naive but widespread assumption that the mere expression of hostility is therapeutic under any circumstances. The operating principle of such groups is not that you should not withhold your *self* but that you should not withhold your surface feelings, especially the type of feelings that the group wants and expects, such as anger and hostility. Trust in technique is essentially irreligious. This does not mean that we should not structure a situation. But it is vital that the structure be one within which spontaneity can come into being. When we reach the place where we are expecting and looking for a certain result, then we have traded in trust for arbitrariness, and willfulness has replaced genuine will. Among those whose whole life work is concerned with freeing others to their potentiality are some of the worst manipulators, some of the most authoritarian figures I have ever met. That is because they cannot trust but have to be sure they get the result they want. Other people join in this spirit, and all the members of the "sensitivity awareness" group become amateur manipulators who tend, as a result, to become more and more insensitive to the unique and concrete happenings *between* members of the group.

We address others not by conscious mind or will but by what we are. We address them with more than we know, and they respond—if they really respond—with more than they know. Address and response can never be identified merely with conscious intent or even with "intentionality." Our resources have to do with what calls us and with the way in which we bring or do not bring ourselves into wholeness in response to this call. The courage to address and respond sees life as a giving and a receiving, but it does not mean a "trust that" life will always be a flowing, even in Lao-tzu's sense.

"In this personal life, probably not one of us will taste the essence of redemption before his last hour," writes Martin Buber. Yet we can glimpse the meaning of redemption by recalling our own dark and silent hours—"those hours in the lowest depths when our soul hovers over the frail trap door which at the very next instant may send us down into destruction, madness, and 'suicide' at our own verdict." At such a moment we may suddenly feel the touch of a hand that reaches down to us and wishes to be grasped. "And yet what incredible courage is needed to take the hand, to let it draw us up out of the darkness" so that we may realize in our own lives that our Redeemer lives and that he wishes to redeem us, but only by our own acceptance of his redemption with the turning of our whole being.[1] This is the courage to respond. It is not the courage of blind faith but the courage of really entering again into relationship.

A newspaper story that has continued to make a deep impression upon me is that of a flood in which a car was washed over the bridge. The husband drowned, but the wife clung for eight hours to a telephone pole. Several boats put out to try to save her, but they were capsized in their turn and the would-be rescuers drowned. Finally, at the end of the eight hours, she was torn away with a shriek into the flood. There are many situations in life where there is a hand reaching out to help and the person in need tries to but cannot quite reach it. It seems as if it is too much to demand of oneself, too much to hope for, too much to ask—too much pain to open oneself again to the possibility of really living, of reentering the dialogue. The last moment with a sigh the person lets go of the hand that is reaching for him and falls. He may commit suicide, but more often he simply gives up ever again trying really to go beyond himself, ever again risking pain and suffering to discover whether there is something there to meet. He prefers to say, "No, I have been through this before. I am not going to expose myself. I prefer to call it all negative rather than move off my base without a guarantee of response." And he is right, in his terms; for there can be no such guarantee.

The courage to respond begins with openness and listening. We have seen the problematic of not hearing that begins with not wanting to hear and ends with not being able to hear. The

---

[1] Martin Buber, *Israel and the World,* "The Man of Today and the Jewish Bible," pp. 101 f.

converse of that problematic is not that it is always easy
to hear even when you do want to or that the address is always clear. It does not mean that one can respond when no
voice calls. Nor can one always find the resources to respond
when a voice does call. We live in an era of existential mistrust, an era that Buber has aptly named that of the "eclipse
of God." This existential mistrust has little to do with whether
people believe in God or with the "death of God" theology
that proved so newsworthy for a time. It has to do with the
loss of trust in our meeting with the other in the interhuman,
the social, and the political realms. We not only expect that
the other is trying to put something over on us; we even
suspect our own motivation as untrustworthy. We no longer
really believe that we can confirm others or they us; for we
do not really mean them and they do not really mean us.

The Hebrew Bible speaks of God hiding his face. This
means, in our terms, that we can no longer find a touchstone
of reality, that we can no longer find a meaning, a contact.
There are periods in history such as the present when just that
existential trust that underlies the courage to respond no longer
seems possible, when the meeting with present reality in the
everyday is lost in a welter of mistrust—psychological, political, social, even existential. The fact that we have a ground
to stand on means nothing if we cannot use that ground to
go out to meet a genuine other. The "Job of Auschwitz" had
to face a reality which is by its very nature unfaceable. *The
Diary of Anne Frank* can move millions, but the extermination
of six million unique persons exceeds our capacity to understand or even imagine. We live in the era of Auschwitz, of
Hiroshima, of Vietnam, and of Biafra—an era in which the
social cement that held society together has been dissolved
and the most ordinary social confidence is no longer present.
We could not imagine, in advance, that people would systematically turn other persons into cakes of soap or irradiate
people in such a way that they would die on the spot *or*

slowly and horribly over a great many years. Yet now that this has happened, reality creates possibility, and the unthinkable is no longer unthinkable. In *To Deny Our Nothingness* I have spoken of a "Dialogue with the Absurd," implying that it is sometimes possible, without making the absurd anything other than absurd, to enter into dialogue with it, to find meaning in this dialogue. But this "Dialogue with the Absurd" does not in any way mean that the inconceivable horror which it has been our fate to witness and live through is anything other than just that. Any view which enables us to be comfortable with the destruction and endless suffering of countless of our contemporaries is surely a deception.

If the Job of Auschwitz nonetheless remains in dialogue with God, or, like Camus' hero Doctor Rieux in *The Plague*, in dialogue with the absurd, it is not an affirmation that really everything is for the best. It is existential trust that just in this terrible world and here only is reality. Rather than leave this "world of illusion" for some supposed oneness with the cosmic All or the God within, it is better to stand one's ground and contend as long as one has life and breath to contend. Once the Quaker economist Kenneth Boulding, the author of the *Naylor Sonnets*, said to me: "If it were not for Christ, I might believe that God was the devil." This was a great statement of faith in Christ. Yet it was also to me a terrifying statement: behind the image of God in Christ lurks the darkness of an evil so great that it is impossible to trust the imageless God who cannot be fixed in any one channel of redemption.

To me the most moving psalm has always been "The Lord is my shepherd": "Though I walk through the valley of the shadow of death, I shall fear no evil, for Thou art with me." This is that biblical *emunah* that Jesus also expressed in the Sermon on the Mount when he said, "Which of you by taking thought can add a cubit to your stature? Take no thought for the morrow. Sufficient unto the day is the evil thereof." This biblical trust cannot mean a guarantee of salvation, nor that death is any less real, nor that we shall not walk through the valley of the shadow. Each one of us must "walk that lonesome valley," each of us by himself. We not only walk *through* it: In a very real sense of the term, we live *in* it. The very border and ground of our life is death. The Psalm says only, "I shall fear no evil for thou art with me." Like the Song of Songs, it claims that "love is stronger than death." This affirmation of trust can only be expressed and renewed in the present. It does not tell me that if, like Katov in Malraux's novel *Man's Fate*, I should be thrown alive in an engine of boiling oil, I should be able to preserve my trust unshaken. Untold millions of people in our day may have met their inhuman deaths engulfed in the darkest horror. Even the idea of immortality cannot do away with the human facts of death, of loneliness, of abandonment.

When the death of others or our own serious illness forces us to confront the reality of death, we discover that we do not in fact know anything but present reality. For all our imaginings of being at our own funeral, we do not know anything except life. We exist as finite selves set over against other selves and other reality that come to meet us. We are given in our lives a ground which is ours. But the reality which is that ground is not done away with by our death; for it is a reality in which we partake and which we share. That does not mean that we can say after a person has died that the reality of the person that he was still exists as such other than in our memory or in the impact that he continues to have upon us. When we live with the death of one who was close to us, the mystery of his having existed as a person and being with us no longer cannot be plumbed. It is part of the paradox of personal existence itself, which has no secure or continuous existence in time yet does really exist again and again in moments of present reality. We tend most of the time to think of death as an objective event that we can understand through our categories. But when we truly walk in the valley of the shadow, the imminence of death tells us something that we have really known all along: that life is the only reality that is given to us, that this reality—and not some continuing entity or identity of a personal nature—is all that we actually know.

I shall never forget a rabbinical student of mine—the class wit whose humor excelled all would-be competitors. Once when he had invited my wife and me over for dinner, he was walking around the living room with his two-year-old son on his shoulders. Suddenly he stopped and said to me, "I wish I could trust in God the way that my little boy trusts in me."

What is it to trust in God? If it is anything, it is like personal trust rather than an attempt to pin down who or what God is or who or what we are. The true trust of a person is not that you already know all about him before you meet him. That is simply defining and delimiting an object. True trust is the readiness to find out where he is moment by moment through address and response. The same holds for our relationship to God. The meaning of the imagelessness of God is that you have no conception, no definition of God, no assurance that he will be merciful but not terrible. Trust in God, like existential trust, is not trust in what God will do for you but simply that unconditional trust that enables one, as long as one has strength to do so, to go forth to meet what comes. It is only trust that gives us the real resources to keep going. It is very much like a man who has a direction and who starts walking in that direction. He is knocked down and the breath is knocked out of him, but when he gets his breath back he gets up and starts walking again in the same direction. Your resources are those that you find at a given moment. Except for freedom from false notions of unfreedom, they do not depend on any conception of "God." Trust in God and existential trust are identical.

Existential trust does not mean trust *in* existence as being constituted in one particular way. It cannot be attained by "positive thinking," and it does not lead to "peace of mind" or "peace of soul." It is not inconsonant with pain, grief, anxiety, and least of all with vulnerability. Where it does not exist, one no longer goes forth to meet others: "The broken heart it kens nae second spring again, thae the waeful nae cease frae their greeting." There are some people who continue to live, yet never really go out again as a whole being to meet anyone. Is there not, says the poet Conrad Aiken, one *"tetelestai"* that can be said for those "who creep through life guarding their heart from blows to die obscurely?" Are not they, in their so different way, like Jesus who cried out his "forsaken!" on the cross? Who would presume to judge them? But our desire for security leads some of us to see ourselves as forsaken simply because life does not comport itself as we think it should. We wish to prescribe what will come to us and, like Kafka's mole, construct a burrow that will make it sure that nothing reaches us except what we want to reach us. Our views of existence are based upon our disappointments, upon the shattering of trust that every child experiences no matter how confirming his parents are. Every child experiences separation and betrayal. On growing up and first entering into romantic relations with the opposite sex, he is already expecting rejection and hurt—the repetition of his early experiences. Time and time again we think that we have "had it"; yet at another moment we are able, like a character in Samuel Beckett's novels, to get up and go on. More than we can conceive, we are sustained from within ourselves, from what comes to meet us, and from the meeting itself. We are not sustained in smooth continuity, to be sure. On the contrary, we constantly descend into the abyss, we walk again and again in the valley of the shadow. Yet our existence is given back to us, we are renewed. We walk over the abyss at every moment, walk in the valley of the shadow every day. Yet moment by moment we are carried, day by day we are given back our ground and our freedom. The smog of existential mistrust through which we move need not prevent our making ever-new contact with reality. If we dare to trust, we can grow in the courage to address and the courage to respond.

[Chapter 18]

A Meaning for Modern Man

"God-talk" is objective; "experience"-talk, whether mystical or simply religious, is subjective: "I have had these feelings or this experience." Touchstones of reality has tried to point toward something which is neither objective nor subjective. For that reason it has a great deal to do with the way we walk in our daily lives but very little to do with the way we *think* about this walking, since our thinking usually remains bound up with the objective and the subjective.

In our search for meaning, for touchstones of reality, we sometimes confuse two quite different things—a comprehensive world-view that gives us a sense of security and the meaning that arises moment by moment through our meeting with a reality that we cannot embrace. Many people when they have a religious or mystical experience move quickly to a metaphysics and identify their experience with one particular philosophy of religion or of mysticism. Not content with having found meaning in immediacy, they want to wrap up reality in some conceptual totality and use their experience as the guarantor of that totality. Perhaps one of the most important witnesses that can be made in our day is that it is not necessary to have a *Weltanschauung*, a comprehensive world-view, in order to be able to live as a man. What is more, our "world-view" may get in the way of our confrontation with the concrete at any given point and just thereby rob us of the real world. This means, in terms of theology, that our stance, our life-attitude, is more basic than the affirmation or nonaffirmation of a "Being" or "ground of being." No intellectual construction, not even the philosophy of dialogue, can ever include the real otherness of the other. In meeting the other, I come up against something absurd in the root meaning of the term—something irreducible that I cannot get my arms around or register in my categories. If this is true of the otherness of every concrete other, it is true by the same token of God, whom we meet in the meeting with the other.

A world-view is like a geodesic dome. It creates a special atmosphere for you, keeps certain air currents up, and gives you a sense of spaciousness without giving you the real world where the winds blow freely and sometimes uncomfortably. A world-view exists within your consciousness, even when you share it with any number of other men. No matter how adequate the world-view is, it leaves out otherness by definition. For that is the very nature of the other—that it cracks and destroys every *Weltanschauung*, that it does not fit into any ensemble of coherences, that it is absurd. You can fit others into your world-view, but you cannot do so without robbing them of what makes them really other.

For me, at least, the ground of trust cannot be sought in theology or metaphysics. We cannot step outside the given of our situation and posit a foundation that is conceptually adequate. Once I wrote to Martin Buber and asked him, "Did God have an I-Thou relationship with man in creating him?" "Now you are talking like the theologians!" Buber replied. "How do we know what relationship God had with man in creating him?" There is something about the whole enterprise of theology, metaphysics, and often of philosophy of religion, which tempts the thinker to see God, man, and the world from above and leave himself out of it. Then one wonders how Bergson got outside the *élan vital* or Whitehead outside the dialectic between God and the world so he could see it as a whole!

There are two different meanings of the word "ground" as we use it in a phrase such as the "ground of being." One of these is found in conceptual, or ontological, formulations. The other is a ground only in the sense of what we can touch on in our situation, in our experience, in our existence—what gives us the courage to take a step forward and then perhaps another step forward and still another. With the former meaning of ground I can have nothing to do because it presupposes removing us from where we are in fact. It presupposes getting behind or above creation. This is the one thing that Job was reproved for and properly so. He was not reproved for questioning God, for contending with God, or for crying out but only, as it says in Chapter 40, "Will you condemn me to justify yourself?" Will you, in that witness for your innocence and for your suffering which you have to make, go further and make statements about the whole of reality? This desire for a comprehensive gnosis may give satisfaction to our minds when we give in to it, but we cannot live our lives from there. It goes beyond the given of our existence, of our finite freedom and our finite-infinite knowing.

The other meaning of "ground" I can and do affirm, for this is precisely what I mean by "touchstones of reality." Existential trust has to do with this second meaning, but not necessarily and often not at all with the first. Existential trust does not depend upon a man affirming that he believes in God or that he has faith in God. What a man believes, in the conscious, rational sense of that term, often has little or even a negative connection with his basic life-attitude, his stance. I have never heard a confirmed optimist talk without shuddering. Underneath his words I can sense that he has such a black feeling of what reality is that he constantly has to erect this rosy superstructure over it to avoid having to face it. The confirmed pessimist is in no better case. He enjoys it when things turn out the way he has predicted. He gets a positive ironic pleasure out of being able to gloat, "Well, it is just as I said it would be." Both the optimist and the pessimist put between themselves and the reality they meet a prejudice—an *a priori* emotional or intellectual view that prevents them from seeing reality as it is. If you are really willing to see things as they are, you cannot say in advance whether they will be good or bad. You may even be forced to revise your notions of what is good and what is bad!

But does not biblical trust rest upon the belief in the existence of God? I do not think so. We have been hung up for centuries on the question of the existence of God, on proofs and disproofs of his existence. This is not a question that biblical man ever asked. A God whose existence could be proved could not be the biblical Creator; for he would be part of an already given order where one thing could be causally or logically related to another since this is the very nature of proof. Biblical man did not live in such a world of abstractions. He did not know about "nature" as some great whole. He just knew the goats, the war horse, and the clods of dust—all the particulars of things. What he was concerned with was the reality he met in his existence. He was not concerned with metaphysics or even theology. He could not ask the question, for that would mean to turn the world into the given and God into the variable. In Proverbs it is the fool and not the skeptic who "says in his heart there is no God." That does not mean he does not "believe" in God. It means he shuts out the reality of the otherness that meets us in each new situation.

What does this say about God? Abraham Heschel says, "God is of no importance unless he is of supreme importance." That means that a "God" who is just a means to our ends is not really God. Jean-Paul Sartre says, "Even if God did exist, that would change nothing." In contrast to both Heschel and Sartre, the vast mass of men want to keep God around for his usefulness—for the national welfare, for successful living, for positive thinking, for peace of mind or peace of soul. In the face of this situation, the truly religious man, or in our terms the man who is deeply concerned with touchstones of reality, must sometimes, like Albert Camus, have the courage to put the belief in God aside in order to try to make contact once again with existential reality. "I want to live only with what I can know," says Camus. I want to find touchstones of reality that I can live by. In our age this man in his atheism may affirm reality more than those who profess the existence of God but, in the language of T. S. Eliot's "Ash Wednesday," "affirm before the world but deny between the rocks." These latter confess belief in order to keep the social integument together but do not let it matter in the least in their lives.

We meet the "eternal Thou" only in our existence as persons, only in our meeting with the other: we cannot know it as if from outside this existence. If we recognize this, we must renounce the attempt to include God in any conceptual system, even the most creative and organic of process philosophies, whether that of Alfred North Whitehead or Pierre Teilhard de Chardin. To say that one meets God in what transcends oneself does not mean that the other one meets is "supernatural," or even that the "supernatural" is in the "between." The term "natural," however, leads us to forget the reality over against us and to see our existence as entirely included in a conceptual totality which we call "nature," "world," or "universe." In our actual experience, reality, including all other selves, is not only within but over against us. It is not some common, undifferentiated, reality that can be seen from the outside. Much modern thought confuses the subjectivity of the person and the subjectivity of "man": it treats man as a totality and what is immanent in him as if it were in a single self. In our concrete existence, however, there is no such totality. The Thou confronts us with the unexpected, takes us unawares. We must stand our ground yet be prepared to go forth again and again to meet we know not what. It is not insight into process but trust in existence that enables us to enter into a genuine meeting with the unique reality that accosts us in the new moment.

There is often a correlation between a thinker's approach to ethics and his approach to philosophy of religion. Those thinkers who feel that religion is solidly founded only when it rests on proofs of the existence of God, proofs that by their very nature put God into a rational framework of universal order or law, stand in opposition to the existential trust that receives only what it receives without demanding that God, man, and world be installed in any objective, comprehensible totality. The security of the former rests on the cosmos that human understanding has opened to it, the "holy insecurity" of the latter on the trust in the meeting with the reality over against one—the meeting with the God whom one can talk *to* but not *about*. Similarly, those who demand a logical, ordered ethics often do so not because they have reason to believe in the objectivity of the moral order, but because they have an almost magic belief that what they posit as fixed, objective and universal provides security and solidity and protects them against the threat of the romantic, the irrational, and the demonic.

To speak of "touchstones of reality" does not imply that we can define what we mean by "reality." All we can say is that we mean the concrete situation, including whatever enters into it from all that we have been. There is a relation between our various truths—our touchstones of reality—both those that we experience in our own lives and those that we encounter in the lives of others. But this relation is not one of an abstract consistency. We cannot stand back and look at those events from which we derive our touchstones as if in the moment of reflection we were outside of time. Rather in a new situation it is possible to reaffirm the old touchstones—not in such a way as to say that they are the same as the new, but they are illuminated by them. If this leaves us with no absolute or truth other than the relation to the moment, into that relation may enter every other truth-relationship that we have made our own. We do not *have* truth. We have a relationship to it. We can affirm certain moments of meeting—not necessarily as having an objectifiable knowledge content but still as not being sheer immersion in the flux. These moment by moment truth-relationships do not yield some higher truth that we can objectify as always the same. All we have is what at any given time we know *and* what we are not given to know. The notion that man is moving toward omniscience, that science will some day know everything there is to know, simply misunderstands the fact that all human knowing is a mixture of finitude and the infinite. All our knowing is partial ignorance. What we should be concerned about is what it is given us to know at *this* time. In each new discovery or re-discovery our earlier touchstones of reality are brought into the fullness of the present. Any reference point beyond that would take us out of the only dimension in which we live and think and know—the dimension of time. We must, of course, act as if we were above time when employing our useful abstractions—from mathematics and logic to engineering and even some parts of law. But in the essential matters of our lives, in our concrete existence as whole persons, we must avoid the illusion that we can rise to a reference point above existence itself—an abstract spatiality divorced from events.

If I meet my friend again, I can recognize him, know him again, only if there really is a new relationship. Otherwise I remember him from our past moments of relationship, but he has not come alive to me again as my friend. If I do recognize him in new relationship, then the old has been given new meaning through being brought into the new without destroying its original meaning. Similarly the God that I *re*-cognize, that I know again, I know in concrete uniqueness, not in any abstract sameness. Objectivizing, structuring, formulating are essential in the carrying forward of our truths. But if you content yourself with them alone, you lose your touchstones of reality. You have to take the further step of bringing the old touchstones into the new. Therefore, our ultimate criterion of meaning and truth is not the objectification of a structure but the lived new meeting with reality.

For this reason we cannot find touchstones of reality by going back to tradition. We can only find them through renewing tradition, through making it living again in the present. I believe, with Saint Augustine, that we live in the present alone—that the past is memory, the future anticipation. In Deuteronomy it says, "Not our fathers, but we here, the living, stand on Mount Sinai to receive the Covenant." This does not mean that there is no difference or tension between our fathers and us. "Over an abyss of sixteen hundred years I speak to you," says Saint Nicholas at the beginning of Benjamin Britten's *St. Nicholas Cantata*. We are aware he is speaking to us, but we are also aware he is speaking to us across an abyss of many centuries. If we attempt to "continue" tradition without the awareness of this abyss, we lose the tension. I once went to a Seder service on the first night of Passover during which I noticed that on one page in the *Haggadah* (the book of prescribed prayers and rituals) it said in English: "May the next year be a year of peace and prosperity"; whereas on the facing page in Hebrew it read: "Next year may Messiah, the Son of David, come." Those who could still read the Hebrew had their choice of the older or the newer meaning. Those who only knew English had the smooth, modern meaning, without any tension. If cutting off from tradition is one danger, there is an equal danger in retaining the time-hallowed symbols yet reading into them new meaning so freely that, like Peter Pan's shadow, it becomes tacked on to the old. The most glaring example that I know of this transvaluation of religious symbols is Mordecai Kaplan's book, *The Meaning of God in Modern Judaism* in which a whole series of traditional terms, like the kingship of God, revelation, sovereignty, and creation, are simultaneously retained and retranslated as evolution, creativity, survival of the Jewish people, and natural process!

Only when we have three elements—our personal uniqueness, the will to be open, and holding the tension with tradition—is there a meaningful dynamic. We must fight and contend with tradition in order to make an honest witness to our own uniqueness and to all the absurdity and incongruity that has entered into our lives. There are two different Pietàs of Michelangelo. The one that was brought from Saint Peter's in Rome to the World's Fair in New York is very beautiful, but it is still the early one in which Michelangelo portrays Mary as a lovely sixteen-year-old girl holding a boyish body of Christ. The later Pietà, which one sees in Florence, is the great one that shows real agony and that was produced in agony out of a genuine wrestling with the marble.

"From wonder into wonder existence opens," says Lao-tzu. To have a touchstone and to touch touchstones means a whole different way of living than is implied by locating the reality "out there" or "in here." Many of us feel that if we only replace the anthropomorphic notion of God with some impersonal concept, we are on the way. But what are we on the way to except another abstraction, unless it lead to greater openness? The only "perennial philosophy" I can espouse is that each of the religions and touchstones that I have entered into dialogue with points toward greater openness. "Alas the world is full of enormous lights and mysteries," says the Baal Shem, "but man hides them from him with one small hand." Prayer is the removal of that hand.

Prayer has to do with discovering each time anew what we can bring and what can be brought—the way we bring ourselves to a poem or a dream or a Hasidic, Zen, or Sufi tale.

That is why my wife Eugenia, without reducing the religious to the aesthetic, can say in all the seriousness of her open and faithful dialogue with the poems and poets she reads and teaches, "Poetry is the liturgy of our lives." My chief advisor for my doctoral dissertation, Professor Arnold Bergstraesser, amazed me when I had finished it by asking, "Do you know Buber's secret? It is prayer." He did not mean by this that Buber spent so many hours a day praying, but that he brought himself every hour of his life in a real openness. Then Bergstraesser demanded of me, "What will keep you from reading this dissertation ten years later and asking yourself, 'Did I know that then!'?" What he meant, I have realized ever more deeply in the twice ten years since, was that all the marvellous insights that I had gleaned from my study of Buber's thought might become lost, closed over as the waters close over the deep. Not because the insights were untrue but because I might fail to authenticate them and make them real by bringing them in openness into my life. The life of prayer can only be sustained if we bring ourselves to each situation with all that we know and have been. We are all like that Hasid on whom the terrible penance was imposed that for the rest of his life he preserve the full intention of every word of prayer!

The kingdom of God cannot be localized in the immanent, or the transcendent, within us or beyond us. It is both the personal—the quality of individual living—and the social—the realization of justice, righteousness, and loving kindness in lived community. It is dialogue, trust, and grace—moving among us. It is the covenant of peace—the task that demands us and the partnership of existence that sustains and comforts us. It is our touchstones of reality—our discovery and confirmation of them in the cruel and gracious happenings of our lives.

About the Author

Maurice Friedman is Professor of Religion at Temple University, Philadelphia, and on the faculty of Pendle Hill, the Quaker Study Center at Wallingford, Pennsylvania. He has taught at many other colleges and universities, including twelve years at Sarah Lawrence. In 1972 he will be Visiting Distinguished Professor at San Diego State. Born in Tulsa, Oklahoma, in 1921, he has an S.B. from Harvard, an M.A. from Ohio State, a Ph.D. from the University of Chicago, and an honorary LL.D. from the University of Vermont. He is the author of *Martin Buber: The Life of Dialogue; Problematic Rebel: Melville, Dostoievsky, Kafka, Camus; To Deny Our Nothingness: Contemporary Images of Man;* and *The Worlds of Existentialism: A Critical Reader.*